SHAGGY DOGS

THEOPHILUS CROUTON LABONZA

Trafford
PUBLISHING™

Order this book online at www.trafford.com/08-0797
or email orders@trafford.com

Most Trafford titles are also available at major online book retailers.

Edited by : Vanessa Weeks Page.
Cover Design by: Jennifer Phillips Lane

Note for Librarians: A cataloguing record for this book is available from Library
and Archives Canada at www.collectionscanada.ca/amicus/index-e.html

Printed in Victoria, BC, Canada.

ISBN: 978-1-4251-8122-2 (soft)
ISBN: 978-1-4251-8123-9 (ebook)

*Our mission is to efficiently provide the world's finest, most comprehensive
book publishing service, enabling every author to experience success.
To find out how to publish your book, your way, and have it available
worldwide, visit us online at www.trafford.com/10510*

Trafford rev. 8/24/2009

www.trafford.com

North America & international
toll-free: 1 888 232 4444 (USA & Canada)
phone: 250 383 6864 ♦ fax: 812 355 4082

TABLE OF CONTENTS

INTRODUCTION

Against my better judgment, which I'll officially consider to be better than a renewed outbreak of cholera in order to eschew the dangling modifier, I feel I should remind you (And, by that, I do not mean the literal meaning of the word: to re-insert a person's brain, as in, "Dr. Frankenstein <u>reminded</u> his monster to take out the garbage.") that the stories in the pages to follow are not of my own making, but, rather, are humble transcriptions of classic tales which, if not an integral part of our grand oral tradition, are at least an exceedingly fractional one.

Anyway, for the benefit of you more discerning readers who want some idea of what you're getting into before plopping down enough money to buy a jeroboam of your favorite malt liquor, the plots of these stories all, without exception, resemble Llewellyn Melville's prehumous novel, *Hubert.*

Hubert was the white whale who haunted the Parisian sewer system (*Le Cordon Sanitaire*). He was ruthlessly hunted by Captain Jan Cheesenbürgermitonionundtomato of the Vatican Coast Guard, who viewed the creature as an affront to his dignity.

Armed only with his faith and a Jumbo Oeconomy-Size can of DrânZero, the captain pursued his ursine prey (Nobody had yet told him it was a whale.) through chapter and a little light verse, until he eventually found himself wandering through the Mariana Trench, considered by aficionados to be the deepest spot in the Pacific Ocean.

At that point (That one, right there→ .), he came to realize he was standing among several thousand soldiers who, they claimed, were attached to the Aqueous Expeditionary Force. Though it seemed fishy to the captain, he had to admit there was a not an inconsiderable bit of warfare occurring around the trench.

"I say," he began, revealing to all present the precise method he chose to communicate his thoughts, "can anyone explain what is going on here?"

"You mean you don't know?" 86,312 of the soldiers asked him.

"No, I do not," replied the captain. "Will somebody or bodies, known or unknown, please inform me?"

"Why, we're fighting the Huns to make Davy Jones' Locker safe for democracy," a PFC Jones informed him.

"Huns?" wondered the captain, whose madcap dashes through the Parisian sewers had caused him to lose touch with reality. "What Huns?"

"Those no-good, baby-killing, bloodthirsty, unpatriotic, Pearl-Harbor-bombing, sieg-heiling, spike-headed guys over there in the grey flannel suits, that's what Huns!" entire regiments explained.

"Which reminds me," a doughboy from Pillsbury, Vt., giggled, "here they come."

Sure enough, the mighty gray horde advanced, led by a masked, caped figure who seemed, well, nigh invincible.

"Oh, no!" moaned a subaltern. "It's Kaiser Bill's Batman!"

Rest assured or, at any rate, in a supine position, the attack was repulsed and soon followed by a crushing victory for The Allies near the quaint undersea village of Vass, where they forced the Huns to capitulate and submit to the Humiliating Peace of Vass.

"Say, that was some war," the captain remarked to his tour guide, a surplus brigadier general, "but I really should be leaving."

"Won't you stick around and watch us drown the Kaiser?" the general suggested.

"Nay," replied the captain, noticing the officer's cavalry insignia. "I have decided to return to my relentless pursuits, and, in so doing, depart from the bottom of the Pacific Ocean, or BOTPO, as I have come to call it for the sake of brevity."

"You know," the general sighed, "if only you didn't talk the way you write, you might have at least a few friends."

"That is so," the captain concurred. "Natheless, I'm leaving. As our recent allies say, '*Auf Wiedersehen!*'

"Now, if you'll tell me how to reach dry land..."

Without a word the general pointed to a gaudily-attired building at "two o'clock" PST. A closer look through a pair of trinoculars the captain had borrowed from a sea monster revealed the establishment to be DRY LAND, The World's Largest Dry Cleaning Emporium, Featuring **99** Press-O-Matic Computers and an Old Guy Who Does Shoes While-U-Wait!!

"No, you don't seem to understand," he protested.

"Understand what?" the general countered.

"Anything and everything, but, in this case, my desire to evacuate the bottom of the Pacific Ocean or BOTPO, as I call it from time to time to save wear and, if you must belabor the point, tear on my vocal chords, which are, I should point out for the enlightenment of generations yet unborn, g#, A7 and a variety of atonal combinations that arise whene're I chance to blossom into song."

"Well," observed the general as he removed his fingers from his ears, "there are two ways that you as a foreigner of extremely unknown derivation can leave the bottom of the Pacific Ocean or POBOT, as we in the military call it.

"The first way," he continued, "is to take advantage of our efficient personnel management system and process out in a duly-processed manner.

"The second way—"

"I'll take it!" the captain chimed (g#, if you remember) in.

"I was going to say" (which he was), "the second and less-employed manner of evacuation (although yours is the only case I know of anyone wanting to depart from our paradise under the Pacific and, in fact, the only known case of anyone ever wanting to enter same, which, I'm sure is very significant and highly suspicious); yes, well, the second and, as I believe I already indicated," (which he did), "less-employed manner of evacuation is to correctly ascertain the daily code. That is: to *guess the secret password!*"

Reminding himself never again to eat so much pizza before going to sleep, Captain Cheesenbürgermitonionundtomato set his mind to the task.

"Pornography," he guessed.

"Negative," answered the general smugly.

"Lust," tried the captain.

"Not even close," he cackled, having set his uniform on fire.

"Licentiousness?"

"Tell me, Cheesenbürgermitonionundtomato" inquired the rank-infested inquisitee."

"That's 'Cheesenbürgermittomatoundonion,' the visitor needlessly corrected him.

"Yes, well, why are you guessing all those filthy words? Soldiers don't talk like that."

"Thanks for the tip," replied the captain with a nudge and a wink. "How's this? Abstention, apathy, chastity, Puritanism."

"Wrong, wrong, wrong, wrong and WRONG!" bellowed the general.

"You're getting ahead of me."

"Very well, you may have one additional wrong guess without comment. Just think of a highly inappropriate word."

"Boner," he tried, positive he would fail.

"THAT'S IT!"

"You mean I guessed the secret password?"

"No, of course not, but that is a highly inappropriate word if I ever heard one."

"Straws," the captain guessed, grasping at straws.

"Negative."

"Wax?" he suggested, beginning to wane.

"Negative," sighed the plucky leader as he prepared another chicken for the spit. "Look I'll give you a hint: it's a word you don't know."

Needless to say, though said it will be, the guessing game had now turned into child's play, for the number of words Captain Cheesenbürgermitonionundtomato did not know was scant indeed. He was able to rattle them off in a matter of days.

"Abecedarian?" he began. "Abdoudikro? Absterge? Acanthopterygian? Aeruginous? Algolagnia? Asyndeton? Axotol? Baboo? Baldachin? Baldwin I? Barbicel? Bedizen? Bistoury? Bubbly-jock? Cacoethes? Caesalpinaceous? Cespitose? Chernozem? Confarreation? Crapulent? Crwth? Cukoo-spit? Dahabeah? Dahoon? Diplostemonous? Dowitcher? Dreegh? Dyspnoea? Ebaunche? Eidolon? Epexagetic? Epicklesis? Esne? Exergue? Febrifugal? Felly? Fossick? Fozy? Frigg? Futhroc? Fyke? Gaboon? Gadroon? Galactagogue? Galligaskins? Gallimaufries? Galoon? Ghat? Gnar? Greegree? Gyve? Hippogriff? Hoopoe? Iceblink? Idioblast? Ixtle? Izzat? Jemadar? Jerreed? Jubbah? Kakapo? Kanone? Kroon? Lakh? Lat? Leaf lard? Limachine? Lissotrichous? Loxodromics? Lumpsucker? Maccaboy? Maenad? Mho? Mirza? Monticule? Mooneye? Mulct? Nagana? Nelumbo? Nomarchy? Nyckelharpa? Nympholept? Obeah? Od? Ogee? Old sledge? Orra? Otiosity? Ouabain? Pachouli? Pagurid? Palinode? Palsgrave? Paragoge? Pasquil? Peavy? Pewit? Pilewort? Pipal? Pish? Pochard? Pood? Poon? Probang? Quagga? Quitch? Quotha? Raffinose? Rat-stripper? Razee? Roorback? Rosolio? Rovaciolite? Rutilant? Saloop? Sayyid? Scatt? Scumble? Shaloon? Shebeen? Simoon? Skirr? Smeek? Snool? Soom? Spontoon? Stoa?

Taeniafuge? Tew? Thurible? Tmesis? Tzigane? Ultramundame?
Vagroom? Vinegaroon? Vug? Vugg? Vugh? Wadmal? Waucht?
Whaup? Xiphoid? Xyster? Yapok? Yerk? Yill? Zaffer? Zareba?
Zingaro? Zoon? Zwitterion? Zymosis?"

"No, you dummy!" stormed the general "The word is
'zymurgy'!"

"I was going to say that next," the captain offered.

"Sure you were."

Right then, a subversive looking individual somersaulted by
and into the murky background. The general abruptly inserted
his thumb into his left eye and, in a snappy motion, plucked it
out.

"Not that I wish to change the subject," the captain wondered,
"but why did you do that?"

"Because," his host explained, marveling at the lesser man's
stupidity, "I was told by higher headquarters to keep an eye out
for suspicious-looking individuals. Well?"

"Well, what?"

"The secret password, 'zymurgy.' Aren't you going to say
it?"

"I've never liked that word."

"If you're not going to cooperate, then get t'hell out!" the general ordered his charge.

Which the captain did.

To this day, no one actually knows whether poor
Cheesenbürgermitonionundtomato ever caught the white whale,
Herbert. In any event, the French government awarded him the
prestigious *croissant d'honneur* and returned him forthwith
to the Vatican, where he later decided to shorten his name to
Cheesenbürgermitdaswerks.

Still, I should point out (since if I pointed in, I might stab myself) that the brave captain came to an unfortunate end. He went
mad, they eventually realized, and passed his final days hunched

over a glass of beer, shouting: "The prince of whales has lost his tales! Hats off, number three!"

To be sure, there is a lesson here somewhere. And, though you may entertain grave doubts, I shall provide the explanation, all in due time. As our friend Mr. Deuteronomy tells us: "To every thing there is a season and a time for every purpose under the heaven

"A time to rip and a time to rend;

"A time to gag and a time to bind;

"A time to cast aspersions and a time to gather aspersions together;

"And all that stuff."

Okay, now it's time. Many readers who pretend not to understand what I am talking about, are left with the same basic question: what are these shaggy dog stories anyway? I am making believe I'm delighted you asked me that question. Let us dwell, first on one thing, then another.

No less a statesman than Lyndon Baines Johnson once had the opportunity to say of such stories, "Never—and I do mean never—in my entire adult life have I been so emotionally drained. I lay on the floor for three days, panting like a beached goldfish."

Lord Beaconsfield (pronounced "Beansfield,"), on the other hand, had little use for the genre.

"I think they're rather meshugennah," the former premier of England said whenever the opportunity presented itself, "and they hardly make me think of goldfish one bit."

As your editor struggles mightily to frame a definition for something so ephemeral as a shaggy dog story, we should take note of an interesting anecdote involving the late Ceasare Borgia and his favorite sculptor, Pasquale "The Ice Pick" Bogiagaloupe. When commissioned by Borgia to create a statue of Jesus Christ, the sculptor asked his patron how he wanted the job done.

"It's simple," explained the Great Man, "You just knock away anything that doesn't look like an elephant."

"Pardon me, Your Holiness," observed a nearby penitent, "I think you are in the wrong joke."

Nevertheless, as E.A. Poe's raven almost quothed, the approach remains sound.

Consider this: a young lady named Mary married a man named Gary. They were quite prolific, having five children in only five years, but then Gary died.

Hardly was the body cold when Mary turned right around and married a fellow named Harry. Mary and Harry were even more prolific, having had six children in five years. Then Harry died.

And despite the more-than-heroic efforts of our postal service, in which we must find ourselves badly swollen with pride, the last of the sympathy cards had not been delivered before Mary had gone off and married a man named Sid. They too were highly prolific, having five more children over the next five years, but then Mary died.

As the multitude of friends and family filed by her open casket, one elderly gentleman said as he stood over it, "Well, now they'll be together at last."

"You mean...Gary...and...Harry...and Mary?" asked another mourner.

"No, I mean Mary's legs."

If that story struck you as both funny and short, then make a note: shaggy dog stories are neither.

Equally important, know that shaggy dog stories are not sung. Ever. And when they are, they are not sung by Creoles, Gypsies, Arabs or lepidopterists. Another helpful hint: tales of this ilk are never conveyed in a foreign language. Anybody trying to fob such a story off on you in a tongue other than your own is probably seeking to sell you more life insurance than you need.

Along that same line, it would be foolish to classify as one, Raphaello Spaghettini's least acclaimed opera, *The Unisex Hair Stylist of Seville, Ohio.* A body might try but, if the fool would persist in his folly, he'd be more foolish yet.

Any notion that such a tale can be a work of non-fiction is patently absurd. How can a cookbook possibly evoke any kind of story at all? That shaggy dog won't hunt, as they say in the ice cream parlors of Grosse Point. As to other works of nonfiction, I defy you to identify the shaggily canine elements in this passage from *The Book On Lists*:

Lean to the left!
Lean to the Right!
(Stand up, sit down)
Fight, team, fight!

Yet another brilliant example of what we are not talking about is illustrated in the following dramatic piece by the notable playwright, Tennessee Tuxedo Jones, to commemorate the digestion of his parakeet by a hungry but otherwise disinterested alley cat.

A Rose By Any Other Name For Esmeralda

A drama in four or possibly five acts

Cast of Characters (In order of disappearance)

The Hand of Providence	An allegorical figure
The Foot of Pawtucket	His not-too-distant cousin
"Two-toot" Tootsie Goombah	His cocaine-snorting daughter-in-law
Big, Fat, Huge, Enormous George	The heavy
Esmeralda Herself	A lady of the mid-afternoon
Sonny Lee Matina	The president of France
Papa Buttone	The town glutton
Orville W. Snorkel	An apparition of the penultimate act
Jive-talkin' Jimmy Slick	The town Notary Public

Various Extras, Stand-bys, Duplicates and Spear-Chunkers to order

Act I

(*Opens in the garbage-out room of a major metropolitan software company.*)

ONE EXTRA: If we're going after the great white smelt, then what are we doing here?

NEXT EXTRA: I know! I know! Woolgathering.

ANOTHER EXTRA: You're right. Let us instead rent a shopping cart and head for the parking lot.

YET ANOTHER EXTRA: I sure hope they're biting today!

SOME OTHER DAMN EXTRA: And why shouldn't they? It's Tuesday, isn't it?

VOICE FROM OFFSTAGE (After a long, embarrassing pause): How quickly we forget!

ENSEMBLE: How quickly we forget!

(Curtain, which failed to go up at the beginning of the act, is raised at last and then lowered.)

Act II

(Act opens in the street, directly outside the actual stage door.)

THE CAST: Let us in, you stupid son of a bitch! We don't know the secret password!

(Curtain is carried up to the roof by living room toughs, filling in for the street toughs on strike, and dropped onto the assembled cast.)

Act III

(Opens in the courtroom. The judge, jury and executioner have

not yet arrived. Enter a stranger, dressed in lederhosen and playing an accordion.)

STRANGER (SINGS):   Ven-a der moon hits-a you eye
                         like eine beeg-a pizza pie, dot's
                         amore!

(*He is hit in the face with a large pepperoni pizza*).

(*The curtain still missing, the audience is temporarily blinded with strobe lights.*)

Act IV

(*Enter Sgt. Snorkel*)

SNORKEL: Audience, tensh HUT!
            Left FACE!
            Fwooord HARCH!

(*All are dismissed. Exit Snorkel*)

Act V

(*Opens on two janitors, sweeping the stage in tandem with push brooms. One stops to pick up an object. Any object will do, as the janitor is blind.*)

1st JANITOR: Look, a rose. I'll bet somebody meant to give this to someone. I wonder who it was for?

2nd JANITOR: Yo' mama.

(They both have a hearty laugh, as the 1st janitor throws the rose, or whatever it was, away. Exit janitors, sweeping.)

(The curtain is retrieved, dragged onstage by pyromaniacal ballerinas on steroids and set afire, in lieu of the house lights coming on).

It is true, as many have noted, that the preceding piece scrupulously maintains the Three Great Dramatic Unities: Unity of Time, Unity of Place, and the Author Wrote the Whole Thing Without Once Getting up to Go to the Bathroom. Still, that does not necessarily qualify it as a shaggy dog story. In point of brutal fact, at no time in recorded history has a shaggy dog story been presented as a stage play.

Finally, shaggy dog stories cannot ever be considered as poetry. Here, just watch what happens:

> Roses are red
> Violets are blue
> Dogs are shaggy
> And...YARRRRGHPFT!

You see, it just can't be done.

There, I have knocked away the pieces that do not look like a shaggy dog, ergo you should know exactly what one is. If you still wish to imagine you're in the dark, there is nothing to do but read on. But that was the idea all along, wasn't it?--tcl

THE SHAGGY DOG

By Theophilus Crouton LaBonza

Fittingly enough, we are beginning this anthology with the original shaggy dog story, as the above title may have led you to believe. Owing to its place in line as the first of the breed, the tale is set way back in the troubling times of the Cold War. What people of our ilk now call "the good old days."

We have elected to tell this story ourselves. About us too little is known already.

I

It had not started to rain yet, but they were expecting some within the coming decade. Such news would have offered scant consolation to Willie McGurk, even if he listened to the news anymore, which he did not, for Willie was a bum, and a damn good one at that.

Not that he had been one all his life, you understand. There had been a time in his past when he worked for a living.. In the army he had been an Acting PFC for a few weeks. The experience and skills acquired in the service enabled him to launch a month- long career in door-to-door encyclopedia sales, but it all went downhill from there. Some blamed the bottle, but others chalked it up to cheap wine, while the failed pool sharks whined about cheap chalk.

Today things seemed worse than ever. The only response to his repeated requests for spare change came when a guy in a convertible pulled over and rotated his tires.

"Thanks for the tip, buddy!" the driver called out as he roared off in a squeal of freshly-situated rubber, for which counsel Willie did not get so much as a nickel.

At least it wasn't raining.

"A little piece of wine would sure help this day out," Willie reasoned. A medium sized dog with a long, dirty coat growled at him. As he backed up to avoid the animal's attentions, he was assaulted from behind by a telephone pole, which had the bad grace, as he saw it, not to have moved. He struggled to his feet and faced the pole to deliver it a well-earned glob of spit, but paused mid-hawk to read a notice somebody had posted.

LOST!
MY ADORABLE WONDERFUL
CUDDLY SHAGGY DOG,
"MAURICE."
I MUST HAVE MY DOG BACK.
MONEY IS NO OBJECT.
$100,000 REWARD

The notice went on to instruct the finder to deliver the pet to Mrs. Leotis van Dandt, Suite #921, at the Exorbitant Towers Condominia.

Just then the dirty, SHAGGY dog that had growled at Willie dashed down an alley and out of sight.

"Wait a minute," Willie said, although the dog did not even wait two seconds, "that must be the dog!"

At a pace faster than he had not attempted since that rumor of the welfare checks running out a few years back, Willie lurched down the same alley. As he came out the other end, he saw nothing of his prey. In an instant it dawned on him that the greedy damn dog was probably heading for the Exorbitant Towers to claim the reward for himself. Enraged, Willie tore off in the direction of the Condominia as fast as his aching feet would allow.

His insight was rewarded as he eventually spotted the dog, which, being a male, had given Willie several opportunities to make up the lost ground. The dog started at the sight of the rapidly approaching figure and ran down another alley. Willie continued the exhausting pursuit. Again he sighted the dog. This time it was chasing a pick-up truck that was carrying a load of garbage. Just before the light pole failed to step out of Willie's way, he saw the dog jump onto the bed of the truck.

"LOST," read the notice on the light pole that towered over Willie's prostrate form, "MY ADORABLE, WONDERFUL SHAGGY DOG, 'MAURICE'..."

Willie was wise to the ways of the street. He knew that, in this town, people rarely hauled truckloads of garbage to their living rooms. Odds were pretty good, the truck and the dog were going to the city dump.

"I got there as soon as I could," he was to tell me later, except he never got around to it. He looked around for some sign of the pick-up or the dog, but saw neither. The man who would be dogcatcher raced all over the dump, hoping to get some inkling of where they went, but nary a clue turned up.

As he plopped onto an empty crate, a trickle of ocular drool rolled down his cheek. Riches beyond his wildest dreams had eluded him, after all that.

Automatically and with a scavenger's instinct, he began to sort idly through the nearby trash. Without paying much heed to what he was doing, he pulled out what appeared to be an old oil lamp. Thinking, as people always seem to do in situations like this, that the lamp could use a shine, he rubbed it on his pants. Immediately a brilliant flash of light and a heaven-shattering roar rent the air. It had started to rain at last.

II

At any rate, one of Willie's wishes seemed to come true. As though the thunder had pealed to announce his discovery, there, amidst a pile of empty paint cans, lay an almost full wine bottle with the familiar bird on the label.

"Hot diggity dog," he observed as he grabbed the bottle and expertly removed the cap. The stuff tasted as sweet as ever as he poured the wonderful nectar down his parched throat. Of course it was impossible for him (as it would be for any of us) to taste the difference between that particular brand of wine and the paint thinner that was actually in the bottle.

"Now that," Willie informed the red-eyed, green-scaled monster sitting next to him, "was some *fine* stuff!"

"And who might you be?" a solid-chestnut zebra with only one horn (a sousaphone) asked the creature.

"I might be Man's Best Fiend," replied the monster with a blast of fire that left the zebra feeling medium well, "And just whom do you think you are...or were?"

Meanwhile, Willie had crawled into the castle and shut the manhole behind him.

"Oooo-WEE!" proclaimed the king when he discovered Willie. "Boy, you hell when you well, butchoo alla time sick! Throw yourself to the lions, boy, and I mean yesterday."

Fortunately for Willie, he lost his way to the lion's den and wound up throwing himself to the piranhas instead. As a careless chambermaid had made off with the drain plug in the belief she had discovered the king's lost crown, not a drop of water remained for the unfortunate fish to swim in. All they could do to Willie was to flop around on the damp floor and make ugly snapping noises at him.

"That was a close shave," he remarked from the barber's chair. "Now how about a manicure?"

"Nope," the barber insisted, "Cash. $3.85 plus tip."

"Sorry," Willie explained as he hurtled through the shop window, "I'm takin' a 'five-finger discount' on this trim.

"Now where did I leave that lion's den?" he wondered.

"Hang a left, down the hall, then you walk smack into a wall. Can't miss it," instructed the king, who was trying to improve his execution. Willie followed the directions to the letter, but ended up in the Autobahn Society headquarters in spite of himself.

"Pardon me," he urged his hosts as he pulled a dead bird from his coat pocket, "I seem to have taken a wrong tern."

"Lions den," they all agreed, "no doubt about it."

"Right on," Willie added as he tiptoed out of the room, down the elevator shaft, and out through the **wine cellar**. He found a path and proceeded along it, "one step," he smugly assured himself, "at a time.

"I must find a farm," he thought as the quicksand he had stepped into fast approached his forehead. Very few farms, he realized, grew quicksand as a cash crop.

In a short while he did discover a farm, where he rooster-in-residence greeted him.

"What t'hell you want, boy?" squawked the rooster.

"Oh, to get out of that quicksand back there and maybe a hot meal," Willie surmised.

"Well, guess what, buster, we don't heat our meal up for anyone around here, least of all a trespasser!" the rooster pointed out.

"Don't mind him," the farmer explained to Willie. "You see, all this excitement makes my cock hard. Say, why don't you come in and wash up?"

"I can't figure out why," Willie admitted.

"Well, send me a telegram when y'do," the guy suggested as he returned to his crops.

"Now, there's a man outstanding in his field," thought Willie.

Soon enough, he came to another place, as people on the move are wont to do. From the scare-pelican in the yard, he figured it was a trout farm.

"Wait a minute," Willie cried out, "did he say somethin' back there about a **wine cellar**?" But by then, kindly hands had started dragging him toward the farmhouse.

"Dot's Kindly Hans," corrected the rootin' Teuton, whose job it was to harvest the spuds.

"Welcome stranger," effused the new farmer, once Willie was inside. "You may stay the night, but if you fool around with my daughter, I'll kill you."

"Oh?" Willie replied, as he surveyed the room, "Where's your daughter at, so I'll know not to go there and fool around?"

"Los Angeles, but YOU BETTER WATCH YOUR STEP, MISTER!"

As he drifted off to sleep, Willie wondered what the farmer's daughter might have looked like.

"Aha!" roared the farmer as he burst into Willie's room and cocked his smooth- bore machine gun.

"Let," Willie suggested rhetorically, "me out of here." He did not stop running until he reached the Big City.

WELCOME TO THE BIG CITY
SEAT OF THE BIG COUNTY
"NON PECUNIA LOQUAT SED IURAT"

Read the sign on the outskirts of town.

"Say, buddy," he asked of the first sphinx he came across, "d'ya think you could spare me a coupla bucks?"

"It depends," spake the sandstoned one, "Solve this riddle and there's a C-note in it for you: what walks on two legs in the afternoon, four legs in the evening, and thenceforth, walks hardly at all?"

"Hey," Willie realized aloud, "that sounds like me when I get ahold of some fine cheap wine."

"You are correct," the sphinx proclaimed. "The hundred's in your pocket," which it was.

Before he knew it, Willie was on his way down the main drag.

"This is as far as I'm gonna drag you, Mac," the trucker explained as he let go of Willie's hair, "from now on, you're on your own."

Fortunately, the guy had dropped him off in front of a classy eatery called, OPEN ALL NITE—ANY KIND SANDWICH U-WANT.

"Whaddya got for free?" he asked the counterman.

"Ain't nothin' on the house but the roof."

"In that case, I'll have the shit on a shingle."

As he waited for his food, Willie looked dully at the placemat. On it was a verse by Leif "The Chief" Monroe, a local poet. As he held a saucer over the mat for better shade, he read the verse.

Ringside and Table Manners

You must roll with the punches,
But roll with the brunch is
Included free of charge
(I'll have you know).
Stroll with some punch
On the promenade,
And your roll with the brunch
Is w/o marmalade.
(Ain't life a bitch? Check one, yes or no.)

Extol with the punches,
Say something nice.
(Don't get hit in the mouth.)
And exhale with the brunch
Is my advice.
(Don't get food in the nose.)

"Ain't it the truth," Willie might have sighed if at that moment
a noisy drunk had not staggered in and interrupted everybody's
train, bus or cab of thought.

"Hey!" the drunk called out as he pounded the counter for
attention, "Hey, gimmie a whale sanwish!"

"Aah, get lost," the counterman advised him.

"Hey, man, your shign says any kinda sanwish you want, and
I wanna whale sanwish!"

"Look, buddy," the counterman snapped, "it's three-thirty
in the goddamn morning. If you think I'm gonna start a fresh
whale, just for you, you're crazy."

"Aha!" the farmer called out, tommy gun at the ready.

"Check, please," Willie proclaimed.

As the farmer continued to blast the diner to smithereens,
Willie went on his way in search of a decent place to bed down.
Soon his eye landed on the marquee of the luxurious Maison
duPhloppe Hotel. Making but little effort to squint, he spotted a
smaller sign underneath that called out to him is alluring neon-
lit tones.

"Vacancies," it said.

"This must be the place," Willie surmised when he determined the farmer was nowhere around.

"Oh, this is the place, alright," the desk clerk assured
him, "unless, of course, you're fixin' to pull off some funny
business."

"Farthest thing from my mind," Willie mumbled as he slipped

the joy buzzer back into his coat pocket.

"And a good thing for you it is," explained the clerk, "'cause we got two house detectives in this here hotel, 'stead of your usual one." Sure enough, even as the desk clerk spoke, the two wily investigators lounged in the lobby, sharpening up their wits.

"Suppose you was locked in a room without no windows and there was a fire?" one of them asked.

"I wouldn't go to it," the other answered like a shot.

Willie walked along the treadmill to his room, entered, and sat for a while on the edge of the bed.

"I think I need a drink," he concluded. He phoned room service and ordered a case of the cheapest wine they had.

While he waited, he stood by the window and looked down at the street. He tried to clear his addled mind by focusing on the mundane scene below. After he'd wasted several seconds watching the huge, virulent octopoid creature at the intersection grab the passing cars and throw them into an enormous dumpster, on which was stenciled, FOR THE PREVENTION OF DISEASE ONLY, Willie grew bored with the conjecture and concentrated on the tap dancing firemen around the corner as they tried to stamp out a small but fierce cobblestone fire. He wondered how they produced such loud tapping from their bare feet until he realized the noise was actually someone knocking at the door. He remembered his order for a case of wine and eagerly yanked it open.

"Very well," remarked an elderly man dressed in white, wearing a pith helmet and clutching a magnifying glass, "show me the carvings, and I'll see what I can do. Twenty bucks a line, you understand."

"What's goin' on here?" Willie inquired. "Where's my wine?"

"I have no idea. You did call for rune service did you not?"

"No, all I ast for was a case of wine. Now where's it at?"

"Well, I'm sorry, old chap, but we are not in the wine business," the old man explained.

Within that very same week, Willie thought he smelled smoke. As he stuck his head out into the hallway, he overheard one of the bellboys on the payphone, calling the fire department.

"That's right," the employee repeated, the Mayzone doo Flop Hotel...yeah we're on fire.

"Whataya mean ya never hearda the place? We're right where we've always been," he went on to explain.

"How do you get here? What about that big red thing you people always drive around?"

"Fire! Fire!" the old gentleman in Willie's room shouted, once he got wind of the situation..

"OK, then," Willie told him, "you're fired."

"Fired? Hell, I quit!" the man raged as he stormed out of the room and into the waiting conflagration.

"Sure enough, the illustrious hotel was ablaze," explained one of the house detectives.

"There you go," grumbled the other as he rolled around on the floor, the better to squelch the flames on his trench coat, "jumping to conclusions again."

"Yeah? Well maybe I should jump on your face instead!"

"You and whose mother?"

"Excuse me, guys," Willie interjected, "but you're blocking the door. Do you mind if I get by?"

"Go fly a kite!" they shouted in unison as they loaded Willie down with silk, sticks and a length of twine.

"How'd you like a knuckle sandwich?" the one detective asked, resuming the conversation with his partner.

"I'm terribly sorry for the inconvenience," the harried proprietor (who had taken a short break from spitting on the flames) explained to Willie, "you see, all this excitement makes my dicks tiff."

Never, as he was, at a loss for an escape route, Willie sped down to the meat locker and slipped out the side entrance.

Once he was back on the street, safely among the giant scorpions, he paused to collect his bearings. Why he had looted that ball bearing factory in the first place was a mystery to him, and easy answers were nowhere to be found. In desperation, he began to run backward, full tilt, until he tripped over (and fell on top of) a large pile of clean, white bones.

"Bones," the learned paleontologist lectured Willie, "do not get to be bones without a lot of practice. I suggest you attend the church or synagogue of your compulsion."

Knowing good advice from a pro when he heard it, Willie ducked into the first available church: The First Available Church of the Holy Mackerel, where morning services were underway.

"Thank heavens you're here!" the organist wailed, clutching Willie in a warm, embracing full nelson. "For weeks, I've been getting nothing but sour notes from this accursed instrument. "Here, just look," he whined as he showed Willie the latest one:

Dear Mr. Organist: You couldn't tickle my ivories with an ostrich feather. You are so inept, you make Handel's *Messiah* sound like *Jingle Bells*. When will you wise up and find something you can actually play? Like maybe the radio.

Sincerely yours,
A. Whirlitzer

"There, you see what I mean?" complained the unhappy man.

"Uh, yeah," Willie answered as he wondered what on Earth this had to do with him.

"If you can't get it fixed by the end of the sermon, I'll have to play the offertory on the bongo drums, and that so antagonizes the congregation."

"Oh, so you expect me to fix it," Willie realized.

"Precisely. We pay in cheap sacerdotal wine, after the job's finished."

"Well in that case, let me at it," Willie enthused as he snatched the pipe cleaners from the worried hymnster. He was still trying to figure out what to do when the Reverend Jimmy Jack Squatt began his sermon.

"Brethren and sistern," he intoned solemnly, "I have come to talk to you today about sin, and I mean sin in a place where you might not think to look for it. I am referring to sin within married life. More to the point, I am talking about the sin of for-no-ca-tion.

"'Why, Reverend Squatt,' you may well ask, 'isn't it all right to for-no-cate if you're married? Don't we have the legal right to *do it* all we want?'

"Well, I have news for you, my friends. For-no-ca-tion is a sin, plain and simple! Oh, sure, the Lord is willin', to look the other way, ever' once in a while, but only so good Christian married folk can produce more good Christians to carry on His work. I am quite sure that the Lord God Almighty did not intend the sin of for-no-ca- tion to become your favorite recreation, second only to television itself.

"Now I bet most of you so-called respectable married people are thinking to yourselves, 'He must be talkin' about some other couple that *does it* more than we do.'

"Am I? Am I talking about your neighbor, or am I talking about you, Christian?

"Let's see who I'm talking about and who I'm not. Let me take a little poll amongst this congregation, and you best be honest because the very salvation of your soul is at stake.

"I'm going to ask the men, just the married men out there,

how many of you supposably respectable Christian men for-no-
cate with your wives three or more times a week?"

A dozen hands went up.

"You're sinners!" the preacher thundered. "Mark my words
and mark them well. Unless you forsake your rapacious ways
and devote your lives to Jesus *right now*, you shall burn, I say
burn, in the everlasting fires of Hell!

"Now then," he continued, after a deep breath, "how many of
you men for- no-cate with your wives only two or three times a
week?"

Twenty hands went up.

"Well you're no better!" he raged. His fist pounded the po-
dium to the rhythm of his words. "Your gross, disgusting dis-
plays of sexual excess are just as displeasing to the Almighty as
that first bunch. Mend your ways, people, or you'll pay dearly in
the afterlife

"Tell me," the reverend went on as he tried to smooth his hair
back in place, "are there any men out there who do it with your
wives once a week?"

As the poll continued, Willie realized he was at a complete loss to fix the massive instrument that had been left in his
charge.

"Three or four times a year?" the preacher called out as
Willie tossed the pipe cleaners in the air and sat wearily down
on the bench.

"Too much!" moaned the unhappy pastor to the three men
who had raised their hands, "Far, far far too much. Oh, Lord, I
implore You, have mercy on these poor misguided sinners, provided they mend their wicked ways, PDQ!

"I am beginning to wonder about this congregation. Are
there any men out there who for-no-cate with their wives twice
a year?"

One very old man in the second pew raised his hand.

"I suppose you think you are a good Christian," the Reverend Squatt told him. "Well, I have some pret-ty disturbing news for you, mister. Your conduct offends the Lord grievously. Repent, or you shall burn with the others.

"Yes, you shall *all* burn in Hell for ever and ever! I am outraged that such sinfulness can go on in this community! It is with the greatest fear and trepidation in my heart that I ask: is there one good, decent couple out there? Is one true Christian present who only for-no-cates with his wife once a year?"

"Me, me, reverend! Hallelujah!" a man in the back of the church shouted, jumping up and waving his arms frantically.

"Hallelujah indeed," the preacher beamed; "At last, I have found a good Christian amidst this pack of sinners."

"Me, me!" the man in the back repeated, "I'm the one!"

"Praise Jesus," the Reverent Squatt responded. "Allow this fine man's example to shine as a beacon for the rest of you.

"Now then," he continued, "let us remember the words—"

"Me, reverend, me! Praise the Lord God Almighty!" the same man, whose flailing had not ceased or slowed a bit, went on.

"Yes, well, that's very commendable," the Reverend Squatt assured him, "but we really must get on with the service."

"Me, me! Glory hallelujah!" the man persisted.

"Tell me, my son," the preacher sighed, "why in heaven's name are you so agitated?"

"Tonight's the night!" he called out.

While the rest of the congregation was giving the man a standing ovation, the organist leapt to his feet and shoved Willie off the bench. He immediately began playing the chorus from Handel's *Messiah*.

"Beautiful, just swell!" the organist proclaimed. "Hasn't sounded this good in months.

"Alleluia! Alleluia!" he sang. Immediately the choir leapt up to join him.

"Dashing through the snow in a one-horse open sleigh,"

All this commotion baffled Willie who, of course, had done nothing to fix the instrument. Just then, the happy man turned away from his keyboard and explained the situation.

"You see," he told Willie, "all this excitement makes my organ swell."

As the man returned his attention to the keyboard, Willie realized there would be no cheap wine forthcoming. He had no sooner finished storming out of the church when two cops grabbed him by the arm.

"I've got this arm already," the sergeant commanded his rookie partner; "You grab the free arm, get it?"

"Right, Sarge," snapped the rookie as he clamped onto the sergeant's free arm.

"C'mon, you," the sergeant snarled at Willie, "you're comin' with us!"

"But I ain't done nothin'!"

"Yeah, yeah, that's what they all say," the sergeant grumbled.

"I say it all the time," the younger cop added, trying to be helpful.

The older cop rolled his eyes as he wondered how he could have been stuck with this guy.

How that came to pass goes back to when his partner, Stanley Dombrowski, had applied for a place in an upcoming police academy class. At that point only one slot remained, and Dombrowski was but one of three candidates vying for it.

"Now, Lt. Flaherty," the police chief said into the telephone, "I just want to remind you people in personnel, that we've been getting a lot of flack from the public and the press lately about ethnic prejudice. Not just the blacks, but lots of the other types as well."

"Oh, yes, sir," agreed the officer, "indeed we have."

"And it's important, lieutenant, very important, you keep that in mind when you interview prospects for this next class of cadets."

"I certainly will, sir."

"So, here's what I want you to do," the chief told him. "I want you to devise a question you can ask these candidates that will ferret out whether or not they may be too prejudiced to join the force. Do you understand what I'm saying?"

"You can depend on me, sir."

"All right, now, Mr. Goldstein," Lt. Flaherty continued, fixing his stare upon the first interviewee, "I have one last question for you: who killed Jesus Christ?"

"It was the Romans! It definitely was the Romans!" Goldstein raged. "Why to the *goyim* still keep blaming the Jews?" I tell you, the Romans did it!"

"I don't know," Lt. Flaherty thought as he wearily rubbed his eyes, "perhaps the lad is one of these here militant Zionists you hear about. Better be cautious with this one.

"Well," he told the candidate, "thank you for comin' in, Mr. Goldstein. We'll be getting' back to you shortly, one way or the other."

As neared the end of his interview with the next candidate, Lt. Flaherty leaned in toward the young man and inquired: "now then, Mr. Fettuccini, can you tell me who killed Jesus Christ?"

"It was the Jews! Don't nobody listen to the Pope no more?" Fettuccini raged, "It was the Jews killed Jesus Christ! What are ya, stupid? Look it up!"

"That's fine, Mr. Fettuccini," the lieutenant assured him as he mentally put the candidate on the 'dubious' list; "We'll get back to you real soon."

Flaherty may have thought that his first two interviews that day had been a little difficult, but they felt like coffee breaks compared to the ordeal of trying to interview Dombrowski. Finally, after a struggle the like of which he had not experienced in over fifteen years on the force, he came to the last question.

"All, right, Mr. Dombrowski," he sighed, "one last question: who killed Jesus Christ?"

"Um, uhhh, I dunno," the candidate admitted. "Can I get back to you on that one?"

The sparkle reappeared in Flaherty's eyes. At last! Here was a lad who didn't go flying off the handle with some kind of bigoted answer. Sure, this was the kind the chief was looking for.

"Well, Mr. Dombrowski, you've done just fine!" beamed the lieutenant; "We'll be getting' back to you real soon, you can be sure a' that."

When he came home that evening, Dombrowski's anxious mother greeted him.

"Tell me, Stasha," she asked, "did you get into the academy?"

"Not only did I get in," he grinned, "they've already put me on a murder case!"

"Look, Willie protested, "whatever this is, I'm innocent."

"Aah, tell it to the Marines," the sergeant growled from the passenger seat.

Right then Dombrowski took a hairpin left turn and brought the squad car to a halt in front of the MarineWorld Water and Self-Amusement Park.

"Here we are, Sarge."

While the sergeant was running as hard as he could in a valiant but vain attempt to kick his partner in the pants, Willie took the opportunity to sneak away.

"God dammit, our prisoner's escaped!" the sergeant roared as he rushed back to the car. By then, Willie had hidden among the rides.

"Hell!" the older cop stewed as they stood by the merry-go-round, "I wish I could turn some lights on."

"Here, I'll throw the light switch," Dombrowski offered, but all was still dark. Then, the merry-go-round began to move.

"Help!" called Willie from atop a wooden horse.

"Sarge, I think he's coming around."

"What?" the doctor asked.

"I said I think he's coming around," answered the intern at the de-tox center as Willie's eyes fluttered, then reluctantly opened.

"Does this mean things will get back to normal now?" the intern asked.

"After a fashion, son," the doctor replied. "After a fashion."

III

"Name?" the nurse snapped at Willie from across the desk.

"Um, uh, William McGurk."

"I see..." said the nurse as she pulled a rectal thermometer from her pocket and began to write. "Now what asshole has my pen?" she fumed.

"You're here from the detox center, aren't you?" she asked him.

"Yes, m'am, for observation."

"Well, why else would you be here?"

"You mean I gotta think of another reason?"

Eventually Willie was admitted to the hospital for what they all came to agree was "observation."

"Tell me," commanded the psychiatrist as he showed Willie a picture of a circle beside a triangle, "what does this bring to mind?"

"Sex," came the speedy reply.

"Strange," the analyst muttered, "and this?" He held up an

image of three parallel lines.

"Sex."

"Hmmm. All right then, what about this?" the doctor inquired as he showed him a picture of a ladder.

"Sex."

"My, you certainly seem to have sex on the brain."

"Me?" Willie shot back, "Hey, you're the one with all the dirty pictures."

"Well lookaheah," Old Johnson chuckled as an orderly wheeled Willie into the ward, "if it ain't my favorite honky! How you is, bro?"

"Uh, I dunno," Willie replied as he studied the man's wrinkled face, "Am I suppose to know you or somethin'?"

"Heh, heh! McGoik, you sho' nuff gotcho haid messed up," Johnson noted. "Least ah know why ah's heah.

"Yeah," he went on, "It was on accounta this dog, you unnastane. I'm hangin' out in the city dump when this big ol' shaggy-lookin' dog run up an' like to bite my leg off Whooee! You wanna ax me 'bout some pain? Boy, ahmo tell you..."

But by that time, Willie had plunged out the window and was stumbling down the road in his hospital gown.

"Mrs. Leotis van Dandt, that's it," Willie recalled as he struggled toward the dump. "The Exorbitant Towers Condominia, suite some, huff, damn, huff, thing, hufff..."

He stopped by a telephone pole and leaned on it, trying to catch his breath. Then he heard a familiar voice behind him shout, "Aha!", but when he spun around in panic, there was nobody there.

Nor was anybody at the dump, but that was okay. If the dog had come there twice, Willie reasoned, he'd probably come back a third time.

"And dat's when I'm gonna make me a big pile of money."

He lay down in the back seat of an abandoned car. As he shut

his eyes, he imagined himself as he would be: a man of respect
with a cool hundred grand to his name...

"Uh, lookaheah, bro, do, uh, monsoor have zee rezzivation?"
inquired Old Johnson, the maitre d' at the exclusive *Pied du
Cochon*.

"S'a mattera fack, I don't, Ace," Willie sneered between
puffs of his fat, previously unsmoked cigar. "Whyn't you remedy dat li'l detail?" he asked with a wink, as he slipped Johnson
a fifty.

"Yassuh, toot sweet!" the host replied as he led Willie to a
table that a dentist and his wife had already waited forty-five
minutes for.

"Carçonne!" Willie called out.

"Oui, monsieur?" his waitress responded.

"Bring me a caraffey of your house wine and a magnum of
the cheapest champagne what ya got."

"Does monsieur weesh to order ze dinnair at zis time?"

"Yeah, I'll have the roast grackle wit' all th' trimmin's"

"But, monsieur, we 'ave no such a thing on ze menu."

"What, no trimmins?" Willie snorted. "Hell of a way to run a
eatery, if you ask me. Well, in that case, change my dinner order
to a bottl'a your second most cheapest champagne."

Willie turned over in his sleep and drooled contentedly on the
tattered seat cover.

"I tell ya, Flanagan, it's true," he taunted the barkeep. His
nemesis, Flanagan, had sworn that Willie would never sponge
another drink off him again, but that was before

WILLIE McGURK AND HIS
FAMOUS ***TALKING DOG***...UM...UM
WHAT'S-HIS-NAME!

"And I s'pose yer goin' ta tell me this here mangy mutt can

talk."

"He sure as hell can," Willie replied as he rubbed the dog's shaggy head. "Whyn't you just put up a little inducement, and I'll have him do his stuff."

"All right, McGurk," the suspicious bartender scowled, "here's a bottle a' the cheapest wine I got. Now let's see what that dog a' yers can do."

"Nothin' to it," Willie told him after taking a big long pull from the bottle.

"Listen now, bwah," he commanded the dog, "I want you to tell all these fine people here, who was the greatest ballplayer ever."

"Roof! Roof!" the dog answered.

"Why ya dirty swindlin' son of a bitch!" Flanagan shouted, although he actually meant Willie. He grabbed the baseball bat he kept behind the bar. "I'll play ball with your head, ya rotten, connivin'..."

Willie ran out of the place with the irate proprietor in hot pursuit, thumping him now and then with the bat.

"Ouch! Hey! Jesus, whatsa matta?" he complained as he tried to put some distance between himself and the principal product of Louisville. Finally, Flanagan gave up the chase and returned to the bar, holding one foot off the ground, for he was hopping mad.

As Willie nursed his bruises, he glared at the animal.

"A fine mess you made outa things!" he moaned.

"Maybe I shoulda said DiMaggio," the dog suggested.

Willie stirred uneasily in the back seat.

"Roof! Roof!" The dog said.

"Aaah, stow it," Willie mumbled.

"Roof! Roof!" the dog repeated.

He sat up with a start.

"Roof! Roof!" It was coming from fifty feet away.

"The chickens is comin' home to roast," Willie gloated.

As he squinted, he could make out the dog's form in the faint light of the dawn.

"Nice doggie," he ventured.

The dog growled.

"C'mon, nice doggie," he implored his prey, "ya wanna yummy dog biscuit?" He smiled hopefully as he held out a wet cigar butt. The dog peered quizzically at him.

The encounter was abruptly cut short by the squeal of tires and the roar of an engine as a sports car tore down the road at top speed. Nothing Willie might have in his hand could hope to compete with the taste of hot wheels on the roll, so the dog tore off in an instant. In the next instant, Willie was running down the highway in pursuit. While it is a topic for hot debate in some circles today (the Arctic and a couple others, to name three) whether the dog lost sight of the car before Willie lost sight of the dog, there remains little doubt in any but the most twisted minds that, lose sight of the dog he did.

Exhausted beyond his wildest dreams (see above), he flopped down onto a park bench to organize his thoughts.

"The hell with it," he concluded.

He sought to take his mind off the disappointing turn of events by swiping a bag of candy from the five and dime and heading off to the grade school playground around the corner. The children, as it happened, were just going back inside after morning recess.

"Damn!" thought Willie, for whom nothing had been working out lately.

He settled under a shady tree to catch a few winks, waiting for the kids to be let out again. Instead, he slept until the end of the school day and would have slept through that if the big wooly dog that had taken a liking to nine-year-old Ira Pitkin and, thus, decided to follow him home, had not been so noisily enthusiastic about the whole thing.

"Roof! Roof!" the dog remarked. Willie came to in a second. Using such stealth as he could, considering the length of time since his last bath, Willie trailed the dog to the boy's home. He had crept quite close in preparation to snatch the dog, when Ira's mother opened the front door.

"Look, Mom, he followed me home. Can I keep him?" the youngster begged his mother.

Mrs. Pitkin, having spotted Willie, rather than the dog, failed to construe her son's meaning and, as a result got a bit flustered.

"You rotten, lousy pervert!" she screamed, then lunged at Willie with the eight iron she grabbed from the umbrella stand, "I'll kill you with my bare hands!

"Police! POLICE!" she shrieked as she chased Willie down the street, flailing away at him with the club in the hope of extricating him from the sand trap of life.

"Hey, Sarge," the rookie cop in the patrol car pointed out to his partner, "there's some broad callin' for the police. Maybe we should swing by and tell her to dial 119."

"That's 911, Dombrowski," the sergeant mumbled half awake. "Can't you get anything straight?"

So relieved was Mrs. Pitkin to learn Ira meant the dog and not the bum, she was only too happy to let her son keep the animal, whom, as Mr. Pitkin was to find out later that evening, the child had decided to name Maurice.

IV

Life had not always been easy for Harold Pitkin, father of Ira Pitkin and recent co- owner of a shaggy dog named Maurice. The youngest of three children, Harold was the only one in the family who was entirely whole. His brother, Neal, had lost both legs below the kneecap while cleaning a loaded machete. His sister, Ilene, had simply been born with a right leg longer than the left. (She would later join the Peace Corps and become the only volunteer ever to serve a tour of duty in Pisa. It is extremely important for the reader to keep that in mind.). Their father, Nick, a barber with a bad case of Parkinson's, was hardly able to support the family, especially after his wife, Annette, lost her job on a fishing scow, due to the floundering economy. By that time, it had become apparent that young Harold would have to find a job to help his family get by.

He secured a position as a produce clerk at Machiavelli's Market, with slim prospect for advancement until, one day, a customer approached him and demanded to know the price for half a head of lettuce.

"We don't have half a heads of lettuce," he pointed out to the man.

"What?" the irate customer shouted, "Exactly what kind of game are you shysters trying to pull, anyway? I'm reporting you to the BBB; no, better yet, my attorneys."

"Now, sir, there's no need to get all worked up," Harold assured him.

"Oh, so you are going to give me the price on half a head of lettuce?"

"Well, like I said," Harold tried to explain, "we don't exactly have—"

"JUST AS I THOUGHT!" the shopper stormed. "I think I'd better expose you con artists to the media!"

"I tell you what, sir, let me go check with my boss," Harold suggested.

"Yeah, you do that!"

Harold walked back to the boss's office and poked his head in the door.

"Mr. Machiavelli, I'm sorry to bother you, but there's some jerkwad who wants to buy half a head of lettuce." Harold turned around and saw that, unbeknownst to him, the customer had followed him to the office. "And this fine gentleman, here, wants to buy the other half."

"Kid, you seem like you're really on the ball," Mr. Machiavelli complimented him afterward, "D'ja ever think of goin' to college?"

"Oh, I don't know, I guess."

"How 'bout Georgia Tech. D'ja ever hear of Georgia Tech?"

"Yeah," Harold said, "I hear all they got down there are whores and football players."

"Hey! My *wife* went to Georgia Tech!" the wise old grocer informed Harold as he reached for a meat cleaver.

"Oh, really?" Harold gulped, "And what position did she play?"

Harold wound up accepting Machiavelli's advice on two key points: 1) that he should go to college and make something out of himself, and 2) that he should get the hell out of the store before he got his goddamn head chopped off.

He studied botany at the state university. Degree in hand, he had no trouble finding work as an insurance salesman for Feelings Mutual Calamity and Casualty Company a mere two and a half years later.

He had not been on the job very long before he came across Carla Fabbrizzio, Secretary to the Vice President of Paper Clip Control. This lady was built, as they liked to say in the business, like a brick, single-family, owner-occupied outbuilding.

Mustering his courage like never before, Harold bought her a paper clip sampler, presented it to her and asked her out to lunch. Eventually they were married.

"Gee, I hope Uncle Luigi makes it down all right," Carla fretted as the day of their wedding approached. Uncle Luigi, the only one in either family with any money, lived in New York and had elected to ride the train down to Miami for his niece's wedding.

"Don't worry," Carla's father assured her as the train pulled into the station, "there he is, getting off now.

"Hey, Luigi," he asked his brother, "How was the trip, eh?"

"It was-a no good," Luigi grumbled. "I'm-a get onna train in New York, okay? Then I light up dis-a nice big cigar, and the condotorre, he come along anna say, Ey! No canna smoke no cigar on dissa train!'

"So, I say, okay, I no smoka no cigar I don' wanna mak' no troble.

"Then, as we leavin' outa Piladelphia, I bring out my bottla *vino*. Before I'm-a tak' even one sip of her, here come dat same condotorre guy again. 'Ey!' he say to me, 'no canna drinka no *vino* on dissa train!'

"And if thatsa no bad enough, when we pull outa Wilmington, I take out my *pannino* I'm-a bring for the trip, an' whaddaya know: here come that same damn condotorre. 'No can eata you sannawich on dissa train. You hungry, you go to the dining car anna you buy somethin', capeesh?'

"Well, I'm –a really gettin' mad now, but what can you do? I no wanna mak' troble.

"But then, when the train come into Washington, somethin' good finally happen to Luigi! Dissa fine, good-lookin' nice young girl, she come on the train and sit down right next to me. Well, we start to talk about one t'ing, then another, anna she's eatin' up everyt'ing I'm-a say! So I tell myself, 'Luigi, dissa you big chance, mak' you move! The train's about to stop at the next station. What if she get off?'

"So I get set to mak' my move when, guess what? There's that damn condotorre again, except dissa time, he no come up tell me in private like before. No, he gotta stand inna doorway an' shout so everybod' can hear: 'No'folka Virgin'! No'folka Virgin'!'"

"Don't you dare laugh at my uncle," Carla hissed as she saw her fiancé doing a bad job of trying to stifle a chuckle. "He's got no kids and a pile of money. You damn well better not get us on his bad side!"

Not long after they were married, Harold and Carla had their first child, a daughter, whom they christened Helga, after one of Harold's favorite hurricanes. The name did not sit well with Uncle Luigi, much to their consternation. Only with repeated assurances that he'd get to select name of their next child did they manage to struggle back into his good graces.

As it turned out, Uncle Luigi was visiting when Carla went back into labor, while her husband happened to be on a business trip.

"I didn't forget," she reminded her uncle as they sped to the hospital, "You decide the name this time."

Harold had not been entirely happy with the whole idea. "You know, your Uncle Luigi's not too bright. I'm afraid he'll stick the kid with some really dumb name."

"I'll tell ya what's dumb," his wife explained to him. "What's dumb is gettin' cut outta his will, which he might do if we don't keep our promise."

That night, Harold phoned the hospital.

"Well, has it happened yet?" he asked the nurse at the maternity desk. "What did we get, a boy or a girl?"

"Mr. Pitkin," the nurse replied, "you are to be congratulated. Your wife gave birth to twins at 11:30 this morning. You have one of each: a boy and a girl. Mother and babies are healthy and doing fine."

"Wow, that's great!" Harold observed. "Tell me, was my wife's uncle Luigi…"

"Mr. Fabbrizzio?" the nurse answered, "Yes, sir, he returned to the hospital as soon as he heard."

"And did he name the, uh…"

"Oh, yes," the nurse confirmed. "Your daughter's name is Denise."

"Not bad," thought the new father of three. Maybe he had been a little hard on Uncle Luigi.

"And your son's name is Denephew."

"Christ on a bicycle," Willie muttered impatiently from behind the bushes where he kept the Pitkin home under constant surveillance.

Five years later they had their final child, Ira, who would grow partially up to adopt the shaggy stray, Maurice.

When Ira was born, the Pitkins were still quite poor. Harold, so far, had failed to make much of a go of the insurance business. Another three years would pass before the light bulb in his thought balloon finally lit up.

It started with the district sales manager deciding to have a little fun at the expense of his worst salesman, the better to pass a tiresome summer day. He put Harold onto a "hot" prospect named Tyrone Schuze. He had neglected to convey that Mr. Schuze was "a major loon."

To the manager's surprise, Harold sold the guy a policy with the greatest of ease.

Two days later, as he waited at his desk in wonderment of where the next lead might be coming from, the receptionist's voice came over the intercom.

"Mr., Pitkin, there's a...er...Mr. Edna Saint...what?

"Excuse me, there's a *Miss* Edna Saint Vincent Millay to see you." When he strolled out to meet this odd-sounding prospect, he was surprised to find Tyrone Schuze in drag. Making the most (and heretofore only) brilliant decision of his career, Harold did not let on there was anything amiss. In even less time than it took to sell the original policy to Mr. Schuze, he had sold an identical one to Ms. Millay.

Two days later, the receptionist advised him there was a Mr. Bonaparte to see him. By this time, Harold was starting to get the idea. He sought out multiple personality types wherever he could find them and dedicated himself to taking care of all, and he meant *all* their insurance needs. His commissions soared through the roof. By the end of the year, he was petitioning the court to have the twins' names changed, and the money kept rolling in.

"Y'know, Honey," he mused one night as he casually lit his Havana cigar with a twenty, "it's too bad I didn't think of this angle sooner."

"You said it," his wife agreed as she dipped another corn chip into the caviar.

"But, even though it's too late for us, I think we oughta see to it the kids pick up some class .Like for instance, I think we should send Helga to that finishin' school we heard about so she can get some extra spit and polish."

Thus did they decide to enroll their firstborn in the most expensive such school around: Miss Swithington's School for Young Ladies of Breeding. The tuition was astronomical. True to its voluminous late-night advertisements on the TV, the course of instruction was thorough and rigorous. Only after a full two years of exhaustive drill was a student allowed to take the final exam, which consisted of hosting a formal dinner party for a dozen distinguished guests. Even the slightest faux pas would result in the student's having her diploma ripped up right before her eyes, emblematic of failure.

Head erect, Helga walked tensely behind Miss Swithington as the headmistress began inspecting the preparations for the party.

"What's this, Miss Pitkin?" the lady demanded to know as she tapped a gloved fingernail (her own) on the table next to one of the sugar bowls. " I see no tongs. You have failed the course."

"Oh, no!" wailed the distraught girl, "I can't believe this! You mean you're gonna rip up my diploma just for some lousy tongs?"

"Precisely, my dear."

"But why," Helga continued to protest. "Why can't people just pick the sugar cubes up? Why do I gotta have tongs?"

"My dear child, you know nothing," replied the exasperated headmistress. "Very well, I'll explain to you how serious your breech of etiquette actually is.

"You see...well...when the gentlemen go to their, uh, bathroom, as it were, well...they must perforce handle themselves, so to speak. No hostess in her right mind would let them touch the sugar cubes with those same fingers. Now report to my office."

Of course Helga's parents were disappointed, but by no means discouraged.

"We all learn from our mistakes Sweetie," Harold comforted her as he wrote another enormous check to Miss Swithington's school. The poor girl endured another two years of close-order etiquette, then prepared once again for the dreaded final exam.

Miss Swithington donned her white gloves and marched forth to begin her inspection. She went right to the nearest sugar bowl and gasped.

"Why, I...I...can't *believe* it!" she squealed in her outrage. "This is precisely why you failed the last time, young lady! I even told you why, and look! No tongs in sight!"

"Apparently," Miss Pitkin replied in her haughtiest tone, "you've not taken the trouble to check the gentlemen's bathroom."

Meanwhile, her father had, by dint of his spectacular sales record, risen to the rank of Deputy Assistant Vice President of the company and been named Insurance Man of the Year by the prestigious Association of Insurance Underwriters and Editors. In addition, he had been awarded a jumbo sketchpad when he asked for a bigger draw on his commissions..

It was during this period that Tyrone Schuze had penned a

letter to the Czar of Russia in which he stated his intention to finish the job he had started in 1812, of burning Moscow to the tundra. Being Napoleon at the time, he had felt obligated to compose the letter in French, a language he did not remember all that clearly from his high school days. Well, nobody said conquering half the civilized world was going to be easy. It was only after a difficult two-day struggle that he was finally able to send this grim message to his Russian opponent:

> Le Czar
> Le Kremlin
> Moscow, Russia 44113
> Mon Cher le Czar:

> J'entre dans la sale de classe. Je prends ma cahier et mon crayon. Le crayon est bleu. Le ciel est bleu aussi. Vive La France.

> Bonsoir,
> "Boney"

Several months of cryptographic endeavor ensued, after which cunning linguists in the Kremlin finally deciphered the coded message for what it was: a clear and present threat to burn their city down.

The extremists on the Central Committee, led by Field Marshall Piztov, called for a pre-emptive nuclear strike. It was the field marshall's own subordinate, Field Deputy Sheriff Takeiteasky, who suggested a more practical plan.

"Comrades," he pointed out, whereupon his finger was immediately frostbitten, "rather than start World War III this far ahead of schedule, let us consider a more sensible approach: fire insurance."

"Fire insurance?" snorted the Premier, awakening with a start, "This is Socialist Workers' Paradise. Who amongst us would stoop to such a filthy capitalist trick as fire insurance?"

"Nobody, of course," agreed Takeiteasky, "but here is no problem! We'll buy such insurance from the Americans. They'll sell us anything." The wily tactician proceded to explain that, if they took out coverage on every major structure in the city, the imminent conflagration could result in a huge claim against the forces of imperialism. "Why, it will cost them hundreds!" he chortled.

After careful and thorough consideration of the matter, the Central Committee chose Feelings Mutual Calamity & Casualty company to write them a policy for the entire city of Moscow.

"These people must be crazy," declared the president of the company when he read the Central Committee's proposal.

"It's the wildest, most hare-brained idea I ever heard of," agreed the executive vice president, a former district sales manager.

"The very notion," he continued, "of us sending over a..." He stopped and smiled.

"Pitkin!" they both said at once.

"Hey, Maurice, guess what?" Ira Pitkin shouted in a voice that never failed to make Willie grind his teeth, "You and me are goin' to Moscow!"

V

The task would not be easy. Willie, who had been turned away at the Mexican border as an undesirable alien, did not move well in your international circles. And now it looked like he was going to have to trail that damn dog all the to Russia if he couldn't find a way to snatch him right here. His chances of success remained slim, as long as Mrs. Pitkin persisted in walking their pet with the the ever-present eight-iron clenched in her free fist.

"If I can't grab the dog here," Willie figured, "maybe I can stow away and take it over there."

To be sure, even if he managed to smuggle himself into the Soviet Union, there remained the extremely difficult matter of smuggling himself out with the dog. But then, he guessed, the Soviet border guards couldn't possibly be more difficult to deal with than Mrs. Pitkin and her sand wedge. But, until he devised a plan, none of that made any difference.

As the family's departure day drew near, Willie finally spotted his chance. He noticed a large steamer trunk standing on its end along with some other bags and cartons, inside the Pitkins' screened-in porch. More important, he noticed that Mrs. Pitkin, the dog and the eight-iron had all gone out for a stroll. Willie crept up to the porch, where he found the door unlocked.

"It's now or never," he sighed.

He made a pass through the kitchen, filling his pockets with whatever food he thought would not be missed . Then, he bored three holes into the steamer trunk, after which, he opened it. The trunk was crammed full of old, smelly, very used clothing. After he had removed the clothes inside, he could see there would be enough room for him inside the trunk, but first he needed to dispose of those clothes, so that the Pitkins would not think there was anything amiss. It was at that point, he noticed two large, empty suitcases. He threw the displaced articles of clothing into the empty suitcases, then shut them. After making sure none of the removed contents of the trunk lay conspicuously around, he climbed in and shut the lid behind him.

Willie had just drifted off to sleep inside the steamer trunk when Carla Pitkin came back from the Happy Pet Doggie Motel, where Maurice would stay, to little Ira's bitter disappointment, during the family's lengthy visit to Moscow.

That evening, Helga, who had acquired a pair of sugar tongs with which to impress the worldly, sophisticated Soviets, was somewhat taken aback when she tried to practice with them. "Very well," she inquired in the genteel fashion she had so painstakingly cultivated, "who hogged alla goddamn sugar cubes, huh?"

VI

"I guess we packed enough to last us three months," Harold calculated as he reviewed the family luggage rolling by on the baggage carts. As ever, he was grateful Carla had tended to of most of the details, including packing his bags. After twenty-one years of marriage, he trusted her judgment. Still, he could not help going over the last- minute stuff they had to take care of.

"Let's see, dog's in the kennel; golf clubs locked in the basement; paper's been stopped...what else?" he thought. "Oh, right, that charity business.

"Dear," he asked his wife, "did you manage to send those old clothes off to Father Gilhooley before we left?"

"Yeah," she answered without looking up from her magazine, "he said he was happy to get 'em too. Said they were goin' to some orphanage at Tierra del Fuego."

"Where's Terradel Foogio, Mom?" Ira asked.

"I dunno, honey, somewhere in Puerto Rico."

"Y'know, I don't mind gettin' rid of those clothes," Harold added, "but it seems like the waste of a perfectly good steamer trunk to send it off to some orphanage in the middle of nowhere."

"Yeah, well, it wasn't all that good," Carla pointed out. "I noticed three holes in the thing when the church people came to cart it away."

The flight to Moscow was uneventful and, like clockwork, as

the Pitkins touched down in Moscow's Sheremetyevo Airport, their luggage touched down in Pittsburgh.

"Rest assured, comrade tourists, a liaison officer commanded the passengers, "your luggage will materialize shortly. Meanwhile, you are invited as honored guests to a tour of our grand and glorious city."

As if on cue, a uniformed officer from the Ministry of Tourism appeared, ready to take the Pitkins and their fellow travelers to see what he assured them were the "hot spots" of Moscow.

"Notice the clean, immaculate tiles," the tourguide pointed out to them as they beheld the wonders of the Moscow subway system, "not covered with filthy graffiti, like in your New York City."

"That's the truth," Harold agreed. "Say," he added, "what do the trains look like?"

"Notice also," the guide pointed out, glaring at Harold, "how entire station is free from crime. As you witness with your own eyes, nobody is being mugged, such as happens in America all the time, yes?"

"Oh, yes, constantly," Harold again agreed, to the great and everlasting humiliation of his children. "Say, when do you suppose we might get to see one of the trains?"

"And here," the guide continued, resolutely ignoring Harold, "is vending machine that dispenses your famous Pepsi Cola. Note, if you will, this major difference: in our stations, Soviet citizen can deposit his money and be confident he will receive Pepsi. In New York, the machines just take your money and give you nothing, *nyet*?"

"You bet," Harold answered him, blissfully unaware of his wife's frantic signals to shut the hell up, "it happens all the time. I'm still curious, though, what about your trains?"

"Yes," growled the exasperated tourguide, "and what about your lynchings in the South?"

Finally, when it seemed that the Pitkins could not possibly

paint the town any redder, they were reunited with their luggage at the hotel suite.

"Good thing for us," Harold sighed, "I've been sweating like a pig in these clothes.

"Hey, honey," he asked his wife, "which suitcase's got my good pinstripe suit? I want to hang it up before it gets too wrinkled."

"How the hell should I know?" she replied. Here the lazy slob had packed his own bags for the first time, like, ever, and still he expects her to tell him what's where.

"Fine," Harold muttered as he hoisted the nearest suitcase onto their bed, "I'll find it myself."

He unlatched and lifted the lid. The first thing he saw was a frayed, dirty halter top inscribed, SOUVENIR OF CYPRESS GARDENS. The rest of the rumpled clothes in the bag were of a similar nature.

"The hell's goin' on here?" he wondered as he swept the one suitcase off the bed and brought up the other, from which he extracted a yellow T-shirt that read, MY MOM AND DAD WENT TO PALM SPRINGS AND ALL I GOT WAS THIS LOUSY T- SHIRT.

"Carla," Harold called out, waving a training bra at his wife, "this is the crap we gave to the church!"

"*Buenos dias, compadre,*" whispered the young revolutionary upon opening the steamer trunk. "The Premier said he would find a way to bring you here. *Viva la revolucion!*"

Willie blinked several times and looked around. This did not look like Moscow.

VII

Let their history books tell you about *El Libertador, Guillermo McGorque.* Let the C.I.A speculate on whatever became of "Secret Agent M." Here is what actually happened.

Willie, who certainly wanted no part of anyone's revolution, was on the verge of telling those foreigners to buzz off, when two very important details were brought to his attention. First, they were too poor to pay him in anything but cheap wine. Second, once the revolution got under way, they would probably need to dispatch him to Moscow.

"You mean where dat dog's at?" Willie asked.

"No, señor," his translator tried to esplain, "I mean Moscow that is in Russia."

The ensuing firebombing and killing tended to go against Willie's grain. Moreover, the miserably cold Tierra del Fuegan climate was doing his rheumatism no good whatsoever. But then he had that good cheap wine on hand to take the edge off of things. More important, there was the prospect of being sent to Moscow, where he could snatch the dog, that spurred him on.

Certainly it's what sustained him the night the authorities arrested and brutally tortured him in an effort to force him to name names. (Willie had generally stayed too drunk to remember the men's names or to learn any Spanish beyond the ever-popular *Mas vino, por favor.*) The dream of finding the dog must have sustained him even further when his own men staged a daring raid to rescue him in the course of which, Willie was only slightly less fire-bombed than the jail itself.

As the struggle continued, hot scraps and fragments of the 200 billion dollars the United States was spending to keep Tierra del Fuego out of the Communist sphere lodged themselves in Willie's much-abused flesh with ever-increasing regularity. It was going to be tougher than ever to grab that dog without the left foot and right arm he was now missing. Perhaps, he mused as field surgeons clumsily attempted to reattach the ear he had lost, he should throw in the towel and write the whole thing off to experience.

Then, he heard a rustling in the bushes. The guerillas fled, leaving Willie alone on the stretcher.

"Oh, Christ," he whimpered, "this is the end."

"Comrade McGorque," the figure within the shrubbery whispered, "it is time to go to Moscow. That is in Russia."

A few miles away, federal agent Angus McPherson Waddy picked up the field phone and rang his headquarters, a hastily-assembled task force known as the Departmental Office Of Direct Assistance.

"This is Scotty Waddy, DOODA! Scotty Waddy, DOODA!" he barked into the receiver.

"Please specify," returned the laconic voice from HQ, "Are you day team or night team?"

"Scotty Waddy, DOODA: day!" the operative snapped.

"Okay, what do you have?" his contact asked.

"I got something really big. I just learned they're sending a chopper for 'Secret Agent M' at 2100 hours tonight."

"Oh, yeah?" asked the HQ operator, trying to sound casual. "You got Zero Perceptual Defects on the site? If so, which Zero Perceptual Defects Plan do you want to initiate, 'A' or 'B'?"

"Roger, that's Z.P.D., DOODA: Z.P.D. 'A'," Waddy replied, "So I'll need some Direct Assistance dispatched to Sector 37, NLT 2030 hours.

"That's a big four-ten, good buddy," the operator assured Waddy, meaning that they were going to send him their latest and best weapon for the mission: the deadly M-410 Wine-seeking Rocket Launcher.

The formidable M-410 Missile System had worked fine when tested under ideal conditions at the Napa Valley Proving Grounds, but those tests had not allowed for the contingency that the target might nod off and drop its wine bottle out of the chopper, after the rocket was launched. As a result of exactly this kind of mishap, the projectile failed to obliterate the helicopter, not that Agent Waddy cared. Enough of the missile had hit and damaged the dorsal propeller to send the craft into a long, wild spiral, ever downward into the none-too-tepid waters of the southernmost Atlantic.

"That's close enough for government work," Waddy noted as he admired the spectacle through his field glasses.

VIII

"Trenton makes, the world takes," Ira Pitkin read from the trestle as the train approached the Garden State's capital.

"You mean, 'the world refuses, Trenton uses'," jeered his older brother, Tyrone.

"Don't be so sarcastic," chided Tyrone's twin, Edna. "Actually, I'm glad we had to move. Now we can make new friends."

"I just don't understand it," Carla Pitkin reiterated for the nineteenth time that morning. "All you done for them and they transfer you to *Newark*, for God sakes!"

"Aw, come on, look on the bright side for once," Harold argued. "There's bound to be plenty of crazies in a place like that."

"Yeah, but I bet they're prob'ly poor or something," grumbled his wife.

"Listen, baby, this is a real step up for us, believe me," Harold assured her as he took her hands in his. "Soon as I make my killing here, you'll have a brand-new Mercedes, a condo at Ocean City and hot-and-cold-running help. You watch and see."

Despite what he was telling his wife, the relocation was no reward for a job well done. Not by a long shot. To be sure, Harold Pitkin had closed the deal with the Soviets, though not without considerable difficulty.

Prior to the Pitkins arrival in Moscow, there had been a month-long run on men's clothing at GUM, the city's most prestigious and only department store. The bins had been completely emptied due to a major tree blight that had hit the area's forests a month before. Without the trees, no cardboard was available from which to fashion any more men's suits. Whatever they had in stock had been had been gobbled up long before Harold set foot inside the store.

Thus, Harold had had to make do with what his suitcases held.

After several weeks of long and strenuous negotiations, the Politburo finally come to terms. The policy was drawn up and the premier himself had presented Harold with a healthy check for the first year's premium. And, while the snapshot of a grinning Harold Pitkin shaking the Premier's hand as he proudly accepted the check was a memento the insurance company would always treasure, a little of the majesty inherent to the occasion was taken away due to the red halter-top Harold wore, on which was inscribed SOUVENIR OF CYPRESS GARDENS.

Not long after the deal had been closed, a delegation of Americans eminent in the arts had arranged to visit the Soviet capital as part of a cultural exchange program. What neither the American guests nor their Soviet hosts had noticed was that one member of the delegation was the late poet Edna St. Vincent Millay. A week after their arrival, Moscow was in flames.

The train slowed on its approach into Newark when "Joe Smith" entered the station with the idea of cadging some "ticket money" from a sympathetic traveler or two. The three-block walk from the welfare office on his one good leg had just about worn him out, so his first order of business was to flop down on the nearest empty bench. He placed his crutch carefully beside the seat and shut his eyes tightly as he waited for the pain to subside. Soon he fell into a troubled sleep and dreamt of being bound to an iceberg while penguins shouted incomprehensible Spanish at him.

Then a very familiar voice cut through his reverie.

"Jesus, Harold, will you look at this place!"

"Aw, relax," the voice's husband answered. "It's a train sta-tion: big deal."

Joe Smith straightened up and cupped his only hand to his only ear. There could be no mistaking that voice. Then he spotted a porter who was pushing a cart filled to capacity with various kinds of luggage. On top of all the bags sat a large plastic cage.

"Roof! Roof!" exclaimed the cage's cargo. Nor, Joe Smith re-alized, was there any mistaking that voice either.

Neither the Pitkins, who had been walking well ahead of the cart, nor the porter, who had stopped to play his number, saw Joe Smith remove the cage, however clumsily, from the cart and hobble out of sight.

It took nearly every dime of his welfare check to book pas-sage for him and the dog on the Greyhound—the Greyhound bound for the Exorbitant Towers Condominia, where one Mrs. Leotis van Dandt waited with a big bag of money.

The cage had been a real bother to haul around, but, as Joe Smith hobbled into the Exorbitant Towers, the angry but shaggy dog in what passed for his grip, he wished he had kept the con-tainer after all, if for no other reason than to have avoided the sharp, vicious bites the dog had laid on him.

After a good bit of difficulty, he finally learned what he had failed to remember: that the Great Lady was to be found in Suite 921. Not necessarily wanting to attract the attention of the secu-rity guard, who might glance up from her supermarket tabloid any moment, Joe Smith elected to lug the dog up the nine flights of stairs instead.

At last he arrived, utterly spent, at Suite 921. Sure enough, directly over the door chime was a nameplate inscribed, L. VAN DANDT. A flush of anticipation coursed through him as he rang the bell. Either that or he had caught something from the dog.

The door opened partway. There stood a sour-looking, blue-haired lady of indeterminate age.

"What do you want?" she greeted Joe Smith and his canine companion.

"Lady, I'm here wit' the dog," he panted.

"My good man, what on Earth are you talking about?" she asked him. Well, it had been five years since she posted the notice. Maybe the old broad had gone senile and needed some coaching.

"Don't you remember, lady?" he besought her. "You was offerin' a big reward for the return of your shaggy dog."

"Yes," she snapped, just prior to slamming the door in Willie's face, "but he wasn't *that* shaggy!"

THE WONDERFUL CAKE
By W. Matlida Whitney

We were a little surprised to have received this manuscript from our terpsichorical friend, who, by now,
must be sick and tired of all those drunken Aussies
singing, "Won't you come jitterbugging, Matilda Whitney?"
We were thusly bewildered because her expertise has generally
thought to have been in the field of poetry; more specifically, that
poetry which, when properly set to music, exhorts us to patron-
ize one fast food chain or another used car dealership. The lady
has been at least as well-paid for her work as Rod McKuen and,
at that, she has probably moved more hearts (and merchandise).
This is not to gainsay Ms. Whitney's more "artistic" poetry. Her
recent volume of same, *I Know Why the Caged Bird Molts*, gar-
nered an award for Best-Hyped Book in a Genre Nobody Cares
About Anymore, allowing her to insist that, henceforth, people
address her as "Colonel."

On the other hand, we are relieved well nigh unto the point
of collapse that her rendition of this story is almost entirely a
work of prose, as any well-meaning shaggy dog story should be.
(NOTE: That's a red herring. Well-meaning shaggy dog stories
do not exist).—tcl

I

She could certainly understand his request. After all, it was
her initial too, and one not many people shared. In fact, Marie
Quennelle decided, she would make a point to prepare the cake
herself. The recipe, seemingly, had been left entirely up to her.

Mr. Quigley's only stipulation was that it had to be in the shape
of a "Q." Beyond the shape, he had said, the details were hers
to decide, and price, as is so often the case in these stories, was
no object. Inasmuch as Quentin Q. Quigley owned the fabu-
lously successful U-KLEEN-IT Holistic Car-Wipe Centres, all
of which he had judiciously located downwind of his brother-
in-law's United Soot Works, he could easily disobject to most
any price he might encounter. Additionally, Marie reminded
herself (needlessly, it turned out), the man maintained a mighty
big tab at her bakery, sometimes accounting for as much as
one-third of her monthly gross, depending on either the sloth
of her business or the immensity of his appetite. This cake, to
put it in something other than a nutshell, had damn well better
be good.

"Elmer Lee," she asked her number one baker, the great-
great-great grandson of the illustrious Confederate general,
Murgatroid "Old Whisky Breath" Hevenstew, "how are we doing on rum extract?"

"Rum extract? Why, it's lak we had a pahp line to Trinidad
and Tobacco," he replied.

"What about flour?" she continued. "Aren't we running a
little low?"

"No, ma'am," he assured her. "It's lak cocaine at a Co-lum-
bian tuppah weah party."

"Elmer Lee, can't you just give me a simple yes or no answer?
Where are you getting all these fancy allusions?"

"Oh, I got them from the Dah-jayest, ma'am. You know thet
ther part called tords more picture-skew speech?"

Well," she advised him, "save it for your literary friends."

"Oh, I wouldn't waste mah breff on them," Elmer Lee spat in
disgust. "Anyone throws they trash on the street is no friend of
mine."

After a good deal of thought, inventory, soul-searching and

then a pinch more inventory, Marie finally selected her Savarin recipe. True, it would be a pain to prepare, but she wanted a cake Mr. Quigley would really appreciate.

To make certain she was on the right track, she consulted with her analyst, her priest, her next-door neighbor, her beautician, her drycleaner, the cop on the corner and her mother. Everybody except Father O'Shaughnessy seemed to agree she had hit on exactly the right cake, whatever it was, to please Mr. Quigley. And at that, Father O'Shaughnessy was not so much in disagreement as preoccupied, due to the sudden demise of his church's bell ringer.

"It's a black day for us all," he told her in response to her query. "Sure, and with the passin' on of poor Brother Glimp, why, we've no one to ring those bells the way the good Lord meant for 'em to be rung, doncha know."

At once Marie's face had lit up, though, in retrospect, she too might have agreed it was indeed a black day for us all. For the moment, she had managed to come up with a solution to the old priest's dilemma. Her least loathed brother-in-law's second favorite aunt had a set of rather eccentric twin sons, at least one of whom had mastered the art of ringing church bells. The cathedral of his employ had eliminated his job with the advent (although not on it) of electronic chimes, and so, he was thoroughly available for the vacancy created by Brother Glimp's venture into decomposure.

Father O'Shaughnessy took Marie up on her offer, thereby laying the church bell issue to rest for the moment. Later, difficulties would arise from the new bellringer's rather unorthodox method of bell ringing . To spare himself the use of his arthritic hands, the man had developed a method for ringing the bells that required him to perch in the tower with them. He caught the rim of each one under his chin on the upswing, then, rolling with the momentum as he did, pushed the bell back out with his forehead.

It was, the bellster explained to Father O'Shaughnessy, far less painful than when he had to grip the thick, scratchy bell ropes from below. The quality of the tone was every bit as good as it had been under the Glimp administration, so nothing more was said of the matter. In time the strange fellow in the belfry slipped the priest's mind until, one day, many, many years later, the bell ringer yawed when he should have pitched and, inevitably, plummeted several stories onto the inlaid stones.

As well-wishers and medivac teamsters gathered around the as-yet unidentified body, Father O'Shaughnessy scurried from the rectory to find out why the bells had stopped ringing.

"Father," asked a nearby police sergeant, "can you identify this person?"

The good father's memory had lapsed over the course of time and, at that, from a state wherein there had been precious little room for lapse. At first, he was as stumped as the others. Finally, after several minutes' study, he announced: "Well now, I'll tell you, the face somehow rings a bell."

All was not lost for Father O'Shaughnessy and his parish, though. The unfortunate bellpusher still had a twin brother, likewise with hands too arthritic to tug a weighty rope, to whom he had passed on the (nearly) surefire facial method. As the twin succeeded in catching Father O'Shaughnessy in a moment of lucidity, he managed to get his brother's keep with no fuss and hardly a feather.

Life in the church proceeded smoothly for about six or twenty-seven months. Then, as if preordained, the very same accident befell the twin, and he also befell "right on," as the young people like to say, the inlaid stones.

Again a multitude gathered, and again Father O'Shaughnessy popped forth to investigate the hubbub.

"Father," inquired the same policeman, who in the interim had become a corporal, "any idea on the victim's identity?"

"Well," the priest admitted, "I can't definitely say who, but he's a dead ringer for that fellah who used to work here."

Finally Marie consulted with Elmer Lee, to whom she had delegated the task of making the Q-shaped mold for Mr. Quigley's cake.

"Ah'd say use whatevah recipe suits your fancy. Jes make shoah y'all use plenty of it. If that ol' boy evah had to haul ass, it'd take him five trips."

While Elmer Lee concentrated on his assignment, Marie applied herself to the preparation of the cake. Every item had been chopped, ground or pulverized to perfection. Then, slowly and gingerly, she blended the ingredients together in just the right time and just the right way and just the right temperature. At the end of this monumental effort, the cake had come out beautifully. Not long after they had finished, Mr. Quigley entered the store.

"I bet my cake's ready," he speculated as he rubbed his hands briskly together.

"Why, yes, Mr. Quigley, and what a cake you have," Marie beamed as Elmer Lee hurried to fetch it.

"Look!" she enthused, showing it off to the customer.

"It's garbage. Pure, unadulterated garbage," Mr. Quigley snarled.

"What? Mr. Quigley, how can you *say* such a thing? Why, you haven't even tasted it," Marie replied, choking all the while back the tears.

"I don't need to taste it to know I hate it."

"But Mr. Quigley," she protested, "this cake really is delicious."

"I'm sure it's peachy, but the shape's no damn good. That's the sorriest, crudest, plainest excuse for a Q I ever laid eyes on. Personally, I'm insulted."

"Oh, Mr. Quigley, sir, believe me, no insult was intended.

Please don't get upset," she begged him. "Now that we know better, we'll bake you a beautiful cake if you'll just give us another chance."

"Very well," Quigley huffed, "have it ready by Thursday morning. And, Miss, if you can't do the job, there must be a dozen bakeries in town that'd be delighted to have my business."

"Don't worry," she promised, "this one will be absolutely perfect.

"Elmer Lee," she told her assistant after the customer had left, "we have got to come up with something."

"Well, ah spek ah kin fix up a Q-shaped mold thet'd make a blind man sing, if only ah had the time to do the job right."

"All right," she told him, "from now 'til Wednesday night, I hereby free you up to do nothing else but fix me a cake mold, and, Elmer Lee..."

"Yes ma'am?"

"Make it picture-skew."

II

"I must say, that mold you made is a sight for sore eyes," Marie proclaimed when she had examined his work.

"A sight fer soah ahs? Why, that's about the best one ah heard all week! Ah do believe ah'll mail it off to the Dah-jayest, if it's okay wif you. Ah just know they'll wanna pick up on it."

"Suit yourself, Elmer Lee. Now, let's get going."

" 'Scuse me, ma'am, but ah been able to put mah own clothes on since ah was *ten*."

In due time they got around to Mr. Quigley's cake, on which they labored for what felt like hours and hours but was actually the merest fraction of a decade.

"At last the two had everything ready," sighed Marie, confusing in her fatigue the narration for her next line. Now then,

Elmer Lee, set your alarm extra early. We've got a big day ahead of us, was what she had meant to say.

"Hi, Christine, sorry I'm so late," Marie whispered as she entered the apartment. "How're the kids?"

"Oh, somewhere off in dreamland," her sister answered.

"Mommy?" called a tiny voice from the bedroom. "Mommy?" called another.

"Oops, I guess not," amended Christine.

"That's all right," Marie assured her. "Thanks a million for watching them."

"Oh, they were no trouble at all."

"That's good," Marie said. "Now that they're up, though, they'll be a ton of trouble to get back to sleep." And so they were, after milk, cookies, various entreaties and even a brave attempt at a lullaby.

"Read book," negotiated her daughter as she thrust a book into Marie's hands.

"Yeah!" her son chimed in, "Read *Elmer and the Dragon* again."

"No, that's too long a story for sleepy children."

"WE'RE NOT SLEEPY, MOMMY!" they corrected her.

"Yes, well Mommy is. Besides, I've had enough Elmers for one day. Now lie down and be still, and I'll see if I can find something nice and short for you. She pulled from the children's bookshelf a story called *Julie Gilhooley's Pizza Pie Dreams* and began to flip through it.

"Oh, look, here's a poem," she happily observed, upon noticing how brief it was, "Let's read this one tonight, okay?"

"Yuck!" the boy enthused. Marie, nonetheless, read to them about:

The Chuckle Fish

Oh, the Chuckle Fish is a mighty strange fish
That lives at the bottom of the deep.
When deep sea divers are around,
He will not utter a peep.
But when those daunted divers
Go back to the land once more,
The Chuckle Fish just laughs and laughs
'Til he rolls on the ocean floor.

Now I ask you what's so funny
That a fish should laugh so well?
The ocean floor is really a bore
As near as I can tell.

Well many have tried for many a year
To spot that Chuckle Fish.
They've tried to gurgle his favorite jokes
Or bring him his favorite dish (fish).
But when those daunted divers
Go back to their vaunted boats,
The Chuckle fish just laughs and laughs
And giggles and snickers and gloats.

Still, I ask you what's so funny
That a fish should laugh so well?
The ocean floor is really a bore
As near as I can tell.

They say the Chuckle fish won't weep,
But that may not be true.

Yet I do believe that he won't keep
Company with you.
And when those daunted divers
Go back to their abodes,
Why, the Chuckle Fish just laughs so hard,
That often, he explodes.

But I ask you what's so funny
That a fish should laugh so well?
For the ocean floor
Must really be a bore
A near as I can tell.

"My my," Marie added, "here's another short poem on the next page," but by this time, the children were either fast asleep or trying to look as if they were.

The next day, Marie found Elmer Lee already hard at work.

"Is the cake ready to pop in?" she asked him.

"Shore is. We're puttin' 'er in at exactly 7:25, lak you said."

"And the oven, is it preheated to 400 degrees?"

"We're at three ninety-nine and climbin'" he assured her.

At exactly 7:25, the cake entered the oven, only to exit at the prescribed time to cool. Like its less shapely predecessor, it was perfect. Marie iced the top and sides with a flourish, then waited for 10:00 and the judgment of Quigley. Sure enough, at 10:37 on the dot, Mr. Quigley strode in.

"Where's my cake?" he greeted them.

"Coming right up," Marie sang as she went back to fetch it.

"Oh, I get it," Quigley surmised after a brief inspection of the goods, "this is a joke, right? Okay, now let's see the real cake."

"A joke? Mr. Quigley, this is the cake and it's *beautiful*," she explained.

" That is the cake?"

"It certainly is."

"Well, I, for one, hate it. If that's the best you people can do, then I'm going to—"

"Shoot, that ain't nothin' to what we'uns kin do." Elmer Lee volunteered. "We never shoulda let that lazy rascal Gastone make this here cake in the first place. Ah tell ya what, Mr. Quigley, if y'all jes let Miz Quennelle here fix y'up a cake her own sef, why, I guaran-damn-tee it'll be a sight fer runny noses. Meanwhile, I best git on back t'the kitchen an' tell ol' Gas-tone his ass is fard."

"Elmer Lee, Gaston left us months ago," Marie reminded him some time after they had obtained Mr. Quigley's very, very reluctant permission to try again. "You could ruin the guy's reputation with a story like that."

"Ah suppose so," Elmer Lee admitted, "but ah had to come up wif a name right quick. 'Sides, ah doubt if ol' Mr. Quigley keeps up a roaster of who's who in the bakin' game."

"I guess you're right," she agreed.

"'Course, the way that ol' boy packs in them ther profee troles, ah wouldn't be the least bit surprised if he did."

III

As trying as Mr. Quigley had been about his special cake, the Quigley tab was always paid promptly, and here in the mail, payment had arrived for last month's goodies.

"This'll take care of a bill or two," Marie thought as she stared absently at the check. Then it hit her. For the first time, she noticed Mr. Quigley wrote his Qs in the old Palmer method of cursive writing, rather like an oversized ornate number 2. The style still lingered to some extent in the Midwest, from whence Mr. Quigley evidently came.

"In any case, here's where our trouble's been the whole time.

When he orders a Q, he means a letter like this," she explained to Elmer Lee as she sketched out the new design.

"Well, hail!" he exploded. "Why didn't he say so in the first place? Ah ain't no dang mind reader!"

"Elmer Lee, the customer is always right, whether we can read his mind or not," Marie advised him. "Now let's get to work."

Work is what they got to all right. While he forged the new cake mold, she prepared the ingredients for a Black Forest cake. It would prove a far more laborious project than the Savarin, but, as Marie figured, a dedicated glutton like Mr. Quigley would find this cake irresistible, whether he was thrilled with the shape or not. And, at that, she was convinced they had finally found a shape that would tickle his fancy.

Thus it was with a profound sense of relief that she dragged herself home that night. With the day's tribulations behind her, the time for rest had come at last. There remained only the matter of the long, badly-situated lamp cord, over which she managed to trip, bringing the lamp down with a resounding crash and the children out with a much less resounding, "Mommy?"

Predictably, nothing would do to settle them down except a story, and, this time, it had to be a real story, her son instructed her, not some dumb old pome.

"Oh my, here's one that's loaded with adventure," Marie told them as she turned to the tale of

Crazy King Kenny and His
Two Clever, Too-Clever Counts

Long ago, in an era that never should have been, there reigned in the Kingdom of Eastfalia a long line of rulers, each named Kenny and each one madder than the one before. In a mild fit of pique, for example, one of them had thrown everybody in the kingdom out of work. After he had disbarred all the lawyers and defrocked the clergy, he proceeded to disband the musicians, deflower the gardeners, debrief the underwear models, detail the kite makers, debunk the bed builders, debate the fishermen, delight the candlestick makers, and finally, he delisted the contractors he had recently hired to build a duplicate Tower of Pisa.

Many odd occurrences, sufficient to drive even the best of kings crazy, had taken place recently, such as a robin chirping at midnight or a partial eclipse of the planet Neptune. But of all the maddening problems that beset the crazy Kings Kenny, none was worse than the stream of nasty notes that continuously flowed from the Kingdom of Phobadelphia, their hated neighbor to the north.

One day, in the reign of King Kenny XIII, known affectionately to his ever-optimistic subjects as King Kenny the Last, a letter rock flew through the royal bathroom window and made contact with the royal noodle as the king was sitting on the throne. He unzipped the letter and read:

Dear King Kenny XIII:
You, sir, are a jaywalking jerk.
Sincerely,
King Herbie the Bad
The Royal Castle, Phoba.

"Eftsoons!" bellowed King Kenny, largely because he'd not had a single chance to say "Eftsoons!" all week.

"This means war!" he added, which was something he only got to say once a month or so. Indeed, this had been a day full of accomplishments.

"We are exhausted," he informed his Council of War and Privies. "Find out what King Herbie the Bad is up to and report to us Tuesday morning."

The council gathered in the Royal Gathering Room at Tuesday morning sharp.

"We are present, sire," they explained to the king as he entered the room.

"So I gather, so I gather," he muttered.

"The news from Phobadelphia is not good," spake the chief among the assembled counts. "It appears that King Herbie the Bad means to attack Your Highness."

"What, again?" the king fretted, "Why, it's not even his turn!"

"'Tis not for nothing he is called King Herbie the Bad," the head count reminded him.

"And to make matters worse," King Kenny pointed out, "two of our number have already deserted our cause. Where are Count Tooten and Count Tootwenny?"

"I know not of their current whereabouts," answered the same count, "but I do know they were with us when we went to sally into Phobadelphia for a look around."

"Who is this Sally and why is she leading my men astray?" the king demanded to know.

Eventually, Count Sheap broke the embarrassing silence.

"Er, if I may interrupt, sire, I believe I heard Count Tooten and Count Tootwenny say they planned to stay behind and spy on King Herbie."

"I think I heard the very same thing," volunteered Count Kaydentz, "except I recall they referred to him by his rightful title of King Herbie the Bad."

"Since you bring it up," Count Dowgn mentioned, "I believe I heard them say something about staying behind as well."

"To spy on King Herbie the Bad, I suppose" the king grumbled.

"Yes, and also to check out the felines there, or something like that."

"Fie!" the sovereign shouted, for it was his turn to shout "Fie!" that day. "If you ask me, they've deserted. We want them arrested on sight."

E'enso, the tiny Kingdom of Eastfalia commenced preparations for another attack from their enemy to the north. All along the border, King Kenny had lined up his forces: his knights, his bishops, his rooks and his knaves; his castles, his vassals, his bucks and his braves. Little did he suspect, King Herbie the Bad had other plans.

The clever counts Tooten and Tootwenny had uncovered King Herbie's scheme by disguising themselves as giant turkey drumsticks and hiding in the rival ruler's icebox. As Bad King Herbie habitually discussed strategy with his leftovers, the two spies were able to get the cold facts, thanks to some nifty legwork.

What they discovered was that King Herbie (the Bad) intended to put all his warriors in boats and sail down the Sea of Eee, which washed the shores of both kingdoms, every Saturday night, whether they needed it or not. The men would disembark some distance behind the waiting ranks of King Kenny's army, while the troops continued looking northward. Then, the invading force planned to steal everything that wasn't nailed down and sneak back to the boats with the loot.

"We must warn King Kenny," Count Tootwenny said to Count Tooten as they changed back into their armor and saddled up.

"That's a big nine-four, good varlet," his partner copied.

Days later, while King Herbie the Tight was still haggling with the owner of the boat-rental marina, the two clever counts returned to King Kenny's army.

"We must see the king at once," they implored Count Ofph.

"Oh, you'll see the king all right," Count Ofph assured them. "Place them in irons," he commanded the Royal Iron Placer.

"Aha!" observed King Kenny shortly following their imprisonment, "Thought you'd sneak away from the battle, did you?"

"No, no, nothing of the sort," the captive counts protested. "We were gathering important information about the enemy." "Bullfeathers," snorted the king. "We say you're AWOL, and that's that. Chop," he directed the royal executioner, "their heads off."

And so it was ordered, and so it came to pass that Count Tooten and Count Tootwenny, for their heroic efforts, received naught but a cold chop.

Naturally the plundering Phobadelphians caught the Eastfalians completely unawares. When King Kenny and his men at last faced around, they found everything gone, even the flies from the flypaper.

There is, of course a moral to this story: don't hatchet your counts before they chicken.

By this time the children were fast asleep.

"If only Mr. Quigley were that easy to please," Marie thought.

Bright again and equally early, Marie and Elmer Lee put the latest of the Q-cakes in the oven. True to form, it turned out splendidly, for these people knew from whence they were doing. After a great deal more effort, they completed the cake, moments before Mr. Quigley's arrival.

"El perfecto," Marie mused as she looked upon her handiwork. "If that man doesn't absolutely fall in love with this cake, then I don't know what's wrong with him."

"Got a real long sheet of paper? Ah'll make you a list," Elmer Lee offered.

Just then, Quigley came in.

"Well?" he inquired.

"*Voila!*" Marie proclaimed as she gestured toward the cake.

Mr. Quigley glared at it.

"I suppose you must think I'm some kind of hayseed," he growled.

"Moah lak a haystack," Elmer Lee muttered.

"Why, no, Mr. Quigley, I'm sure you're a very sophisticated person," Marie answered.

"You bet I am!" he barked. "Now throw this abomination in the dumpster where it belongs, and bake me a cake that looks like a goddamn Q!"

"But I used my Black For—"

"And be advised, young lady, be advised: this is positively your last chance. I cannot emphasize enough how crucial it is that you get this cake right. You blow it again and you've seen the last of me in this store forever! You understand?"

Inasmuch as his patience was wearing thin, Mr. Quigley had demanded the cake be ready the next morning. Marie had assured him she would be only too happy to take care of it. After he left, she summoned the whole staff.

"All right, now," she told them, "we've got a really big rush project and we must do it right. Elmer Lee and I will be too tied up to handle anything else, so it'll be up to the rest of you to pick up the slack. I know some people have been extending their lunch hours and coffee breaks, but we can't have you taking such liberties now."

"Give me liberty or give me death!" called a voice from the kitchen.

"Who said that?" Marie snapped.

"Patrick Henry, right?" another voice answered.

"Christine, you're a doll for watching the kids so long," Marie said in the quietest of all possible tones.

"Well I certainly wouldn't leave them here alone, but, my God, Marie, what's been keeping you at work so late?"

"I'm working on the cake to end all cakes. You wouldn't believe me if I told you. If I can think to do it, I'll take a snapshot for you tomorrow."

"This is tomorrow," her sister reminded her, "and has been

for several hours."

"I guess you're right," Marie replied.

Suddenly the phone rang. Christine pounced on it before it could ring a second time.

"Hello?" she spoke quietly into the mouthpiece.

"Um, uh, do, uh, Leroy be dey?"

"No," she hissed, "You've got the wrong number.

"Some drunk old colored man," she explained to her sister.

"I'll bet it's my ex."

"You mean the tennis player?" her sister asked, guessing it was Marie's second husband.

"Yeah, love meant nothing to him. Anyway, that's a favorite trick of his. Whenever he'd get loaded and sappy sentimental, he'd want to phone someone up and tell 'em his troubles. And, if it was real late, like it always is, he'd call first, disguising his voice, and pretend to be a wrong number. Then, he could call right back and say, 'Oh I didn't wake you, did I?' The jerk."

"Well, if that is what he's up to, shouldn't you take the phone off the—"

Too late. The phone rang again. Christine tried to pick it up, but Marie pushed her hand aside and grabbed the receiver.

"Listen," she informed the caller, "you so much as say peep to me again and I'll make you rue the day you were born!.... DON'T TELL ME NOT TO SHOUT, I'LL SHOUT AS LOUD AS I GODDAMN-WELL PLEASE. DO YOU HEAR ME?"

"Mommy?" came two little voices from the bedroom in perfect harmony.

"Well, now, here's a tale we haven't heard yet," Marie announced.

"Mommy read?" inquired her daughter several seconds later.

"Huh? Oh, sure, Sweetie, Mommy read," Marie mumbled as she forced open her eyes and proceeded to read the story she had selected, titled:

Hot as Summer and Cold as Winter

Some time, well after the invention of the dinosaur, but long before the discovery of tin foil, the most boring man in Europe came to rule the Grand Duchy of Earl. Grand Duke Ellsworth or "Bland Duke Ellsworth," as his subjects, who preferred things that way themselves, secretly called him, would have nothing to do with loud clothes, loud music or the Metropolitical Visitation of 1633. Most of all, he opposed loud food.

"Everything I eat should be easy on the tongue and easier still on the tummy," he lectured his cooks. "What is more, all my food must be served at the proper temperature: not too hot and not too cold."

"Luke warm, then?" asked Pierre, an assistant chef.

"No," cautioned Sven, the head chef, "I dun't t'ink it shude eeffen loook varm."

As his subjects were ever eager to please the Bland Duke, a basically kind and reasonable ruler, only the very plainest of food came to be served throughout the duchy. Room-temperature gruel was the all-time favorite, not only for breakfast, but for lunch, dinner and high tea as well. As for the duke's own family, his choice of cuisine was perfectly okay with Mrs. The Duke and their three daughters, Beatrice the Ordinary, Louella the So-So, and Willadine the Just-All-Right. Only the young dukeling, Quentin the Quarrelsome, longed for a better way.

For one thing, he wished his father would get busy and become a king. A little war here or (more drastically) a big marriage there, should do the trick.

"Prince, Prince, Prince, Prince of Earl; I am the Prince of Earrrrullll," he would sing to himself over and over.

Far worse, though, than the pain and heartbreak of lacking a kingdom to inherit, was having to put up with all that plain, boring food the duke's chefs served up, day in as well as day out.

"I'm about to go out of my tree," young Quentin complained as he prepared to climb down from his favorite branch. "I had better have a word with the kitchen staff.

"See here," he addressed the assembled chefs and galley-washers, "I want you people to invent me a dish that is as cold as winter and as hot as summer at the same time. If I like it, I'll put you boys in for a ten-pfent-an-hour raise. If I don't or if you fail to produce, heads will roll."

"Oh dear, what ever will we do?" they fretted, all except Bump, the village idiot, who had been hired as a plate wringer under the duke's Exploit Ye Handicapped program. So popular was this program among the merchants and tradesmen desirous of staying on the duke's good side, a great demand arose for workers possessing any sort of handicap whatsoever. It had been a real task to locate them, as most of the citizens were distressingly whole and healthy.

"A hangnail, you say?" beamed the cobbler. "Well, I've been looking for an apprentice with just your qualifications."

"And how long have you had those sniffles?" inquired the blacksmith as he led the recruit to a vacant anvil.

"You say it takes you *how* many strokes to play the back nine?" asked the barber.

Thus it was no surprise that a genuine idiot like Bump held a second and even third job, which would explain his sleeping through this particular crisis.

"Somebody wake up that simpleton and order him back to work," snarled one of the chefs. "We can't have all that snoring going on whilst we're trying to rack our brains."

Ponder as they might, though, the chefs did not have a clue what to do, so accustom were they to preparing food to the duke's taste.

"We're in deep chocolate," they concluded.

Meanwhile, Bump had finished his chores and gone off to his next job as an alchemist's helper for Fred the Wizard, who was away from the laboratory when Bump stumbled in. The boss had left a note for his helper:

"Don't just sit there, do something," it read.

With that advice in mind, Bump guessed he'd take a stab at spinning gold from cream at extremely low temperatures. "What a silly idea!" the Wizard could have told him, and, sure enough, all Bump got for his efforts, even after attempting to speed the process up by adding a little vanilla extract, was some sort of frozen cream. Why it did not turn into gold, as it properly should have, was a mystery to Bump.

"Eeeyoutch!" he proclaimed after trying to see if it at least tasted like gold. "This stuff's as cold as winter!" Then the words of Quentin the Quarrelsome wafted to him as if in a dream, which, in fact, they had been: "As cold as winter and as hot as summer..."

"Yoohooga!" the lad rejoiced, meaning (to him), "I have found it!"

All this while the chefs had created nothing as the young duke of tomorrow grew increasingly impatient.

"I've drummed my fingers long enough," he announced. "Now I expect results or it's off with your heads. You have until five o'clock, and, remember, the dish had better be yummy. No yummy, no noggins."

"What are we to do?" they stewed. "Everything we concoct is hot as springtime and cold as the month of May."

At the very instant their time ran out, Bump, the village idiot, came huffing and puffing into the kitchen.

"Huff," he said, "and puff. I have saved the day."

"What do you mean knuckle-brain? The day is lost for us all."

"Au contrarywise," Bump informed them. "I've just come

from delivering to the Dukeling a dish colder than winter and hotter than summer."

"But 'ow can such a thing be?" asked Chef Pierre.

"Well," Bump elaborated, "you start by trying to spin cream into gold like I did, and you wind up with this." He showed them the iced cream.

"Delicious!" they all exclaimed after looking the stuff over thoroughly.

"And then," Bump continued in language that even an idiot could understand, "on top of it you add—"

"But of course! You mak' ze sauce!" Chef Pierre interjected. "It was ze 'ot fudge, *n'est-ce pas*? Ah, *le petit duc* will adore it! We should name such a marvelous dish after ze day of its invention, *non*?"

"No, it wasn't exactly hot fudge," Bump said.

"Vell, den, perhaps hot butterscotch, yah?" guessed Chef Sven.

"No," Bump answered after thinking it over. "it wasn't hot butterscotch neither, but it was hot as summer. I do recall that."

"Please, please, try to remember," the chefs implored. "We simply must have that recipe for the next occasion."

"Cayenne pepper!" he yelled triumphantly, as the guards began breaking down the kitchen door. After all it was only Tuesday.

Marie reached the shop as soon as she could that morning. At any rate, everything seemed to be going smoothly enough, short of Elmer Lee's upset stomach.

"Why don't you take a couple Alka-Seltzers?" she suggested.

"Druther dah!" he replied. "Last time ah tried to swaller them monster-size tablets, ah liked to choke half to deff!"

A little later, Elmer Lee removed the last part of the cake from the oven. Today Mr. Quigley would get a pyramid of beautifully rendered Q-shaped cakes, each a different flavor and each with its own exotic, rich frosting. And all around the cake, which was half again as large as the largest wedding cake Marie had ever baked, were as many candy garnishes as she could lay her hands on. Where there was still room on the cake's surface, she applied cherries and maraschino strawberries. All the while, the other employees had been working frantically to finish constructing an immense wooden crate.

"Mmm, mmm, MMM!" Elmer Lee declared as he inspected the final product.

"I don't know," Marie fretted, "I'm still worried sick about what he'll say."

At any rate, her period of sick worry would be mercifully brief. Mr. Quigley was walking through the door.

"I'm here for my cake," he reminded them.

"And your cake is here for you," she answered in as cheerful a tone as she could muster. Meanwhile Elmer Lee and the others struggled to lug the cake to the counter.

"Viola!" Elmer Lee proclaimed.

A hush fell over the store as Mr. Quigley cast a fish eye, first up, then down, then clockwise, then counterclockwise the length and breadth of the cake. His mouth hardened as he looked it over again.

"Fine," he said at last.

"Oh, wonderful!" Marie gushed; "I knew you'd like it. Now if you'll just tell me where to deliver—"

"Don't bother," he instructed them, "I'll eat it here."

THE HORSE WHO COULD HIT
By J. Morton O'Vash

"**M**ort" O'Vash made it clear from our first conversation, he did not want us to use his full name, Jellyroll Morton O'Vash (after the self-proclaimed inventor of the jelly doughnut), so of course, we won't.

Mort works chiefly as an historian, although he does overhaul the occasional transmission to maintain a steady cash effluvium. His books, noted for their simple, direct style, include the two-volume series, *Boer War* and *More Boer War*. He told us about his present work on a biography of the man who discovered Pike's Peak.

This fellow, we gathered from reading Mort's manuscript, did more than just discover the peak that bears his name (which, one might suppose, made it all the easier to find). It seems he was quite a "reformation man."

For example, experts credit him with inventing the first motorized bicycle, which many called "Pike's Bike," except for those hooligans who chose to drive the souped-up version, which they referred to as "Pike's Pig."

Prior to the discovery of his famous elevation, he befriended a microcephalic albino dwarf, whom he adopted as the expedition's mascot, for good luck. Insofar as they eventually succeeded, much of the credit went to Pike's Freak. In fact, so strongly did the great man believe in the efficacy of his new mascot's powers, he felt free to discard his former, rather smelly good-luck talisman: a banana skin he had been holding onto for several weeks thereby putting an end to the imagined powers of Pike's Peel.

And while nobody would be so foolhardy as to claim the mighty mountaineer invented the game of volleyball, few could deny the importance of his contribution to the sport. As we should know by now, the game itself was invented by Professor V. Oliver Bahl, D. Phys.Ed., who devised it to replace varsity lawn darts so that his athletes could keep in condition during that portion of the spring when the playing field was set afire. Actually, the good doctor had intended to introduce bare-knuckle gouging as the desired lawn dart substitute, but he'd mistakenly grabbed the wrong blueprints to show the dean. By the time he realized his error, the game of volleyball had become established far and wide.

It is fortunate things developed that way, for, while the doughty explorer's contributions to the world of bare-knuckle gouging amounted to so little of consequence as to make most historians simply give up, he will live forever in the hearts of volleyball aficionados as the inventor of Pike's Spike. That, of course, is that spectacular and devastating stratagem whereupon a front-line player jumps far higher than the oncoming ball, then slams it with his nose into the opponents' court. The maneuver resulted in its inventor developing a large and well-muscled proboscis that everyone referred to as Pike's Beak (although most people took care to avoid saying that to his face, lest they incur Pike's pique).

The town of Fall River, Mass. also owed a debt of everlasting gratitude to the legendary explorer. The recent Borden murders, on one hand, had had the salubrious effect of inspiring tune-smiths the world over to crank out ballads, the least of which was certainly this:

Lizzie Borden took an ax,
And gave her father, forty, wax.
"Thanks a lot," said her dad

With an air of panache,
"I'll smear a big glob of it
On my moustache."

And when she saw what she had done,
She gave her mother, forty-one
And so desperate to
Fight off the ravages of oncoming
Middle age, this advice:
Think twice.

(Hit it.)

Although it has its price,
It must be awfully nice
To think twice about whatever may befall you.
And if you don't approve
Of who you are, you can remove
Yourself to someone else who may not gall you.
So a man like Mr. Hyde
Might not have had much pride
In his crimes which, for the times, were pretty ample.
But later in his lab
As Dr. Jekyll he could grab
The chance to be his own worst example.

Now there's lots of different ways
To take leave of your mind.
Whatever you pick
Is whatever you'll find.
Ah, but if I can have
Only one way to lean,
Let me be a schizophrene!

Life must be awfully void
For a simple paranoid;
There's just one of you to fear what they will let you.
And just because they say
You shouldn't act that way,
Doesn't mean someday some guy's not going to get you.

And if you think you're Jesus,
Remember, when Hell freezes,
A lot of crazy things are going to happen,
But if you're someone else besides,
Then whatever else betides
Ought not to catch the both of you nappin'.

Oh, there's lots of different ways
To take leave of your mind;
Whatever you pick
Is whatever you find.
Ah, but if I can have
Only one way to lean,
Let me be a schizophrene! (That's two.)
No, I don't mean a trampoline. (I guess!)
Just a simple complicated,
Highly motivated,
Ordinary schizophrene!

On the other hand, fear of axes swept over the townspeople. Most of them favored outright confiscation.

"When all the axes are taken away, only crazy ladies will have axes," others tried to argue, but they were hacked to death on the spot. Eventually all the axes in Fall River were confiscated.

Only then did it dawn on the populace, they had failed to consider a crucial detail: what about Sunday dinner?

That first week, the women tried serving the chicken with its head still attached.

"How gross and disgusting! Never," every paterfamilias in every household stormed as they beat their wives senseless with whatever fireplace utensil was handiest, "again do we wish to see such a vile and obscene sight on our dinner tables."

About this time, the Climber of Great Cliffs arrived in town.. The people of Fall River made him aware of their dilemma and begged him for help.

"Pike, speak!" they chorused. He arrived at an answer right away.

He would, he said, assign one of his mountaineers, whose major avocation involved the handling of poultry in a way that could be of service to the people of the town, to stay there and ensure the chickens were once again roasted headless. Thus was a crisis averted by Pike's Geek.

Between good deeds, the noted and quoted trailblazer kept a garden that was the envy of the civilized world. Pike's Peas did especially well, as did Pike's Peaches, but every one of the crops thrived under the green thumbing of his Puerto Rican gardener, Luis Gonzalez, also known as "Pike's Hispano-American."

At last, we put Mort's historical manuscript away and began the tedious process of negotiating a price for this story. We looked him rectangularly in the eye and said to him: "Let's talk Sick Man of Europe."

We were fortunate to catch Mort at a time when he was low on funds.

"That doggone AAMCO place down the block's just about put me out of business," he confided to us from his bucolic one-bedroom estate up in King's County, New York. Needful to say, he was delighted to accept our generous stipend for the surrender of his favorite shaggy dog story.

"Now at last I can put a down payment on them foam-rubber dice I've had my eye on," he gloated.

We can only hope that, when he flips his car into a ditch after trying to take a turn on 1.5 wheels, he will have rolled a "natural." What your crapshoot crowd calls "seven the hard way."

Presently, Mort's only automotive luxury is the vanity plates.

"What do you have on them?" we asked unthinkingly, some would say, as usual.

"BK 5487," he replied.

"And that means...?" we wondered aloud..

"Not a damn thing, except I get to decide what goes on my license plates and not some fat-ass bureaucrat at the DMV."

By his own admission, Mort hardly qualifies as much of a social lion. Nor, would he be equally quick to admit, is he even much of a social gnu. He was once sponsored by his betters for membership in New York's prestigious Union League, but, when he attempted to rally the members to join him in a rousing chorus of *Solidarity Forever*, he met with only indifferent success.

To compound matters, the heated upbraiding he lent his new comrades for their astounding lack of enthusiasm pretty well put the kibosh on his welcome there.

Let us, on the other hand, thoroughly wear out his welcome in the pages to follow.—tcl

I

Clarence Dylan "Crazy" Strangle had the worst team in the majors. Given the chance, he could have undoubtedly had the worst team in the minors as well. Only yesterday, the Senators had pounded them, twelve to nothing. And this was not the Washington Senators baseball club, but, rather, a junketing quorum of Senate Democrats who had been practicing for their annual tilt with the Republicans.

After a mere two weeks of spring training, Crazy had concluded this year's team was going to be every bit as bad as last year's and probably a lot worse. Not without substantial reason did he fear for his job.

"I dunno what I'm gonna do," he lamented to his favorite barkeep, Baseball Billy, owner of Baseball Billy's Bullpen, a colorful saloon festooned with memorabilia from the Green Bay Packers' glory years.

"What?" shouted Billy, cupping his hand to the ear hole in the Packers helmet he wore.

"Doomed!" Crazy called out, "I said I'm doomed!"

"Naw, you're not so dumb." the barman assured him. 'It's just your team's so lousy. Ain't a one of 'em can block worth beans."

"The hell with it," Crazy sighed, "how about another double?"

With a wink and a snappy thumbs up to the skipper, Baseball Billy proceeded to blow a magnificent bubble from the wad of gum he had been eating. Its progress into infinity was stopped only by the helmet's faceguard.

"Another DOUBLE, you goddamned doorknob!" Crazy elaborated as he shook his empty glass at him.

Later that afternoon, things went further downhill for Crazy in a golf game with his usual foursome, consisting of himself and three guys he had struck up a friendship with. He didn't really know much about them. The lone fact he knew, to his considerable relief, was that none of them was involved with professional baseball.

After the first three holes, Crazy, who usually beat these guys with the greatest of ease, found himself in trouble after a few unlucky bounces, while the absolute duffer of all the duffers in their group was actually leading.

"Boy, I'd sure like not to lose for a change," the duffer thought, "but wouldn't it be terrific to win?" His lead was not large, and when he hit the sand trap on the fourth hole while the others reached the putting green in a hurry, he began to get discouraged.

"I knew it would come to this," the duffer moaned.

"It doesn't need to come to this," the imp, who appeared at the bottom of the trap, wearing a burnoose, told him.

"What? HEY!" the hapless golfer shouted.

"Quiet, fool," the imp hissed. "Those other guys can't see or hear me, only you. I'm here to help you, get it?"

"What do you mean?" he mumbled out of the side of his mouth.

"That's more like it," said the imp. "Okay, here's the deal. You're on the green and into the hole on your next swing, but it comes at a price: no sex for a week."

"Yeah, sure, it's a deal," mumbled the duffer. He swung and the ball soared up from the trap, dropped onto the green and rolled seventy feet into the hole.

"Christ a-mighty!" Crazy muttered.

The duffer's miraculous shot so unnerved the rest of the group they played lousy golf for the next three holes, as did he, but at least he wasn't losing much ground. Then the inevitable happened. Crazy and the other two players made beautiful drives off the tee, while the duffer hit into the woods.

"Here it comes," he thought. "I'd of hoped I could stay on top for at least the front nine, but now I can't even find my ball. I guess this round's going into the dumper too."

"Not so fast, there, son," spake the imp, who reappeared amidst the trees, wearing a coonskin cap and squatting over the guy's seemingly lost ball, "Do you want to make a deal?"

"What do you have in mind?"

"A double eagle with your next swing, but it's gonna cost you."

"How much this time?"

"Heh, heh, heh," the imp remonstrated. "No sex for a month!"

"Fine!" the duffer snapped. And then, just to make sure he was going to get his money's worth, the guy closed his eyes and swung with his putter. Somehow, he managed to dig the ball out of the leaves, send it between countless tree branches, get it to bounce three times onto the green, then roll into the cup. Meanwhile, his freshly discombobulated opponents four and five-putted the hole. He succeeded in holding onto the lead, but just barely. At the end of the seventeenth, he found himself tied with Crazy, who was making his move at last. On the final hole both he and Crazy hit the green in three shots, but, while he found himself 85 feet away, atop a steep slope that dropped off into a pond, his opponent was six inches from the flag.

"I knew this would happen," the duffer muttered. "Was it asking too much to win one lousy round of golf in my whole life?"

"Certainly not," the imp, now dressed as a frogman, agreed from a lily pad in the adjoining pond. "I think you know what you have to do or, rather, not do."

"Suppose you tell me."

"NO SEX FOR A WHOLE YEAR! NOT FOR ONE LONG YEAR! NONE! NADA! ZILCH! EL ZIPPO!"

"Yeah, yeah, I get the picture," the guy told him; "All right, I'll do it." Then he tapped his ball and saw it roll 85 tortured feet into the cup. And to make matters better, Crazy blew his easy putt.

As the other two golfers carried off the winner on their shoulders, the imp appeared on the guy's own shoulder.

"And now it's time to pay the piper, Mr.....uh...what did you say your name was?"

"I never did," the duffer reminded him with an impish grin of his own. "It's Father O'Malley."

"What the hell," Crazy decided. Baseball Billy was an idiot, but a drink was a drink, and that's what he needed more than anything right now.

II

Badly hung over as he was, even by his own liberal standards, Crazy had managed (After all, wasn't he the manager?) to drag himself onto the field for the following morning's practice. To be sure, things were no better than they had been since the first day, when the team's only real slugger, Orville "Mad Dog" Starkweather, broke a leg while attempting a jumping-jack.

The sight of bodies colliding as they ran after balls they would never catch and the constant sound of errant throws rattling the old wooden seats in the grandstand were not as daunting to Crazy as they might have been to a less experienced manager. He knew this marked the high point of the day. The really awful part would come in the afternoon, during batting practice.

Crazy grimaced as "Wheezin' Wally" Willoughby, the 73-year-old coach, slowly and deliberately lobbed pitch after pitch right over the plate, only to have them all popped up, dribbled foul or, more frequently, missed altogether.

"That last kid got a pretty good piece of one," offered former outfield great, Willie "Say What?" Washington, the team's batting coach.

"Forget it," Crazy sighed, "That's Willoughby's granddaughter, battin' for the helluvit. Besides, he always goes easy on her."

"How about lettin' me hit a few?" asked a mottled, worn-out-looking horse that had ambled up to Crazy's side.

"Say WHAT?" queried the batting coach. Crazy, who had fainted, said nothing.

That night found Crazy at Baseball Billy's, throwing down drink after drink

"Another refill, Mr. Strangle?" asked the backup barkeep who filled in on Billy's night off.

"Sure, keep 'em comin'," Crazy told him.

The young man was happy to oblige, even though he himself had been totally abstemious, ever since his college days. Back then, he had been a very heavy drinker, to the extent that he would stagger into his dorm room nearly every night and vomit, long, loud and hard, into the room's sink, as the lavatory seemed too far away.

This did not sit at all well with his roommate, a reasonably sober pre-med student. He could seldom sleep through the loud vomiting sessions. Then, in the light of day, guess who wound up cleaning up the sink? Time and time again, he tried to caution his boozing roommate against the perils of heavy drinking, only to be laughed off. Finally, when all other warnings had failed, the roommate warned him, "If you keep drinking so hard and throwing up so hard every night, you will literally puke your guts out."

"Yeah, right," the guy snorted as he headed out on his rounds, "tell me another."

Finally, the pre-med decided the time had come to scare his drunken roommate straight. He sneaked into the biology lab and helped himself to a heaping handful of cat guts. He waited until he was alone, then put the guts into the sink.

"This ought to be good," he thought.

Perhaps because he had accustomed himself to the noise or perhaps because he was sleeping the sleep, not merely of the just, but the just on the verge of sweet revenge, the pre-med actually slept through the usual reversal of peristalsis.

When the scheming roommate awoke, he found the guy on his knees, pale as a sheet, his lips quivering fervently in prayer.

"Well, well," the pre-med observed, "it looks like somebody got religion all of a sudden. I wonder why?"

"You were right!" the frightened penitent moaned, "You were

absolutely right, I coughed my guts up, exactly like you said. But, with the help of God and a long-handled spoon, I got 'em back down again!"

"Y'know," Crazy said to the bartender, "if you stay out in the sun for too long, starin' at a godawful ballclub, you can start to imagine some mighty strange things."

"Like what?" the guy asked.

"Aaah, you wouldn't believe me if I told you, but I believe I'll have another drink. Make it a double."

Crazy was more than hung over for the next day's practice, he was still drunk.

"Which was just as well," he pointed out, "considerin' what I gotta go through every day with this team."

Afternoon batting practice was still more demoralizing than it had been the day before. Even Willoughby's granddaughter seemed to have lost her "eye."

"Jeez, I dunno, maybe I better quit before they fire me," Crazy said to his batting coach.

"Aw, hang in there, Skip," Washington replied. "You never know what might turn up."

"Like me, for example." It was the horse.

III

"Gentlemen, you are my witnesses," Crazy proclaimed. "From this day forwards, I take the pledge to stay stone cold sober for the rest of my life, and I am *not*, repeat, *not* going to hear from any more talking horses, ever!"

"Sure thing, Skip," agreed one of the coaches.

"Right on," added Washington, although, for a minute there, it had almost seemed to him that the fool horse talked.

Crazy had forgotten how miserable it felt to suffer through a night in this stinkhole excuse for a town without so much as the taste of a drink. The following day, though, he approached the practice field with a renewed sense of purpose. Such zeal as he had mastered from his newfound sobriety carried him through the expected morning disasters with a brave smile riveted to his face. In spite of a shortstop's errant throw to first base that struck him in the head as he stood talking to his third base coach, he kept up a brave front.

By the afternoon, his spirits had sunk back to their normal abysmal state.

"Maybe I should just hang myself," he suggested to his batting coach as Willoughby threw pitch after pitch past his best hitters, "and be done with it."

"Maybe you oughta let me hit the ball," said a voice from behind Crazy.

"Somebody oughta hit the ball, that's for damn sure," Crazy agreed.

"So how about it, Skip?" asked the horse.

"Huh? How about WHAT?" roared Crazy as he turned to face the speaker. "Washington, did that nag just talk to me?"

"Uh, I wasn't payin' attention," the coach mumbled nervously as he studied his shoelaces.

"I sure as hell did talk to you, babycakes," the horse explained to Crazy, "and you both better start payin' attention."

By this time the animal was attracting a crowd. In fact, the whole team had assembled behind the backstop.

"I'm the best hitter you ever seen," he elaborated, "and I'm ready to prove it."

"But you're a *horse*," Crazy pointed out.

"So?" the horse answered, "What the hell difference does that make? I'm a long-ball hitter, sport, and you need a long-ball hitter like a wheelchair needs gimps."

"C'mon, Skip, let the horse hit!" laughed Pops Upsom, the veteran left fielder.

"Sure, whattaya got to lose?" remarked Lefty, the catcher, who had acquired his colorful nickname from Baseball Billy.

As the players continued to mill around making cracks about the horse, Crazy came to realize there would be no getting any work out of these clowns until they'd had their fun.

"All right, the damn horse can bat," Crazy snarled as he stomped off toward the dugout.

Amid cheers and considerable laughter, the horse picked up a bat with his teeth and strode to the plate. He cocked his neck so as to draw the bat back in readiness. Wheezin' Wally, who couldn't for the life of him see what harm a tired old horse could do with a bat, served up the kind of pitch he would toss to his granddaughter. The horse whipped the bat around, and the ball shot like a rocket down the third base line.

"Wow, that woulda gone for extra bases," Lefty shouted as the other players began to razz the old coach unmercifully.

"Aaah, stuff!" the old man raged. "I'se just goin' easy on the dam nag, that's all. You watch and see what happens when I give him my fast one."

All eyes turned to the pitching coach, for no one except Crazy had ever seen him throw overhand. His first pitch sailed well over the horse's head, and the next one landed in the dirt. On his third attempt, Wheezin' Wally found the range. The ball was heading right down the pipe. With another violent twitch of its massive neck, the horse jerked the bat around. The ball disappeared against the clear blue Florida sky.

Crazy heard that sound, heretofore missing from the team's workouts, of bat meeting ball with some real authority. He scrambled up the dugout steps and squinted into the sun. To his immeasurable displeasure, he saw the horse plaster another one against the fence.

"God dammit, Willoughby, stop playin' with that horse!" Crazy shouted. "We got no more time for foolin' around."

"Skip, I ain't playin'," Wally protested between wheezes. "This here horse's good!"

"Good my ass!" Crazy snapped. "Santiago! Get the hell out there and pitch."

Hector "Espitball" Santiago was far and away the best pitcher on the staff. With any other team, he could have won twenty to twenty-five games easily. He glowered at the horse from the mound. Then, after he had thoroughly intimidated the strange batter, he threw an inside fastball. The horse ripped it down the third base line. Santiago tried his best curve, and stared in horror it soared into the seats. This nonsense, fumed the pitcher, had gone far enough. The moment had come to give that *loco caballo* his famous espitball. He threw the horse a beauty, then found himself face down in the dirt, after the ensuing line drive had nearly removed his head..

As the pitcher stayed put, praying to every saint he could think of, Crazy walked quietly back to the clubhouse and picked up the phone.

"Hello, Mr. Weitzenheimer?" Crazy began in a noticeably shaken voice, "I think you better come down here and take a look at something. Yes, sir, this is very important."

IV

Wilbert P. Weitzenheimer, multimillionaire heir to the Weitzenheimer Near Beer fortune, had long been unhappy with the performance of his ball club. He had fired a dozen managers before Crazy and was about ready to give him the sack as well.

"All right, Strangle," the boss snapped, "I'll come down there if you say I absolutely have to, but this had better be good. So, what have you got?"

"Well, sir, I don't hardly know how to put this, but we've found a horse that can...uhhh... sort of hit."

"What? A horse? Strangle if you're trying to trifle with me, I had better warn you, you are trifling with the wrong man."

"Yessir, I mean no, sir," Crazy stammered, "I mean I'm serious as hell, sir. This horse really does hit."

With the help of his coaches, all of whom backed up every word he said, Crazy finally persuaded the reluctant owner to take a look at the strange prospect.

As things turned out, the horse performed brilliantly, facing all the pitchers on the staff (except Santiago, who, for some odd reason, was nowhere to be found), and knocking the daylights out of their best pitches.

As soon as the exhibition ended, Weitzenheimer phoned his attorneys. Within a short space of time, they had drafted a contract satisfactory to all parties.

"There's just one thing," Weitzenheimer instructed the group, "It could get real embarrassing if word of this leaked out too soon. And, gentlemen, I will not stand for my team being made into a laughingstock.

"I want you to keep a very low profile, Mr. Horse," he said, turning to the animal, "until we're ready for you. Someone'll be around to transport you up north when the season starts.

"The rest of you gentlemen had best zip your lips if you value your jobs. Understand?"

"Yes, sir," they chorused.

"Oh, Strangle," the owner mentioned to Crazy as they were all disbanding, "one more thing. It's not going to be easy introducing a horse into our national pastime. I think you better wait for a real big emergency before you actually put that animal in a ballgame."

"I thought you was on the wagon," Baseball Billy questioned Crazy as he poured him a double.

"Hell with the wagon. Turns out I'm not seein' things after all," Crazy gloated.

"And,. what…you're celebratin' on accounta you went blind?"

"I'll tell ya what else," Crazy continued, ignoring the bar-keep's inquiry, "but ya gotta keep this under your…uh…helmet. I think I found me a top-notch hitter."

"Hey, that's great," Baseball Billy enthused. "Tell ya the truth, your team genuinely needs a hitter."

"You said it," Crazy agreed.

"Yeah," surmised the bartender, "there's been way too much arm-tackling goin' on there."

Just then a man who stunk unto high heaven entered the place. He slid onto a barstool while everyone else, including Baseball Billy, scooted as far away as they could.

"Look, I'm not sure if stink is on the list," Crazy whispered into the ear hole of Billy's helmet, "but I think maybe you gotta serve this fella or you'll wind up with some civil rights beef on your hands."

Baseball Billy edged as close to the new customer as he could bear and, pinching his nose as he did, inquired: "Can I help you?"

"Gimmie a beer please, whatever you got on tap."

The bartender drew the beer, then retreated to the far end of the bar. In a little while, though, Billy's curiosity and his need to gab overcame him. He forced himself to move just close enough so the guy could hear him.

"Hey, buddy," the bartender began, "I don't wanna get per-sonal or nothin' but—"

"Yeah, yeah, I know," the customer cut him off, "It's on ac-counta I'm with the circus just came to town, OKAY?"

"The circus, huh?" the bartender marveled, "That sounds like fun. So what do you do?"

"I useta be a roustabout, but then I got 'promoted' to assistant elephant trainer."

"Promoted in the circus, congratulations!" Billy beamed.

"Congratulations, my foot!" the guy spat. "All that means is I'm the one has to give the elephants their enemas before the show, so they don't leave a big pile in the middle of the ring. Boy, I'll tell you what: you just can't get down offa that step ladder fast enough. I get splattered every time. Every God damn time."

"Jeez, that's horrible," Baseball Billy commiserated, "but cheer up. Some day you may find a job in some other line of work, where you don't have to alla time get splattered on by elephants."

"What," the guy said with a start, "and get outa show biz?"

Spring training continued while the horse grazed in a nearby pasture. Things looked mighty grim for Crazy's club in the coming season.

"Except for that horse," he thought with a sly smile.

V

The team's attendance figures had been pitiful for the last several seasons consistent with its poor performance on the field. More than once, Weitzenheimer had sought to relocate the team, only to discover there was not a city in the entire nation that was willing to take them. Still, any club could count on a good crowd on opening day, no matter how dreadful the previous season had been. After all, this was the first baseball the fans had seen since the previous autumn, and they always seemed willing to forgive and forget. Sure enough, fully 2,000 people packed the stands. It was the biggest crowd they had drawn since Fake Rubber Vomit Day, three years ago. If the team won today, Crazy realized, a lot of those people might come back to see another game or two. That could put him in real good with the boss. But if they lost, most of those fans would stay away for the rest of the season and Weitzenheimer would very likely ask him to do the same soon after. Well, Santiago had always pitched well against Chicago, so maybe they stood a chance.

True to the manager's prediction, Santiago threw brilliantly against the visitors, striking out the side in the first inning. In nine innings, he had given up only two hits and one unearned run. Unfortunately, his own team had failed to score at all, so in the bottom of the ninth, Chicago led, 1-0.

Before Crazy had much time to think, the first two batters had grounded out on the first pitch. As Pops Upsom headed toward the plate for their last chance, Crazy shouted to the umpire.

"Time out! I got a pinch hitter for Upsom." For a second he hesitated, remembering Mr. Weitzenheimer's injunction not to use the horse unless it was a real emergency.

"Hell," Crazy figured, "if this ain't an emergency, I don't know what is.

"Washington!" he called to the coach, "Get that horse out here."

The opposing team divided equally between those who wanted to dispute the point and those who thought the idea was hilarious. As they discussed the situation, the home-plate umpire studied the animal's contract, which Crazy had been kind enough to hand him as soon as the horse appeared.

"Hey, come on," the Chicago pitcher argued with his manager, "if they wanna waste their last out on a horse instead of a real batter, I say, let 'em."

"Aah, it just ain't natural!" Crazy's rival griped.

"I'm afraid it's legal, though," the umpire interrupted. "From what I can tell, you guys'll have to pitch to the horse."

"That's fine by me," the pitcher smirked.

The crowd finally settled down as the horse assumed its stance. While the pitcher chuckled and shook his head, all three of the outfielders approached the infield for a closer look at the farce that was about to play out.

The pitcher, not knowing any better, served up an underhand pitch, fit for Willoughby's granddaughter. A loud crack rent the air as the ball sped like a bullet to deepest center field, where it took a freakish carom and rolled to the farthest corner of the stadium. The horse stood proudly at the plate, admiring his handiwork.

"Run, run," Crazy panted, clenching his fists with excitement. The horse continued to stand at the plate.

"Run! Run!" Crazy shouted as one of the outfielders finally grabbed the errant ball. The horse, meanwhile, had started bowing to the crowd.

"You God damn stupid nag, RUN!" he raged.

"Run?" the horse snorted, turning to Crazy, "Hey, if I could run, I'd be at Hialeah."

THE TRUE MEANING OF LIFE
By Lewis Crews

The author of this piece is a shameless hack whose inclusion into this anthology is due only to a lost wager on the part of your editor.

We had hauled our clubs out to the local public golf course, hoping to ruin a little real estate, when Mr. Crews approached us. Oddly enough, he seemed to have enlisted a rather large gorilla as his caddy.

"Care to make it interesting?" he inquired.

"We don't think so," we replied. "We're not any great shakes at this game, and, for all we know, you could be a hustler."

"No, no," he was quick to assure us, "I don't mean for you to play me; I'm offering to bet you can't beat my gorilla, here."

"Ha!" we opined. "You somehow imagine this ape is going to beat us? And what do you propose to play for?"

"How's this: if you beat my gorilla, I will pay you the sum of five hundred pounds, Turkish. If you fail to beat the gorilla, you'll have to include my story in your next anthology."

"Deal!" I chuckled (as did the others) in anticipation of easy money.

The first hole was a real challenge: about five hundred yards long, with opportunities a-plenty for sand or water to get in your shoes (or between your toes if you are the ape).

Crews graciously let us drive first, and we hit a beauty: plenty of distance, right down the fairway. We were only about four hundred seventy yards from the pin. He then teed up the gorilla's ball. The animal gripped an iron in one hand and swung. The ball took off like a shot and did not stop until it had bounced off the pin and plopped down about a foot from the hole.

"So that's the way it is," we mused. "Very well, Sir, if you imagine we are going to allow ourselves to be publicly humiliated by your conniving anthropoid, you have exactly one other think coming. You win, we are going home.

"By the way," we inquired of Mr. Crews as we entered the clubhouse, "how does that big ape putt?"

"Exactly how he drives, five hundred yards a pop."

Having been forced to accept this man's services, as we most regrettably were, we explained to him we were looking for a Shaggy Dog story.

"How perverse," he observed. "The tale I had planned to submit is just such a story. I call it *The True Meaning of Life.* So should you."

Mr. Crews tells this one on himself.

As well he should.—tcl

A few years ago I asked Antigone, the brightest of my nieces, if she would like to hear a Shaggy Dog story.

"What's a Shaggy Dog story?" came her quick reply. "Is it some specimen of horribly-convoluted so-called poetry that neither I nor anyone else can understand?"

Henrietta was pretty sharp for a five year old.

"Hardly at all," I assured her. "I am going to tell you the archetypical Shaggy Dog story about the elephant and the one-eyed pirate, and it goes a little like this.

The Elephant and the One-Eyed Pirate

once there was an elephant
who tried to use the telegraph,
oh no, i mean the Dictaphone,

while all along the tree-lined racks
of sneakers, loafers and clods, not
a creature was
stirring, not even a moose. go,
then to the widowmaker and bid
her make one for me.
if it's not too
much trouble, size
thirty-eight. d. yet the sayers
of nay and
the doubters of gray
nuance still haughtily say,
horsefeathers
and tethers and
buttons
and booze. but all
the while, that voice in my
head sends me a coded
message: what've you got (aside from the trifle of your life)
to lose?

"That was nowhere close to a Shaggy Dog story," Ophelia complained, "but it was awfully funny." So, I had failed on two counts.

"I'll tell you what, Ashenputel," I offered, "let me hunt around for five or six years and see if I can locate a Shaggy Dog story that's a little more archetypical and a lot less funny."

"Oh, that would be peachy, Uncle Wilbur!" she squealed, possibly with delight.

My first impulse was to consult a wealthy industrialist, figuring (rapidly and in my head, which I rather excel at. In fact, I once beat a slide rule flatfooted in the pen relays, but that was in another incarnation, when I was Louis-Philippe, the *Citizen*

King) that these people could find me such a story if anyone could.

My eventual choice fell to one Leotis van Dandt, a prosperous subcontractor who produced inclined planes for the aircraft industry. I drove up to the van Dandt Slant Plant, strode into the head man's office and asked him: "Point blank?"

"How the hell would I know?" he volunteered. "Maybe you should consult a specialist."

I took his advice to heart and inquired of my ornithologist, who told me the reason I was having such trouble with this project was that I didn't know the true meaning of life. There could be, I realized at once, no better way to discover said true meaning of life than to ask the wisest man in the world, a most sagacious lama, whose philosophical treatise, *The Sound of One Foot Stomping*, had received the Nobel Prize for confusion. The problem (surely a minor one) was that the lama lived in the Himalayas, high atop the fearlots peak, Mt. Kanchenjunga, named after Sir Hilary Kanchen-Junga, best remembered for having routed Kuklafrannan Ali and his Wooly Bullies in the Battle of Tashkent.

I caught a flight to Nepal on Tijuana Aero Taxi Internacional, or would have if the plane had not crashed into the Pacific Ocean.

Fortunately, a passing frigate rescued us, although where it was passing to, I had no clue. I decided to go right to the top for some answers. Then, as I clung for dear life to the top of the main mast, I realized I might be better served if I sought out the captain and cajoled him into confessing the ship's destination or, failing that, into lending me one of the many towels he had no doubt swiped from the Secaucus Sheraton, for I was highly wet at the time.

Soon my dauntmore efforts (I'll admit I did not try very hard.) were rewarded by the sight of a closed cabin door, on which hung a nameplate inscribed, "MR. BIG." I knocked, after which

I heard a voice exclaim, "Whaddya want? Get t'hell out!"

The voice, it wound up, belonged to the ship's midget, in whose combination picnic basket and sleeping quarters I had unwittingly stepped. He recounted to me as best he could that the captain, who at the moment sat crouching inside the cabin, behind a Gatling gun, would see nobody until his bodyguards got back from their vacation just off the Bahamas. Since they had journeyed thereto *en bloc* (of cement), he doubted they would be returning any time soon. Furthermore, there were no towels to be had, as the Secaucus Sheraton had long since been demolished to accommodate a pig sanctuary, and would I please stop standing on his face?

"You said a mouthful," I congratulated him upon noticing the heel of my shoe was missing.

"A man's gotta eat," he philosophized.

At that time, a violent storm blew up. The gale knocked over several barrels of tar, which caused the ship to pitch considerably. To mark this special occasion, our captain briefly left his sanctuary to lean o'er the rail and cast his lunch to the wind. Having done so, he quickly returned to the cabin, triple-locked the door, and, as an added precaution, stuffed himself into the mattress. He never did trust the banks.

How ironic, then, that after our recent buffeting this way and that by the storm, we came to a point where we did not move at all.

"It's cause the engine's on the fritz," the ship's mechanic informed the first mate (The captain, remember, was a polygamist.).

"Damn!" she intoned, "We never should have accepted that free engine from Fritz in the first place!"

"Whew, it sure is hot," observed the second mate some months later, after the sturdy little craft had become embroiled in a severe heat wave.

"And there's nothing on TV!" wailed the boatswain, who had, in fact, eaten the TV a few days earlier.

"There are many tales," spoke a camel driver, who seemed to know.

"Since we now have no TV, why don't you tell us such a tale?" the first mate requested, making what was possibly the worst decision of her career.

"So be it," declared the wily raconteur, as a gleam mounted in his eye and rode into the sunset.

"In the wilds and woolens of the Tanezrouft Desert, there once dwelt a poor but piebald camel driver named Ali Ben Ali.

"He worked as a camel driver at this time, but, in happier days, he had been a servant to the potentate of an oil-rich emirate. It became Ali's good fortune that he alone, among the Emir's staff, had been chosen to accompany the Great Man to America, where His Highness had received an invitation to dine at the American president's white house.

"Now, the Emir deeply mistrusted foreigners in general and Americans in particular. Although he agreed to attend, he was very, very wary. No, I shall not say that fast three times, now please, let me return to my tale.

"At the dinner, His Highness was distressed to find the dishes they served were unexpectedly spicy, far too much so for his taste. He reached for his water glass, then froze. For all he knew, this could be exactly what the crafty American devils wanted him to do: drink the water they had laced with their insidious drugs, thereby turning him to silly putty in their hands.

"'Ali, you pig-dog, go and fetch me a glass of water. I do not trust the one set in front of me,' the Emir commanded.

"Ali obeyed time and again, but the Emir's thirst knew no quench. Just when Ali thought his boss must surely be waterlogged, he called him for still more.

"'Ali, you bastard offspring of a wanton camel, fetch me another glass of water, immediately!'

"A few minutes later, Ali returned, empty-handed.

"'What is the meaning of this, you avid sniffer of goat dung?' The Emir bellowed.

"'A thousand pardons, Your Highness, but there was someone sitting on the well.'

"Thus, do we find Ali Ben Ali, preparing to drive his camels across the desert, and his adventures thereupon, which I shall now relate.

"After the camels had been heavily laden with travail and other such cargo, including exactly the right number of straws, Ali headed out into the burning sands, stopping eventually at an oasis, where he paused to refresh himself. He did not bother to water the camels, as they were ships of the desert.

"He continued on his trek for several more days before he came to another oasis, where Bedouins, Druids and people of that ilk besieged him. They each held a basket of red dirt that they presented to Ali and for which he was obliged to pay them a bounty, it being a well-known fact that Ali cashes clay. Following all that folderol, he availed himself of the waters. The camels, who were ships of the desert, remained in the background.

"And so Ali and his staunch bestiary pressed forward (actually sideways if you consider that he had strayed 90 degrees off his course. Since the custom in that part of the world is to base the direction one is traveling upon the direction one's feet are pointed, the exception being if one is wearing shoes that one has put on backwards, we can safely say he *did indeed press forward*).

"Nobody, Ali realized, ever said camel driving was easy. But as difficult as his lot may have been, he felt grateful he was not beset by such troubles as plagued his cousin, Hakkim the undertaker.

"There had been a greater than normal harvest for the grime reaper—Excuse it please, will you hold steady the cue card? Thank you—in the town where Hakkim plied his trade, and vast was the quantity of bodies awaiting his attention. Finally, well past midnight, he reached the last corpse. He gave the dead man's body a cursory glance as it lay on the gurney. Then he flipped it over to check the back side. He noticed instantly that the cheeks seemed too far apart for such a state of repose. Closer examination revealed the cause: a rather large cork had been inserted into the sphincter.

"'This,' proclaimed Hakkim, bringing to bear all his accumulated years of wisdom in the trade, 'does not belong.' He deftly withdrew the cork. As he did so, a voice from beyond the sphincter began singing, 'Hello, Dolly, well hello, Dolly. It's so great to have you back where you belong.'

"Hakkim reinserted the cork and smote himself atop the head as shortly after as possible. 'It is a sign,' he concluded, 'that I have been working too hard. Let me go gag down a cup of strong Turkish coffee; then I shall finish my work with no more interference from these strange voices.'

"Hakkim took his coffee break and returned, somewhat fresher, to his work. Obviously the first order of business was to remove that cork. He did precisely that, and the voice began to sing the same song: 'Hello Dolly, well hello Dolly—' 'I am agape!' Hakkim decided. 'Never in all my years of practice have I seen such a thing!'

"He extracted the cork repeatedly to confirm what he had heard, and, without fail, the same song reverberated from within the bowels of the bowels. 'This is phantasmagoric! I must show my beloved wife and family,' he reasoned.

"It grew later yet as Hakkim showed off the wonders of this corpse, over and over again, to his family.

"Soon it was 3:30 in the morning, which did not deter him

from calling his cross-town rival, Mustafa, to boast of his news. Over many, many years, whenever Hakkim had attempted to impress him with a rare and unusual find he had uncovered in the course of his work, Mustafa, always seemed able to top him with a story of his own. Not now, he couldn't.

"'Mustafa, you must come here at once!' Hakkim plored his drowsy counterpart. 'But it is half past three in the morning,' Mustafa protested, 'and besides, it sounds like a sandstorm is brewing. Surely this can wait, whatever it is.'

"'Absolutely not,' Hakkim told him. 'It is vitally important you get here right away.'

"'Nonsense, nothing in our business is vitally important,' Mustafa pointed out.

"'Very well then, it is mortally important that you get over here right away, cheop-cheop.' Hakkim insisted. 'All right, I'll come over,' Mustafa reluctantly decided, and come over he did, following a most laborious journey across town.

"He finally arrived at the house of his rival, Hakkim, in the first hazy minutes of the dawn. 'So?' he stared at his host. 'Come down to my laboratory and see for yourself,' Hakkim responded as he led his grumbling guest thereto. 'Now observe what happens when I draw out this cork.'

"The laboratory fell silent as he gripped the cork one more time. Then, as had occurred every time before, the words, 'Hello Dolly, well hello Dolly' issued forth. 'There!' proclaimed a triumphant Hakkim, 'What do you think of that?'

"Mustafa yawned and rubbed his sleepy eyes. 'Do you mean to tell me' he mused, 'that you woke me up at 3:30 in the morning and caused me to drag myself all the way across town, through a blinding sandstorm yet, to hear some asshole sing Hello Dolly?'

"Now where were we before I was so rudely interrupted? Ah yes, Ali Ben Ali, plodding along happily through the searing desert as he belted out the Arabian Camel Drivers' Anthem, which, for reasons I have failed to divine, is sung to the identical tune as the famous American motorists' hymn, *Plastic Jesus*, but goes instead like this:

Oh, I don't give a hoot and a holler,
'long as I got my plastic Allah
Ridin' on my dromedary's hump.
But I'm a-feared he'll have to go,
His magnet does not work, you know,
Besides there's no room left there for my rump.

"On that triumphant and only slightly off-key note, Ali wandered into an oasis, where he lingered briefly to drink the water and ignore his camels (who were ships of the desert) before proceeding.

"Having twice forgotten to pack the lentil beans, Ali pressed relentlessly onward to German Southwest Africa, stopping only to refresh himself at an oasis. Naturally, he did not water the camels, since they were ships of the desert.

"It was not short before Ali encountered an isolated area of vegetation and potable water, known as an *oasis*. He stopped thereat to draw in long draughts from the wine- dark sea and was sorely disappointed when it turned out to be a metaphor after all. By this time, I should mention, the camels had become rather thirsty. They began offering subtle hints about their condition, chiefly by allowing their dry tongues to hang out at great length, as camels (especially thirsty ones) are inclined to do. One of the beasts added a bit to the pantomime by dying, but all this had no impact on Ali, who knew perfectly good and well that camels were ships of the desert.

"Onward marched the camel driver until at long last, he came upon an oasis. He had started to drink when, oddly enough, one of the camels cleared his throat (which in itself in not an odd thing for a camel to do) and spoke (which is) to Ali in the following manner: a high pitched whine with a slight Arabic drawl. What the camel said was, 'Ali Ben Ali, we are very thirsty. Can we have a drink of water?'

"'You can but you may not,' snapped Ali, who used to be an English teacher until everyone passed his course, and he was pronounced obsolete.

"'That's life,' he sighed.

"The little band continued on and yet again on until they finally reached an oasis, where Ali stopped to refresh himself and flatly refused, due to his prone position as he drank, to give his ships of the desert any water.

"By now, the camels realized they had to make clear to Ali the extreme severity of their thirst. At the very next oasis, they collectively bargained: 'Ali Ben Ali, we are so very thirsty. May we please, please, *please* have a drink of water?'

"'No, camels,' Ali warbled. 'Remember, you are ships of the desert.' And so the matter stood until the group wandered upon one of the very few oases in North Africa.

"'Say there, Ali, old buckaroo,' cooed one camel, (That's nothing: have you ever heard a pigeon bray?) 'howsabout lettin' us have one for the road?' Ali, essentially a kind man, smiled and told them, 'No, camels, you may not, owing to the irrefutable fact that you are ships of the desert.'

"The ship's crew stirred restlessly as Ali trudged deeper into the heart of the desert, until the monotony was broken by, of all things, an oasis.

"'Hark,' one of the camels called out.

"'No,' replied Ali.

"Yea verily and hip hip hooray, my friends, the North African desert is a brutal place. For no small reason our very wisest philosophers call it, The Land of the Dead. Even the terrifying sight of two ghosts playing jinn rummy failed to halt Ali in his quest for kilometry, although an oasis did.

"As he stooped to take in a long drink of water, he heard one of his camels beseech, 'Ali Ben Ali, we are still very thirsty. Please may we have some water?' Ali in his turn (he often enjoyed a pirouette as he spoke) replied, 'Sure, camels.'"

"Man overboard," remarked the third mate, several hours later, but since it was only the camel driver, and since he had been placed there by some outraged members of the ship's company, any memory of the matter quickly vanished.

"Who else can tell us a tale?" the second mate wondered aloud.

"There once was a man from Nantucket," began the nuns' priest.

"Please!" interjected the first mate. "This is a *children's* story.

"I should like to point out," I pointed out, "That your decameronesque antics are holding up my mission to enlighten the huddled masses."

"Which reminds me," said the ship's chaplain, "since today's Sunday and our ship seems to have drifted onto the Alaskan coastline, I suggest we go ashore and masses in de cold cold ground."

"And so," I mused, "we all departed from the ill-fated vessel (not to be confused with the Italian battleship, *Il Fetid*) and worked our way inland.

"Pardon me sir," I later asked the ticket clerk at the Fairbanks transcontinental bus station, "could you tell me when I might catch a bus to San Francisco?"

"Busf'safrasisca leavesfourofive s'mornin'" he enthused.

"And arrives?"

"Two months even."

"Uh," I inquired, "does that not strike you as an unusually long bus ride?"

"Oh, a trouble-maker, eh?" the clerk remarked, depressing simultaneously in a thrilling burst of oral-digital coördination that elicited a smattering of applause from the enthronged eyewitnesses, an alarm button. This not being an actual armed robbery, it summoned two very large policemen on the double.

"Is this the one?" growled the cop who held me up by the throat.

"Yep, I'd know him anywhere," the shrewd ticket broker calculated.

"Let's go, buddy," snarled the one who didn't. "We're going down to the station."

"But we're at the station already," I managed to say, though suspended in the other cop's grip, "Thanks for the lift."

I hardly impressed them with that logic and, in the end, I was sentenced to thirty- eight days for impersonating a vagrant and, of course, resisting arrest, the sentences, like many of my own, to run concurrently.

"There once was a man from Nantucket," began the cagy camel driver, who had swum the entire distance to the Fairbanks hoosegow, changed his repertoire and caught me as soon as I came out the door.

"I'm sure there was," I readily concurred, "good bye and good luck."

I returned to the bus station and bought a ticket for San Francisco with further adon't.

On board the bus, I found myself sitting across from a newly-wed couple en route to Vancouver for their honeymoon. At one point, when nobody appeared to be paying attention, the eager young groom thrust his hand down the front of his bride's dress, then abruptly withdrew it.

"It's all right, eh?" she said with a smile. "We're married now. You can go farther."

So he stayed on the bus all the way to Seattle.

As it turned out, we were only thirty minutes late getting to San Francisco, whereupon I booked passage to India, then prepared to get through the mountains and into the archdiocese of Nepal.

In anticipation of my assault on the formidable Mt. Kanchenjunga, where dwelt the wisest man in all the world, I had assembled a vast troupe of Sikhs, Jats (whom I had finally forgiven for Pearl Harbor), Nepalitans, Gullahs Gurkhas and Gherkins, all of whom I had outfitted at Bombay's prestigious Wogge Shoppe. In addition, I packed an assortment of ropes, picks, shovels, struggling hooks (or whatever it is they're called), manicure scissors and mountain spikes that one normally brings when one attempts seek the wisdom of the ancients (The Grand and Venerable Lama was almost 40). On top of that, I squeezed in some bats, gloves and a resin bag, just in case I had to play ball with the local authorities. As an afterthought, I packed a rifle.

A problem I had not counted on arose from my decision to ascend just after the second great hailstorm in the Year of the Gangzall ("Hail, hail, the Gangzall Year," spake the prophets, and the multitudes heeded not). I discovered that the irregularities on my mountain had been pelted away, leaving it smooth as glass on every face.

"It is the work of the Great Non-Existent Entity," remarked one of my guides, a devout atheist.

"Yakfeathers," I assured him. "It's just a small freak of nature that we'll overcome with no trouble at all," although I'm sure I don't know to whom I was speaking, as the entire group had stolen away (and most of the supplies) upon sight of their slippery assignment.

"Very well, I'll göit alone," I decided in my most memorable and precedent- shattering decision since Presley v. Marimba (the essence of which is that a suspect may not be assailed with a rubber or polyurethane hose for more than five minutes without getting a break to hear the Bill of Rights read aloud in a language no more incomprehensible than Esperanto). Unfortunately I had next to nothing left save the rifle and the baseball gear. Thinking fast (most of the food was gone, remember), I figured I could smear a coating of resin on my hands and slap my way up the mountain, palm by palm. Difficult, I surmised, but worth the ordeal to learn the true meaning of life.

Progress, need I add (If so, see tables on p. xiv.) was slow, and, on the third day of my ascent, the resin lost its endearing qualities, causing me to tumble seventeen feet to the ground.

With the realization that I did not need for this unorthodox method of mountain climbage the two ankles I had broken, I smeared on an extra-heavy coating and shot back to from whence I came. After five days, I caught my first indication I was on the right track. It so happened I had the good fortune to be climbing up the side on the mountain down which the Most Holy Lama disposed of his garbage.

"Eureka," I proclaimed upon taking a direct hit from a Most Holy Banana Peel, which I then ate. A bit later, when I found myself in a face-to-face confrontation with a ferocious-looking yellowjacket, I decided that, in the final analysis, there were probably better sides of the mountain to scale, so I promptly descended.

"Third time charm," I postulated as I began my next assault on the mountain. I did not consider myself charmed in the least after I lost my grip and tumbled down a mere three feet later.

I felt but minute traces of despair as I undertook another attempt, which, after a cruise of two and a half weeks, brought me to the summit of Mt. Kanchenjunga. It only remained for me to seek out the cave where the All-Knowing One dwelt. I was interrupted, incidentally, by the arrival of Frosty the Abominable Snowman.

Fully prepared to inflict casualties of Asiatic proportions, I whipped the rifle from my back and fired, or would have if the gun had not failed to function.

"Damn!" I thought. My bitterness was justified, for, as Chekhov had once said, if you are going to put a gun in your story, that gun must go off before the story ends, and this one had failed to go off, unless you count going off the side of the mountain, down which I threw it in a fit of peak.

Fortunately, I was then able to throw myself into a nearby briar patch, thereby foiling Br'er Snowman. When the creature finally drifted off to sleep, I extricated myself from the thorns and snuck back down the mountain. The next several years I roamed the countryside in avoidance of thug and dacoit alike, begging for scraps (You should see my scrapbook) on the way to New Delhi. Once there, and I was there once, as you shall see, I caught a flight from Suraja Dowlah Airport to the airstrip that lay atop Mt. Kanchenjunga. When, much in the manner of a dog with surgically removed vocal chords, we disembarked, I noticed a sign that read:

LIMOUSINE TO THE LAMA'S CAVE

Upon arrival, I had penetrated the cave but a few feet before I happened upon the Most Holy Lama himself.

"¿Como se llama?" I greeted him.

"Ça va bien," he replied.

"Could you please tell me," I began.

"Yes, very much so," he volunteered.

"The true meaning of life?"

"Life," intoned the lama, and the lama answered, "life...

"All of life," he went on to elaborate, "is like a deep, dark hole."

"WHAT?" I raged, "Do you mean to tell me I endured shipwrecks, exhausting treks, crocodile-filled swamps, frostbite, a storm of locusts and a Mexican jail just to hear you say that life is like a deep, dark hole?"

"All right," conceded the Most Sagacious Lama, "then it isn't like a deep, dark hole."

So there you have it.

THE FRUIT PEELER
By Buck "Buck" Bacaw

Buck or "Buck," as he prefers to be called, is the self-styled King of Tetrazzini in his hometown of Henway, Oklahoma, being the proud owner of a string of Chicken Tetra Shax. He seems to have made quite a success out of the enterprise.. We believe we heard him say he had eleven "chapters," as he calls them.

For the most part, Buck—excuse us, "Buck"—has left the vending of Tetrazzini to hirelings, while he lives the life of a gentleman farmer. It was in such a context we first met him. We found ourselves driving along the road that ran past his farm one wet, miserable day when we saw him struggling mightily to lift his prize pig up to eat apples from the tree in his front yard. This was not only hard on his back, it would seem, but rather a waste of valuable time. Always, as we are, eager to stick our nose into somebody else's business, we pulled up in front of his house and walked over to where he was still struggling with the pig.

"Pardon us," we said, "but doesn't it seem like a big waste of time to hold the pig up to the apples like that when there are plenty on the ground that he could eat?" "Aahh," he strained to answer, " what's time to a pig?" In his own spare time, "Buck" collects Shaggy Dog stories. So far, he has one. We offered him the usual fee for his story, but he would hear none of it.

"Keep your chump change," he said.

"You mean we won't have to pay you?" we asked him.

"Not one thin dime."

"Hot dig," we added.

"But," he said, "there is a catch. I have some friends who are looking to get a little free advertising for their wares. On the other hand, they would hope to avoid the potentially unpleasant glare of publicity that a major ad campaign might bring. I think your little story collection, there, would be just the ideal outlet for folks like my friends who don't want to get too well known. All you got to do is let me intersperse a few commercials in my story."

"Gosh," we sighed, "for a minute there, we had hoped we could launch your story into the world of literature for free."

"Son," he said, "there ain't no free launch."

In any case, we are indeed fortunate that "Buck" decided to give his story to us instead of the recycling bin, where, some might say, it rightfully belongs.—tcl

I

Vladimir looked everywhere up and down the decrepit train as he prepared to board for the interminably long trip to Vladivostok. The Tsar's secret police could be anywhere, he reasoned, and in any disguise. It was of paramount importance he get a coded message to Ivanov in that far-off city, and there could be no slip-ups. Just in case anything went the slightest bit wrong—even the tiniest misstep—he had a cyanide capsule in his breast pocket. He would swallow it immediately, rather than compromise the mission, which was to tell this fellow Ivanov (whom he had never met), "The fog is especially thick." Presumably Ivanov could take it from there.

In every compartment he looked, there was somebody who could very well be a policeman in disguise. In the first compartment, he saw a fat peasant woman with big, hairy moles on her face.

"Secret police," he figured. "That disguise wouldn't fool a dog."

The next compartment contained a little boy in short pants, being lectured to by someone who seemed to be his grandmother.

"Ah, but looks are so deceiving to the untrained eye. Clearly that is a good-secret- cop, bad-secret-cop team," Vladimir mused as he gave them the go-by.

A third compartment featured a dancing bear, got up in its circus gear, and an Italian-looking trainer, who cranked a hurdy-gurdy as the bear went through his paces.

"Please," thought Vladimir, "do they think I was born on the turnip truck?"

Next there was an earnest-looking student with wire-rim glasses, reading that day's copy of *The Hammer and Sickle*.

"Nice try," Vladimir muttered as he kept on walking.

The following pointless, distracting diversion from the plot is sponsored by Sistah Latiqua's Jive Turkey Parts.

Say, brother, has the old lady put you on a vegetarian diet because they told you your ticker's about to give out, but you're ashamed to be seen in one of those health-food stores with all the long-haired freaks, buying their wimpy Thanksgiving "tofurkey?"

I hear you, man. That's why the lovely Sistah Latiqua decided to make her fabulous, nutritious, healthy and absolutely righteous Jive Turkey Parts for those of us who need to watch what we eat these days, but nothing else has changed. You hear what I'm saying? It's the same bogus stuff as that other junk, but without the sissy name.

In the following compartment was a man dressed as a Japanese warrior, who was quite obviously not Japanese.

"That is a strange outfit, if you do not mind my saying so," he told the man.

"Not at all," the man replied, "for I am the personal Samurai to the Emperor of Japan. I am returning to His Majesty's court by way of Vladivostok, even as we speak."

"But you look like a Jew," Vladimir protested.

"And with good reason," the oddly-dressed man answered, "I am a Jew."

"So how did you get to be the Emperor's bodyguard?" asked Vladimir.

"It is a very interesting story," the Samurai began.

"I'm not sure if I have time to..."

"Of course you do," the man explained. "Many years ago, the Emperor's faithful bodyguard died of food poisoning from eating cooked fish.

"'I must have a replacement,' the ruler decreed, 'and he must be every bit as skilled as the man he would presume to replace. Put the word out.'

"And so the word was passed, high and low, to and fro, for a Samurai to win the coveted job as the Emperor's personal bodyguard. Knowing how rigid the requirements would be, almost every Samurai in Japan considered himself unworthy and, thus, declined to apply for the position. Only one Japanese man, considered to be the finest warrior in the country, came to the imperial palace to apply. After him, came a Korean, who evidently thought very highly of himself, and, of course, there was me.

"Clearly the Emperor was disappointed to see only one Japanese warrior and two evident imposters showing any interest in such a high honor. Naturally, he addressed the Japanese fellow first.

"'Show us your reputed skills as a warrior,' he instructed the candidate.

"With that, the Samurai, produced a matchbox that had been holding a fly. He opened the box and freed it. Before the poor insect could gain much altitude, the Samurai had unsheathed his great sword and sliced the fly, midair, in two.

"'Excellent,' the Emperor proclaimed. 'I daresay, you will be hard pressed to surpass that feat,' he told the Korean.

"'With your majesty's permission,' the candidate replied, 'I will demonstrate my skill.' He then produced a matchbox that held a mosquito. With equal aplomb, he served the bug in exactly the same way his predecessor had served the fly.

"'That was even more impressive,' the Emperor observed. 'Although I had believed that, being of the inferior Korean race, you did not have the right to call yourself a Samurai, it seems that you do after all. Congratulations.'

"'Excuse me, Your Highness, but I too am a Samurai,' I told the Emperor.

"'What, you?' he said with a laugh. 'And how is it you think you are qualified to be so considered, Mr. Round Eyes?'

"'Please, bear with me,' I asked him as I produced my own matchbox, this one containing a gnat. I released the gnat and made a few deft strokes with my sword. The insect seemed to wobble a bit, then flew off.

"'Ha! Fool, you did not even kill your bug,' the Emperor was quick to point out.

"'Ah, but the act of circumcision is not meant to kill...'"

"Only a secret policeman could concoct such a tale," Vladimir reasoned as he bade the so-called Jewish Samurai good day.

And so it went as he passed the remaining compartments by, until he came to the last one in the train. In it was a large, sinister-looking fellow with a nasty scar on his face. Vladimir figured that a man who looked so obviously forbidding would be a poorly disguised secret policeman indeed, so, despite the aura of menace that surrounded him, he was probably not one of "them."

"Excuse me, sir, do you mind if I join you?" Vladimir asked the stranger.

"Shut your mouth," the stranger instructed him. Since the man had not actually told him to get out, Vladimir decided to chance occupying a seat opposite him, taking, all the while, great pains to keep his mouth shut.

This portion of our story is brought to you by the Harry Kirshner Breakfast Products Conglomeration, makers of Kirshner's Naturally Hydrogenated Corn Fakes. And now, here is Mr. Harry Kirshner himself:

Hello, my name is Harry Kirshner, president and inventor of the Harry Kirshner Breakfast Products Conglomeration. Are you bothered by tuberculosis? Well then, let me tell you about Kirshner's Naturally Hydrogenated Corn Fakes.

Folks, these golden delicious flakes of crun-crun-crun-chewy corn substitute are made from polymers so sophisticated, we haven't even learned how to pronounce their names yet. Fact is, we've barely learned how to say 'polymers.' But we do know how good they taste. Yes indeedie!

Mmm MM! Now that's *tasty*! Now I just want to emphasize, this particular cereal is not going to get soggy in the bowl any too soon. Why, I had even written up a nice little jingle to say they wouldn't wilt when you poured on milk, but then my attorney pointed out to me that some upstart outfit over to Battle Creek had already beat me to that particular slogan.

Well, that's all right with me, I go and figure. You see, I'm connected to a certain Minnesota folk singer who owes me a favor or two. Bobby, I told him. That is, I mean, whoever you are, on account of how he doesn't want us using his name, see if you can't compose me a jingle to educate the people about the many fine things this product can do besides failing to wilt if you pour on milk, and, folks, that's just what he did.

Won't you try our Corn Fakes,
Taste just like corn flakes.
Well they won't scream
When you pour on cream,

And they won't spin

When you pour on gin,
Nor will they shine
If you pour on wine.

Now they won't sag
If you put 'em in a bag;
Won't bring you disgrace
If you stick 'em in a vase.

They will not crawl
Into your hall,
Nor will they creep
Into your sleep

Won't you try our Corn Fakes?
Please try our Corn Fakes.
They're always crunchy
And they taste real good.

On the third morning of his journey, Vladimir awakened to a great commotion. Some unfortunate passenger, about his own age and build, had been found dead from multiple stab wounds. It had happened at a time when nearly everybody on the train, Including Vladimir himself, had been asleep. Instinctively, he slapped his breast pocket to make sure the poison capsule was still there. For all he knew, this murder could have been a case of mistaken identity with him as the real target.

Then he noticed the sinister fellow who had been sitting across from him had vanished. Could he, Vladimir wondered for an instant, have had any connection with this bloody business? It seemed he would have to go on wondering, for the Tsar's secret police were not about to blow their covers by investigating anything so trivial as a murder when there were subversives to be found.

Before Vladimir could speculate any further, his compartment-mate came back to his seat.

"That was quite a terrible thing," he volunteered to the man.

"Do you by chance recall the conversation we had in St. Petersburg?" he asked Vladimir.

"Conversation? All you did was tell me, shut my mouth."

"Precisely."

II

Dawn of the fourth day brought an even more unpleasant surprise. Two more passengers had been stabbed to death overnight in the same brutal manner. Again Vladimir had slept through the whole business and, like everyone else on the train (except, one would hope, the killer), he knew nothing of how and at whose behest this had happened. One difference he noted from yesterday's slaying was that neither of these victims looked anything like him. Then, he saw that one of them was still clutching a bag that contained a fish, liberally sprinkled with paprika. "Hmmm!" he thought. "A red herring if there ever was one."

Once more, Vladimir checked to make sure his cyanide capsule was readily available, just in case this ruthless assassin had been looking to silence him before he could get to Ivanov and tell him the fog was especially thick.

This time, his scary compartment-mate had not seen fit to return to his seat until mid-morning. Why, Vladimir asked himself, was this fellow nowhere to be found when these murders took place?

This chapter is sponsored by your friends at the ThriffTee-Kleen Banks and Dry Cleaners.

My friends, are you sick of the way those big mega-banks both nickel and dime you to death with their so-called service fees? Gosh, I know I sure am. Well, now you don't have to put up with it any more. Yes indeed, for the low, low semimonthly charge of $47.50, you can write all the checks you want, up to a baker's dozen a month, and never have to worry about what each check is costing you. Are you also tired of the way your desk is cluttered up with those annoying bank statements? Well, get set to join the clean desk club, because at ThriffTee-Kleen Banks and Dry Cleaners, you will never have to worry about getting a bank statement, ever again. And, hey, if you decide you want a statement every now and then, your friends at the ThriffTee-Kleen Banks and Dry Cleaners will be only too happy to tote one up for you with a mere three months' notice and a nominal service fee of $55.75.

And for you savers out there, we at ThriffTee-Kleen Banks and Dry Cleaners pay a whopping eight percent—that's right, eight percent—of the rate those big conglomerate banks are willing to pay you for your hard-earned money. How can we afford to be so generous? It's because we aren't weighted down with those ridiculous overhead expenses like FDIC Insurance and all that bureaucratic hogwash. Yes, indeed, friends, it's like the man says, government is not the solution to our problems. Government is the problem.

Say, did I see some dirty clothes in your other hand? Well, you know, we *are* the ThriffTee-Kleen Banks and Dry Cleaners. Just say the word and one of our dedicated staff members will be happy to take you to the cleaners!

(BranchesinDryGulchOklahomaandBiminionlywithdra-walssubjecttoeigthty-sevendollarsurchargenotresponsiblefortorn-soiledlostordamagedgarments.)

Vladimir had a thought. If the foulard who sat across from him wanted to do him in before he could deliver the message, he knew right where to find him. Perhaps, then, this fellow was not the murderer, despite his murderous demeanor. But then another less reassuring thought struck Vladimir. Maybe the first three killings were some sort of decoy, and he was the intended victim all the while.

He realized he had better start learning what he could about this suspicious character, before he became the next target of the murderer's deadly blade.

"Care for a cigarette?" he offered in a crafty attempt to feel his mysterious companion out.

"Care to shut your yap?" the stranger replied.

III

On the morning of the fifth day, the commotion worsened, as four more passengers had been found in various parts of the train, each horribly mutilated and dead.

"Wait a minute," Vladimir realized, "I think I'm beginning to see a pattern." First one, then two, now four. The fiend was obviously doubling his murder total every night. Vladimir whipped out his abacus and began calculating. At this rate, by the ninth day (of a *fifteen* day journey), he will have killed 511 people. That was more than were on the train. In all probability, the killer would have gotten around to him, perhaps twice, by that time. And again, the stranger was nowhere to be seen when the bodies were discovered.

"Maybe if I swallowed the capsule now, this assassin might see there was no further need to set up all these decoy victims." Vladimir reasoned. After all, his instructions could not have been more explicit: if *anything* went amiss, take the poison and die quickly. He pondered a while, then decided to wait just a little bit longer to see if he could not figure out some way of keeping away from the murderer's blade. This portion of the tale is, once again, brought to you by the Harry Kirshner Breakfast Products Conglomeration.

Hi there, I'm Harry Kirshner himself. You know, folks can get pretty set in their ways, especially around breakfast time. Seems like whenever a slice of toast pops out of their toaster, why nothing will do but to grab it and spread some kind of fruity preserve on it or Lord knows what else. But whatever people are spreading on their toast these days, nobody seems to give much thought to peanut butter. "Peanut butter?" they'll say, "Why, that's something you eat for lunch or maybe when you're taking the family on a long trip, like to Columbus or Rio de Janeiro." I hear people say that all the time. Well now, what about peanut butter for breakfast?

"Okay," you might allow, "I've always trusted your breakfast advice before, Mr. K., and I might be inclined to go with you on this one, but I'm worried sick about all them calories."

Yes, calories were something to worry about, that is until the boys in our research lab here at the Harry Kirshner Breakfast Products Conglomeration came up with our latest development: Kirshner's Extra-Chunky Peanut Margarine. It's a full 4% less fattening than your average run-of-the-mine peanut butter and nearly every bit as tasty. It's always extra-chunky because there's just the one speed left on our blender.

And now, to sing the praises of this fine product is fine crooner in his own right, who owes me a favor or two and who's agreed to sing us a commercial of his own composition, providing we don't reveal his identity. All right, Bob, or, uh, whoever you are under that paper bag, hit it.

I had a bad dream the other night
That me and my bedclothes got into a fight.
They bloodied my eye and blacked my nose
And all in all left me in the throes
Of bein' about to get a fat lip,
'Til I rolled out of bed and said, I'm hip!

Since the sun was comin' up at last,
I went lookin' for a way to break my fast.
But first I heard from my pet dog, Floyd,
Who had learned to talk but was still paranoid.
Listen man, I heard him say,
Most of what's in your kitchen ought to scare you away.
Alien creatures with three or four eyes
Have taken the trouble to poison your pies,
And the frosting on your cake of soap
Is laced with some kind of killer dope.
That scrapple you were gonna eat today
Was scrutinized by the C.I.A.
I guess the peanut butter's safe to eat.
With that, he went to chase a cat in heat.
Now the moral of this whole bad dream
Is not so simple as it may seem.
Keep some peanut margarine well out of sight,
So when your pantry's poisoned, you can still grab a bite
And not have to worry 'bout gettin' too fat:
Kirshner's Peanut Margarine, that's where it's at.

That's Kirshner's Extra-Chunky Peanut Margarine, folks, available wherever it's at.

It went without saying that Vladimir was not going to permit himself drift off to sleep until he got to the bottom of all these shenanigans. Staying awake became even more vital when the malevolent figure he had been riding with returned to their compartment.

Hours passed with Vladimir silent, per the stranger's instructions, but keeping an eye cocked and an ear peeled for any sign of trouble. Day passed into night as he struggled to stay awake. In the small hours of the morning, Vladimir finally lost the battle and drifted off to sleep. He dreamt he was having an eye exam, during which he was having unusual difficulty reading the eye charts.

"What is the problem?" he asked the optometrist when the exam ended.

"Well, to begin with," the doctor said, "you simply must stop abusing yourself."

"Or else I'll go blind?" Vladimir sneered.

"No, of course not, but the other patients find it very disturbing."

He did not know how long he had been unconscious, but something inside him made him awake with a start. There, sitting on the seat opposite him, was the menacing stranger, methodically wiping the blade of a long, sharp knife.

IV

The stranger fixed his glare on Vladimir, then pulled down one of his suitcases. From it he took an apple. Next, he set the apple upon the suitcase that he was now holding on his lap. With the greatest care, he peeled and cored the apple and cut in into neat, identical slices. Vladimir stared transfixed as the man produced a clean, white handkerchief. He placed the slices into the handkerchief and carried them to the last door on the train. Next he opened the door and let the apple fragments fly out of his handkerchief. Following that, he returned, put the hankie back in his pocket and sat down.

"Is this fellow trying to tell me something?" Vladimir wondered.

The stranger did not let on that anything of a suspicious nature might have occurred, but, in another hour, he once again had the knife in his hand. This time, he selected a tangerine from his suitcase. Again using the flat of the suitcase as his laptop counter, he peeled the tangerine and easily bisected the individual slices with his very sharp blade. As he had done before, he put the slices into his handkerchief, then flung them outside through the same door.

"Whatever message this guy is trying to send me," Vladimir told himself, "I'm not getting it." Even the process of smiting his forehead several times with the heel of his hand failed to bring enlightenment, although why that should be so, he did not have a clue.

Chapter IV is brought to you without commercial interruption by the good people at The Happy Harvest Weight Loss Clinic. Want to lose weight, but can't discipline yourself to diet and exercise? Don't have a strong enough heart for amphetamines? The helpful people at The Happy Harvest Weight Loss Clinic have just the answer for you. If you are looking to shed those unwanted pounds, they only ask you to ask yourself, how much do I need that spare kidney or that second lung? Am I not carrying around a lot of redundant weight? And aren't we are all carrying far more blood than we need to survive? Think of how much thinner you'd be if you lost a mere quart of that weighty fluid. At the Happy Harvest Weight Loss Clinic, where for a price that must be seen to be believed, our highly-skilled mechanics will remove whatever organs, fluids or appendages are making you feel so heavy, quickly, painlessly and permanently. You will probably gain back that ten pounds you lost on someone else's fad diet, but you will never gain back another kidney. What is more, you will have the satisfaction of knowing that your spare parts will be sold to some desperately wealthy individual who needs them far more than you. The Happy Harvest Weight Loss Clinic: doing well by doing good.

Another hour passed. The stranger had been napping, but he woke up and reached for his suitcase. This time he pulled out a banana. After peeling it, he took out the same menacing knife and cut the banana into several slices. As Vladimir had come to suspect he would, the stranger withdrew his handkerchief and placed the banana slices inside of it. Then, also true to Vladimir's prediction, he opened the rear door and let them fly from his handkerchief.

All very well and good, Vladimir reasoned, he was beginning to figure out what this sinister fellow was going to do, but he could not, for the life of him, figure out why. Was it to lull him into a false sense of security? He knew, just as surely as if it had been written in a book, if he drifted off to sleep again, he would wake up eviscerated.

Later that afternoon, the stranger would yank out a cantaloupe. And, while it required a little more effort to prepare the slices from this fruit, place them into the hankie and pitch them, that is exactly what he did.

"What is he up to?" Vladimir continued to wonder.

As dusk approached, the stranger brought out a small bunch of purple grapes. With the care and precision of a surgeon, he peeled, halved and pitted each one When he finished, he put the grapes into his handkerchief. Next he held them up to his face as he carefully looked them over.

"Aha," thought Vladimir, "do I detect a change in this strange pattern?" But then the stranger got up, opened the same door, and let the grapes fly from his handkerchief onto the vast Russian tundra.

Desperate as he was, both from curiosity and lack of sleep, Vladimir could contain himself no longer. "I am terribly sorry, good sir, to disturb your tranquility, but I will surely go crazy if I cannot find out: why have you been peeling and slicing all this fruit?"

"Had I known," his compartment-mate sighed, "that I had to have to put up with this incessant yakkity-yak, from the time we left St. Petersburg, I would have cheerfully moved to a quieter compartment.

"Very well," he went on, "I have been, as should be obvious to all but a complete dolt, making a fruit salad. Are you now satisfied?"

"Yes, that certainly seems to make sense," Vladimir admitted, "but why do you keep throwing out the fruit?"

"Idiot," the stranger snarled, "I hate fruit salad."

Epilogue

The Epilogue is proudly presented by the makers of My Homework brand Dog Chompies.

How many times has your youngster tried to weasel out of his missing homework with the sad and sorry excuse that the dog ate it? Did the teacher buy it? No, I guess not. Well, Mom and Dad, now that grouchy old teacher is going to have to take it and like it!

Yessiree, Bob, when you feed Fido a few generous handfuls of My Homework Dog Chompies, then when Junior says, "The dog ate My Homework," he'll be telling the gospel truth. Get it? You can get it at your friendly neighborhood grocery, so put down this book and get it!

Vladimir eventually arrived intact in Vladivostok. He hurried to the address where they had told him he could find this Ivanov fellow. When he arrived, he saw it was a five-story walk-up. In the vestibule, he noticed two Ivanovs listed in the building: one on the ground floor and one on the fifth. He nervously fingered his cyanide capsule as he tried to figure out which one was the right Ivanov.

"I may as well save myself an exhausting climb," he finally decided, as he knocked on the first-floor door.

"Yes?" said the old man who answered the door.

"Ivanov," Vladimir replied, as he fixed him with his hardest stare, "the fog is especially thick."

A smile of recognition played upon the man's face.

"Ah, you want Ivanov the spy. Fifth floor."

And the brutal stabbings? They all turned out to be suicides, committed by recently converted teetotalers on their way to the Orthodox Christian Temperance Union Convention in Vladivostok. When it dawned on them that the rest of their respective lives would be lived without vodka, they opted for the easy way out.

THE TEN DOLLAR SUIT
By Tatheglio Greensward deTroppe

W e are delighted nigh unto the point of giggles to have received this tale from "Tad" deTroppe, who normally writes under the name of Urban VI. Inasmuch as this story pertains to a suit rather than a vestment, we have elected to use his right name and let the chips fly where they may.

Tad or "Tatheglio" was so named because his parents said they "wanted to break the pattern."

When Tad's parents met, his mother had told his father, in answer to his question, "My parents called me 'Sunset,' because that's the first thing my father saw, out of the hospital window, right after I was born."

"How strange," Tad's eventual father answered, "my dad also named me for the first thing he saw, right after I was born."

"Why, that's fascinating, um...what did you say your name was?" Sunset asked him.

"Bill."

Tad attended the University of Southern California at Onofre, on a T-ball scholarship. He graduated with Lowest Possible Honors, having made the Custodian's List twice, once in succession.

Today Tad, a nuclear engineer, eagerly awaits the invention of the nuclear locomotive, so he can at last get a job in his chosen field. For now, he must content himself with working in the hydorelectrolysis department at Tinker's Dam, widely considered to be the most worthless public works project ever devised. In the meantime, and for the most trifling of pittances, he has been kind enough to submit to us his rendition of *The Ten Dollar Suit.*

We like to think that Tad drew on fond memories of his summers as a haberdasher's devil, between college terms, to compose this story. In fact, thinking thusly practically makes our day. Now let us see if we can make yours.—tcl

CHAPTER I

He had high cheekbones, narrow lips and a nasty glint in his eye—his third eye at that, for his pilgrimage to open same had only been a partial success. The Most Holy Wise Guy, Guru Lou McAdoo, had done his best to enlighten the guy up, enlightenment finally coming to the disciple when he realized he was being played for a sap and parted, not only company, but Guru Lou's head with a Louisville Slugger, and a doctored one to boot because that's the kind of guy he was.

"Whaddaya mean, I'm a beautiful human bein'," he thought as he rummaged through his disguise kit. "Still, it's a shame I gotta go incognito for this gig."

He and his buddies had a long list of successful jobs to their credit, and quite a reputation, at least until their last assignment. They had been told to go out to San Francisco and take care of Louie "the Trigger" Bonura and Pasquale "the Ice Pick" Bogiagaloupe. When they barged into the wrong hotel room and blew Joey "the Finocchio" Linguini and Tony "Pretty Boy" Frangipani—away, that is—they earned a new tag as The Gang that Couldn't Shoot Straights.

"Very funny," he mused, not over the line, but what he'd done to the clown who thought it up.

"Ho, ho, ho, ya little bastids," he muttered as he took his accustomed seat on the red velvet throne at Dingleberry's Department Store, "Merry Christmas."

*****

"Deathless, flat-out deathless," Walter J. Fnortner, budding novelist and Junior Systems Analyst *pro tem* for the Departmental Office of Direct Assistance, observed as he re-read the beginning of what he knew for sure was the next blockbuster bestseller ever to hit the presses.

In the meantime, money continued to be tight. While his part-time sinecure with DOODA provided him with enough revenue to pay the rent, keep his car running, and maybe do some eating here and there (hardly ever there), it did not leave him with nearly enough to live on in the style to which he was fully prepared to become accustom, come the blockbuster.

"You could at least get some help for your wardrobe, and, by the way, what does the 'J' stand for, Walter J. Fnortner?" Elroy Bean, his fellow junior analyst *pro tem* of the selfsame system pointed out to him one day.

"Johnson" replied Walter, "I was named after the famous ballplayer."

"You mean Lefty Fnortner? Never heard of him. Seriously, though, you really do need to get some new threads."

"Go shag yourself," Walter thought. What he said out loud was: "What're you talking about? I'm a real snappy dresser, if I do say so."

"Well," Elroy elaborated, "I say you can't make it, day in and day out, with the same two suits. I mean what are you going to do if one of 'em goes on vacation?"

"I suppose you're right," Walter admitted, "but right now I got bigger fish to fry."

"You'll probably get grease all over your clean suit."

Later that day, Walter settled down to lunch in a nearby park. Following a quick ransack of his freshly-dyed brown bag and the almost equally quick boltage of a plantain and peanut margarine sandwich, he found himself with almost thirty-five minutes to kill.

"Somebody stop me before I kill again," he murmured as he set forth to dispatch those minutes in as aimless a manner as possible. This left him standing, a short while later, in front of a store window, whose sign proudly proclaimed: INVENTORY CLEARANCE SALE! SUITS AS LOW AS FIVE DOLLARS! WE MUST BE LOSING OUR MINDS!

"Here," Walter J. Fnortner realized, "is my chance to shine."

"Do we really have suits for five dollars?" the salesman repeated to Walter. "Is the Bear Catholic? But I tell ya what, if you can part with a ten-spot, I can putcha into somethin' fine."

"Well, okay," Walter agreed. "What have you got for ten—"

"Right here, Sport," the haberdasher told him as he snatched a snazzy lime green number from the rack.

"Go ahead, try it on," he urged Walter as he pointed him toward the dressing rooms. Almost before he knew it, Walter had emerged in the ten dollar suit.

"Looks good onya," the salesman observed, "but, remember now, all sales final. No refunds, no alterations. Still, for ten bucks, how can you go wrong, eh?"

"Yeah, I guess this is all right," Walter finally decided. "Mind if I wear it back to the office?"

"Hey, just hand over the ten, and you can wear it to the Inaugural Ball."

CHAPTER I

January came in bitterly cold that year on the reservation, yet the wind-whipped chill would have been something to ignore, even to laugh at, for the chief, were it not for the calamity that had befallen his privy. It lay on its side, his very own personal outhouse, at the bottom of a steep and rocky embankment.

The chief did not become chief by being a fool. He knew that, cold as the wind had blown, never had it been strong enough to dislodge an outbuilding, his or anyone else's. He realized his privy had been pushed down the embankment, and he was pretty sure he knew who was behind it.

"Son," he said to his youngest child, who was getting to be that age, "somebody push over privy. You know who do this?"

"No, Pop, me have no idea," the boy was quick to reply.

The chief sighed and motioned his son to sit down. "Me want to tell you true tale," he explained.

"When Great White Father of whole country, George Washington, was little boy, him chop down his father cherry tree. George Washington father very sad to see this.

"'George,' his father ask, 'you chop down this cherry tree?'

"'Me no can tell lie,' George Washington tell his father, 'me chop down with hatchet.'

"Do you know what happen then? George Washington father no punish George Washington, because him tell truth instead of speak with forked tongue.

"Now tell me again," the chief asked his son, "you know who push privy down the hill?"

"Me no can tell lie," the boy beamed. "Me push."

With that, the chief grabbed his son by the arm. With his other hand, he grabbed a belt and whaled away at him until the wampum beads began to fly. When he finally stopped to rest his arm, the boy was in tears.

"That no fair!" he protested. "You say when George Washington tell truth about cherry tree, his father no punish, but when I tell truth, you punish bad. Why me get different deal?"

"Because," the chief told him, "when George Washington chop down cherry tree, George Washington father *no sitting* in cherry tree!"

*****

Mercifully, Walter's boss came in before he could progress any further with what was, definitely, for sure this time, the opening of his new best-seller, soon to be a major motion picture. Noting only the suit and not what Walter had been doing on the government's computer, his boss opined: "Nice suit, Fnortner."

"Thank you, Mr. Dingleberry, I just bought it today. Pretty okay, huh?"

"I guess," Dingleberry elaborated, "but it appears your right sleeve's longer than your left."

"Suffragan catfish, he's right!" Walter realized somewhat later, after studious observation of his coat sleeves' behavior.

"I've got to take an hour of personal time," he informed the human resourceress, prior to heading back to the store from whence his suit had come.

"Look here, my sleeves are all wrong," he explained to the salesman who had sold him the goods.

"Now, remember, it's like I told you before: no refunds, no alterations, all sales final."

"Sure, I understand," Walter told him, "but can you maybe help me out with this sleeve thing?"

"Well, if you don't wanna spend a lotta dough on altera-tions—and somethin' tells me you don't—then whatcha wanna do is pull your left sleeve down and hold it in your hand, sorta like this." The salesman proceeded to give the left sleeve a tug and then folded Walter's fingers over it.

"There," he explained, "now if you just hold the sleeve like that, it'll seem like it's as long as the right, right?"

"Right!" Walter was quick to agree.

With a high heart and his other internal organs presumably raised to a concomitant level, Walter returned to the office.

"Here I am," he announced to no one in particular.

"Hey, Walter, nice suit," Delores, the girl of at least some of his dreams, noted as he strode past her desk.

"Why, thank you," he beamed.

"Too bad the lapel's all bent out of shape."

Walter checked himself out. Sure enough, his left lapel was looking noticeably perpendicular to the rest of the jacket. .

"Hell with it," Walter thought as he removed the offending garment and hung it up, "I got work to do."

CHAPTER I

"It is said, Sahib, that only mad dogs and Finnishmen go out in the midnight sun," the guide advised him.

"Yeah, well, thanks for the tip, there, Sven," he growled as he chomped angrily on his cigar @ twenty-one chomps to the bite, for his mom had raised no fools.

"Neverthegod damnless," he decided, "out is the direction I'm goin', so let's make like horse-guano and hit the road."

Just like that, they were on their way to the lair of Lars Danfoond, the Heavyweight Turco-Roman Style Taffy-Pulling Champion of the Last Known Universe.

"And I want you to know," the determined explorer explained, "these are the days when taffy pulling was completely on the up-and-up or at least on the out-and-out."

Over the woodlands and through the fjords they tromped until they had reached the secluded hut where the great man retired to shun publicity betwixt title pulls.

"Mr. Danfoond, sir," the explorer besought as he dangled by the ankles over the champ's garbage disposal—a hungry polar bear in a pit—"I've come to bring us fame and fortune. Please don't let me down, and I really mean that."

"Glaaak ♪ beep beep ♫ fnf ptweeng ork," the guide began translating into fluent Fin.

"I hereby waive consecutive translation," the champ interrupted with a waive of his massive hand; "Go ahead, what's on your mind?"

"That bear's jaws, if you don't lift me outa there.

"Thanks, that's better," he told his host. "Okay, now, I'll give it to ya straight."

"Actually, I prefer mine with soda," Lars counseled him.

"I gotcha covered," he replied as he pulled a box of Arm 'n Hammer from his pocket and sprinkled the contents over the champ.

"All right, here is my proposition. We got this wrestler back in America, named Undefeated P. Branscombe, who's been livin' up to his reputation, mainly by stayin' undefeated. In fact he's the world champeen...at wrestling, that is, Mr. Danfoond, sir."

"You may call me 'Big Lars, Sir' if you wish. Now tell me, why would this be of any interest to me?"

"Well, I tell ya, Big, I think you're the man to beat him. I should warn ya, this guy Branscombe has a certain stratagem he calls the Pretzel Hold. Nobody to this day knows how he does it, but, once he gets his opponent into the Pretzel Hold, there's no gettin' out. On the average, it takes a team of chiropractors eight to ten weeks to untangle the victim. Some of 'em are still eatin' off the floor and peein' on the ceiling to this very day.

"Anyway, this here Branscombe and his backers, they've put up a sizeable purse for anyone who can beat him, one fall to a finish."

"It sounds intriguing. Just how much money are we discussing?"

"Let's just say you'll be lightin' your panatelas with ten-spots for a long time to come."

"And how many of these ten-spots would that be?" inquired the champ.

"How many panatelas ya got?"

"Right now, two. I am to risk a lifetime of paralysis for a mere twenty of your dollars?"

"Hell no, I'm talkin' three, four times that much."

"In any case," the champ went on, "why would you wish to enter me for this singular honor? My field is the pullage of taffy."

"True enough, but Branscombe's wise to the ways of all the wrestlers on the circuit. I need a big, strong guy who can throw some moves at him he's never seen before. That's where you come in."

"Indeed, it does sound interesting," Big Lars admitted, "but I would require considerable time to prepare for such an effort."

"You got it, Big. I got a two-year program all mapped out, once we get to America. Believe you me, when we step into the ring with Undefeated P. Branscombe, we will be ready."

"You will be joining me in this ring?"

"Well, uh, not necessarily," explained the man who would be manager. "It's what we Americans call a figure of speech."

"Beps ptang auggght blubblubblub," the ever-helpful guide began translating in an effort to dispel the confusion.

"Thank you just the same," Big Lars replied. "I'll take your word for it."

"Do we have a deal then?"

"It is then that we have a deal."

Suffice it to say, Big Lars and his manager labored patiently for two long, hard, sweaty years, literally learning the ropes. For two years, interrupted only for a brief oatmeal cookie-and-lemonade binge on Groundhog's Eve, the doughty contender trained, strained, ran, walked, lapped, slurped, jogged and even did a few pushups. From time to time he would punctuate these endless calisthenics with wrestling matches against lesser opponents, none of whom took very well to being handled like a clump of taffy. (It should be noted that, during this era, Big Lars had let his taffy-pulling title fall into the clammy but otherwise strong hands of Ali the Terrible Turk, born Ollie the Incredible Jerk, in Sophia, Bulgaria's sister city, Ellie Mae. Despite such questionable origins, he always prayed to St. Peter—the patron saint of taffy pulling, for reasons little understood nor long remembered—before each match and his cigarette lighter as well.)

As fortune would have it, Undefeated P. Branscombe still held the championship, and the rich prize that would go to the man who could beat him was still available. It was with the utmost confidence that the Branscombe camp accepted the challenge of wrestling Lars Danfoond.

Once the date for the contest was set, Big Lars and his manager intensified their efforts to prepare for the bout. Hour after hour they poured over stereopticonic images (Remember, Tommy Edison had yet to invent the training film.) of the champ's past matches, trying to determine how to avoid the dreaded Pretzel Hold.

"He always grabs the left ankle. Keep that in mind," the wily coach told his charge. "Keep your left leg away from him, and he'll have t'fightcha fair and square. When he does, you jump right in and turn him into Jack the Beanstalk."

Come the big day, the two opponents squared off at mid-ring. At the opening gun, they both circled one another feinting sporadically. All the while, Big Lars was careful to keep his left ankle out of his opponent's reach.

"Two fifty! No, make that three hundred! I got three of the best and brightest on my man, Big Lars!" his manager called out.

"Five hundred? Sure I got five hundred. Whaddya think I am, a piker?" he continued as Undefeated P. Branscombe's supporters deluged him with wads of cash.

"A thousand? I got a thousand, it's right in the bottom of my shoe. Don't worry, I'm good for it...yeah? Well, your *mother's* moustache! What? Now you're talkin', now you're talkin'!

"Another grand you say? You're on, sport. Now who else wants a piece a' this here action?"

Meanwhile, Big Lars had been concentrating on his opponent. Just as his manager had placed the last thousand-dollar bet, Branscombe leapt straight up with the spring of a trained pogo-stickler. When he came down, he had Big Lars firmly by the left ankle. Seconds later, he had him in the Pretzel Hold.

"Oedipus Rex (or words to that effect)!" Big Lars' manager cried out. "I'm ruint!

"Let me out of here," he added as an afterthought, not necessarily needing to have any further discourse with those who had bet against him. He was just about out of the arena when he heard his protégé erupt with a mighty bellow. Then he heard the crowd roar even louder than it had when the Pretzel Hold was applied.

"Christ, what's that bastard done to him now?" the manager wondered. He decided to allow himself a quick peek at the ring before resuming his place on the lam. What he saw coming down the aisle toward him were two men bearing a stretcher on which lay a very bruised, battered and bloodied Undefeated P. Branscombe.

"What the—SOMEBODY OWES ME MONEY!" Big Lars' manager marveled as he bounded up the aisle. He ran up to the new champion and asked him, "How in the blue-eyed hell did you get out of that hold?"

"I'm not entirely sure myself," Big Lars explained as he torched his Hav-a-Tampa with a clean, crisp ten dollar gold piece, "but here's what I remember.

"All of a sudden I find myself getting thrown and twisted, this way and that. Before I know it, I'm on the floor, staring right at a pair of trunks, front-wise. Not having any better idea what to do, I thought I might bite the son of a bitch on the testicles."

"Yeah, so?" the manager asked. "How did that get you out of the Pretzel Hold?"

The new champ stared at his manager for a moment and then asked him: "Do you know what you can do when you've bitten your own balls?"

*****

"I can't stand it," Walter exclaimed, referring, not to what was, this time, without question the up-and-coming buster (if not pulverizer) of blocks, but, rather, to the perpendicular lime green lapel that continued to mock him from the coat rack. With a speed that could only bedazzle, Walter was on his way to the haberdashery.

"I know I should of mentioned this earlier," he explained to the salesman, "but I got another problem with this suit. The lapel keeps—"

"Now, I'm not gonna tell you again," the salesman told him again. "Our policy is strickly no refunds and no alterations, period, end of story, *chiuso, fini,* 23 skidoo."

"I know, I know," Walter agreed, "but I thought you might have some idea how to fix the damn thing so it won't stick out and all."

"Hmmm," the salesman piped up, "let's see now...I guess if you tilt your head over a little, like so, you could hold it down with your chin. Give it a try."

Walter gave it the old college try, and, sure enough, the pesky lapel pesked no more.

"I think we got something here," the salesman enthused. "Yes, I think we definitely got something here."

" 'ts okay?" Walter managed to ask

"It fits you like a glove," the salesman assured him as Walter strode gleefully from the store for what the salesman, treating himself to a rare moment of sincerity, sincerely hoped was the very last time.

CHAPTER I

"Now listen carefully," the veteran bellhop instructed young Todd Griffiths, an initiate into the same calling. "You gotta be discreet. Without you got discreetitude, you got nothin'.

"Y'know what that means? It means, f'rinstance, when a guest don't want us around, we ain't around."

"How about when he does?" Todd wondered aloud.

"Well, most likely, we ain't around then neither, but that's okay, see, long's you're discreet."

"So how do I go about bein' discreet?" asked the newcomer. "I'm not sure I get what you mean."

"Can't explain it in so many words, but, I tell you what. By the time you get done studyin' my technique for a week, you'll know from discreet all right."

"Hey, where you guys been?" the floor manager snapped, "Nine twelve's had a room service order in from the dawn of time. Now let's hustle it up there."

With nosebleed speed they were at the door of room 912.

"Here, quick, take my hanky," the old bellhop said to Todd, "before you mess your uniform up."

"Thags," Todd answered as he pinched his nostrils to stem the flow.

They knocked on the door several times and got no answer.

"Must've stepped out," the wise old hopster concluded.

"So what do we do with this stuff, take it back?"

"Are you nuts? If we don't deliver the goods, they don't get charged for 'em. Now what the hell kinda way is that to run a hotel?" the veteran explained as he let them into the room with a passkey.

Once inside, the two of them saw the bathroom door was wide open and, standing at the sink with her back to them, was a shapely young lady wearing only a towel around her wet hair.

"Oops," the senior bellhop observed. Then he called out in a loud voice: "Excuse me, sir!" As he did, he grabbed Todd by the arm and hustled them out of there.

"Um, uh," Todd pointed out, "I don't wanna sound like I'm tellin' you how to do your job or nothin', but that was no guy, that was a broad. You sure your eyes are okay?"

"Boy, you got a lot to learn," the old-timer chuckled. "Now listen real careful, and I'll lay it out for ya. This here is what we mean by your discreetousness. You seen it was a broad, and I seen it was a broad, but the broad don't know exactly what we seen, y'get what I mean?"

"Well…"

"So you call out 'Excuse me, sir,' like I done, and the broad thinks we was in and outa there so quick, we didn't get a good look at her. That way, she won't get all worked up and give us a hard time."

"She's still giving me a hard time."

"Cut the wisecracks, kid. Someday you'll be glad I learned ya this stuff."

"Captain, I'm afraid we've developed a bad shimmy at warp-5."

"You're right, Kate," the captain responded. "It's sort of like what happened once on our sister ship, but it's not quite the same thing."

"I guess if it were, you could fix it."

"Yep. I wish I could shimmy like my sister ship, Kate."

"Earth to Rumblestar Five. Earth to Rumblestar Five. Come in, Five."

"This is Rumblestar Five. Go ahead Terrafirm."

"Please advise as to your present situation, Unit Five. We are unclear as to the nature of this exchange."

"Wise up, Planet E., it's a space break."

"Oh, Johnny, isn't this great? Us in the honeymoon suite!" Doris Cappuccino marveled as her brand new husband continued to case the jernt.

"Yeah, yeah, this'll do fine," he allowed, "but right now, I'm lookin' to tie on the old feedbag. Christ, they don't hardly letcha eat nothin' at your own wedding."

In a matter of minutes, he was on the house phone, ordering up a sizeable chunk of food, while his bride repaired to the bathroom to change into her birthday suit. As it turned out, she was ready well before the food was.

"Food? What food?" Johnny asked as he jumped between the covers. And, as luck would have it, they were not singly but dually (and none too silently) on the very threshold of climax when young Todd, to whose knocking they had been understandably oblivious, came barging in with their order.

"Ulp," he said as he took in the scene before him. Then in a flash of inspiration, he called out, "Excuse me, gentlemen!" and got the hell out of there.

"Am I good or what?" he asked himself as he cruised down to the lobby.

*****

"Saay, get a load of the new duds," Elroy Bean observed. "When did this happen?"

"Lunchtime," Walter answered, putting the latest best seller on the back burner for a moment, "and I got a real good deal too."

"I bet. So, let's see what you got."

Walter stood up and performed a three fifty-eight to model

the new pants, having decided to leave the problematic jacket out of the picture for now.

"Not bad," his co-worker said, "especially if the pants weren't so baggy in the crotch, or were you surprised to see me?"

"Huh, what? These pants are baggy? Let me take another look," Walter fretted as he sped off to the department's Hall of Mirrors. Sure enough, the pants did seem to sag, very badly, now that he thought about it.

"This will never do," he decided.

"Cover for me, will you?" he called out to the roofer as he grabbed his jacket and hurried out the door, back to what he had come to regard as the scene of the crime.

The salesman's eyes grew wider, then glazed over as he saw Walter approach the store yet again. His mouth twisted into an idiotic grin.

"Dee dee deedle dee dee dee dee dee, DEE DEE DEE DEE!" he began singing as Walter came through the door, "Good bye, cruel world, I'm off to join the circus."

"Say, I hate to be a nuisance," Walter called out over the din of the salesman's headbanging, "but I've got another problem with this suit."

"Well, it better not involve a refund or an alteration, 'cause if it does, you're outa luck!" the helpful salesman paused to remind him.

"Oh, no, I'd never ask you to do anything like that, but I was hoping you could maybe—"

"Give me some advice," they both said.

"What is it this time?" the haberdasher sighed.

"The pants. Don't they seem a little baggy to you?"

"Some days everything seems a little baggy. This one here's a good example. All right, let's have a look.

"Now even if they did hang down a bit in the crotch," said the salesman, "and I'm not sayin' for one minute they do, but even if in theory they did, whatcha could do is reach behind you, just below belt level, say, and pull 'em up some."

"Like this?" Walter demonstrated.

"Yeah, that's the ticket," the salesman assured him.

"Now, let me get this all straight," Walter said, "I pull on my left sleeve like this to make it even with the right."

"That's right."

"Then, I'm supposed to hold the lapel down with my chin like this."

"Exactly."

"And then," Walter went on with some difficulty, "I pull the pants up from the back with my other hand."

"Bingo!"

On a faded green bench in the park where Walter often ate his lunch, two elderly women sat and watched as he made his way back to work.

"Oh dear," one of them said, "wouldja look at that poor crippled man."

"Yes," sighed the other, "but don't his suit fit nice?"

THE RED HORSE
by Henry Worthwads Widefellow

Henry, though unspeakably wealthy from an inheritance, does not like to flaunt his fortune. So, rather than take the snobbish, aristocratic approach we would have expected him to take by declining payment for his shaggy dog story, he insisted on triple the price, just to show he was "one of us." We welcome brother Widefellow to the ranks of the downtrodden, of which we suddenly discover ourselves prominent members, after paying him his royalty.

We find it remarkable and more than a little bit suspicious that he has been able to write so voluminously about college life (where this particular tale is set), when his own stay within the halls of academe lasted only two weeks. Ah, but, when you write as well as Henry, by which we mean, when you write checks as well as he can, who needs four years of college?

In our capacity as editor, we did take the liberty of altering the name of a frequently-mentioned fraternity, which was meant to be fictional, to the extent that one of the letters is not a true member of the Greek alphabet. Please bear with us. We are perfectly well aware of what the correct letter is, but had we used it, we would have bungled onto the name of an actual sorority. Rather than risk the hell that hath no fury, we decided it would be better to play dumb, which some would maintain is far less of a stretch than we think it is.

By the way, we urge you in the strongest possible terms not to confuse this story with "The Horse Who Could Hit." There is a horse in this one, true enough, but you will note that it can neither hit nor talk. Even so, we would ask you to stifle your bitter disappointment and read on.– tcl

I

Lyman Pendergrast Bumpo III could hear the dog barking, even through his headphones.

"Must be the mailman," he thought as he rose and turned off the music. "Shut up, Ralph," he snapped at the dog. Sure enough the mail had arrived.

The first few things he flipped through were plainly addressed to Lyman Pendergrast Bumpo, Jr., his dad. Then he spotted an envelope addressed to him from Persons University.

"Uh-oh," Lyman thought. If this turned out to be another rejection, his parents were going to be plenty sore. After the perilous closeness of his graduation from high school, the family dentist had referred him to the family dermatologist for skin grafts to his teeth. Still, Lyman had applied to dozens and dozens of colleges at a cost in application fees of $850.00, and every one turned him down flat, even the state schools that had to take him, but went to court to get their charters amended so that they would not. This letter represented his last chance. Persons University was his "escape" school, as it was not necessarily known for its rigorous admissions criteria. Still, Lyman held his breath as he tore the envelope open, the dog having passed some wind. He unfolded the paper and read:

Dear Mr. Bumpo III:

It is our pleasure to inform you that you have been accepted for admission to Persons University.

To insure your place in this year's freshman class, please to send us $3,000.00 in small bills. No check, please.

Cordially yours,
Alonzo LaPeche
Director of Admissions

Lyman dashed out to the back yard.

"Guess what, Junior?" he shouted to his dad, "I got accepted by Persons!"

"About damn time you got accepted somewhere," his father grumbled. "Now see to it you graduate."

Of course he would try to graduate, that went without saying. After all, he had no wish to lose his student deferment and wind up getting drafted. But of far, far more importance to Lyman was a matter beside which the prospect of being yanked into the army and sent to war seemed the most trifling of details: getting into a good FRAT! From such a stroke of good fortune, Lyman sensed, would come virtually limitless partying and perhaps even loss of his virginity. For starters, he would plough the proceeds from his summer job into a set of wheels, thereby assuring himself instant acceptance by any reasonable frat. The rest, up to and including graduation, would be a lead pipe cinch.

*****

"So, Bumpo, when's ya job start?" his buddy, Stu, asked as they sat around a grimy table at Snarlin' Ed's Dew Drop Dead Hostility Howse, their least favorite hangout, but the only one in town where the proprietor couldn't be bothered to check your ID.

"Monday, Gatz, at eight sharp," Lyman answered him, "and I'm makin' two and a half bucks an hour."

"Hey, that's pretty good for the mid-sixties," observed Chuck, who had been brought in all the way from Wilkes-Barre for precisely that purpose.

"I don't know," Stu cautioned. "Rumor has it they're a pretty weird bunch." Indeed, the Harry Kirshner Breakfast Products Conglomeration, that had hired Lyman for the summer, was about as strange as they came in those days.

Fortunately for Lyman, his involvement with the business was limited to the crating and shipping department. True, the taste-testers in quality control got paid a good deal more, but, as Lyman came to realize, they probably earned it.

"Don't worry, Gatz," he snapped, "I know what I'm doing."

In a nearby booth Tony Scoreggia was expounding his thoughts to Linda Poughbalz, the new light of his life.

"Y'know," Lyman heard him tell her, "some things, they sound, like, real poetic, even if they're ordinary household words. Take f'rinstance, you got a word like 'cellar door.' Now, if you didn't know the difference, you'd prob'ly think it was somethin' real special, right?"

"Oh, Tony," she sighed, gazing fondly into his acne, "you're so sensitive."

Suddenly, the shrill blast of a police whistle shattered the air. It was Snarlin' Ed.

"Alright, people, it's 9:48. Last call's in two hours! I want that you should all finish feedin' yer faces, pay yer tab and get t'hell outa my place!" Lyman looked at his watch. Sure enough, it was 9:48 on the button.

"Wow, Ed musta been in a really great mood tonight," he told the others as they began bolting their food.

*****

PLEASE DO NOT THROW
CIGARETTE BUTTS IN THE URINAL
It Makes Them Soggy and Hard to Light

read the sign in the washroom. Lyman finished drying his hands and went out to join the group in the stockroom, where they were waiting to begin the first day of their summer jobs.

"No kiddin'?" one of the college guys asked as Lyman took a seat on the bench.

"Sure as I'm standin' here," Old Pete answered.

"You were a pilot in the cavalry?" asked another of the new hires. "I don't get it."

"Well, y'see," Pete explained, "It's like this. Back in 1918, durin' the first war, I was assigned to cleanin' out the stables, and alla time, it was pile it here, pile it there, then wheel it out, heh, heh, heh."

"So, d'ja shoot down any Japs?" Lyman asked.

"Okay, gennulmen, off an' on!" barked the foreman as he marched into the stockroom. "I want you college guys to go with Pete, there, and start fillin' them cartons. Then you put 'em on this here conveyor belt, so's they can be put inta crates and banded up. Any questions?"

As there were none, the group got down to work. A little later in the shift, a squat swarthy man drove up in a fork lift.

"So," he said to Lyman, from whom he had just bummed a smoke, "you go to college, ha? Is goot idea. Get to be foreman that way for sure. But first, you gotta be smart like me, Stavros Papadopolous. Someday, I am foreman too." Before Lyman could explain to Papadopolous that he didn't necessarily plan to study foremanship in college, the driver took off to fetch another load.

"Was that guy for real?" Lyman asked the other forklifter, Rosenfeld Smith, born in November of 1932 and named for the man who, according to his father's disgruntled Republican boss, had just been elected president of the United States.

"You mean ol' Papa Hoomaumau?" the driver chuckled. "Yeah, he thinks he's gonna own the place someday, on acounta he's so smart." With that, Smith had a good laugh and sped off.

Eventually Papadopolous came to reveal the whole secret of being smart.

"When I am first come here," he confided to Lyman, "I work very hard for only little money. Then I see this guy, just stand around and smoke pipe. 'Hopa!' I tell my friend, Dmitri, 'I bet he don't make *scata*. He don't do no work at all.'

"'You kidding?' my friend say. 'He make planty. He's the foreman.'

"So I say, 'How come he make so much money to stand around and do nothing?'

"'Because he's a smart guy,' my friend say.

"'Okey dokey,' I decide, 'I go find out what is this smart stuff.'

"First chance I get, I ask him, 'Hey, Mr. Foreman, how come you so smart, ha?'

"He tell me, 'Here, I show you.' Then he put his hand on a brick wall. 'Hit this,' he say and point to his hand. I take big, hard swing with my fist, but then he pull his hand away, make me to hit the bricks.

"'Hey, why you do that?' I say while my hand is killing me.

"'Because I am smart,' say the foreman; 'I pull my hand away, just in time, before you can hit, okay? So you hit the wall instead. That's what smart mean.'"

" So, what's this about being smart?" asked one of the college guys, an All-Big-Ten linebacker and star shot-putter.

With a smile and a wink to Lyman, Stavros answered, "Okey dokey, I show you now." With a sly cackle, he held his hand up, six inches in front of his nose.

"Here," he challenged the athlete, "hit this!"

For the most part, though, the job was pretty routine. Work continued more or less without interruption, except for the one day in late August, when the crew that prepared the crates for shipping discovered that their banders had somehow vanished.

"I don't know what to make of it," admitted the foreman.

"For all we know, it could be the work of a frumious bander-snatch," volunteered a fellow named Lewis.

"Yeah," the foreman nodded absently, "I better check that out."

II

"This one's for Jesus, ya stinkin' sonuva bitch!" raged the Destroyers' skater as he smashed the wheels of his boot into the ribs of his prostrate opponent while Lyman took in the action. *Holy Roller Derby* was his favorite Sunday morning TV show by far. He hoped he would be able to get it on the Persons University campus, but he was not overly optimistic. It was all well and good that he was continuing his militarily defermented education, but it meant giving up the comforts and familiarities of his home in the urbanely renewed community of Wiggleton Acres and shipping out to some college town in the middle of nowhere. On top of that, he was going to miss most of this week's episode thanks to that damn plane he had to catch.

"Lyman P.," his mother called from downstairs, "Daddy wants to get underway. Are you packed yet?"

"I'll be right down in a flash, Mom," Lyman answered as he began looking around for more stuff to throw in with the tooth-brush and the pair of socks he had already packed.

Amid admonitions to dress warm and make the dean's list, Lyman's parents finally saw him onto the plane.

"That's one down," sighed a frazzled Lyman Pendergrast Bumpo, Jr., meaning Lyman III, "and one to go," referring to his youngest son, Nathaniel Edward Bumpo. Ralph, the dog, had long finished with obedience school.

*****

"Good morning, freshpeople, and welcome to Persons University," intoned the speaker, a distinguished-looking gentleman in a tweed suit. His eyes were an abundantly clear blue and not a hair on his head was out of place. "I'm your M.C., Dean Martin. Uh, that is to say, my name is Dr. Herbert Martin, and I'm dean of students here at P.U... Uh, that is to say, Persons University, as it were.

"It is my job to start your orientation off with an explanation of the rules by which your conduct here will be governed. While we are justifiably proud of the work our deportment committee has done in eliminating most of the hidebound ideas and picayune regulations that ought no longer be deemed appropriate to the modern quest for knowledge in today's academic atmosphere, we do consider it extremely important that the few rules we have chosen to retain be obeyed to the letter and without exception.

"These are the rules, and it would behoove all of you to pay close attention, as even the smallest breech thereof can and will result in your expulsion, I assure you. The rules are as follows.

"One: all tuition and related fees are to be paid in advance, *prior*, and I emphasize that, *prior* to each semester.

"Two: all such fees are to be paid via cash or certified check. Personal checks *will not be accepted*.

"Now then, before I turn you over to the activities chairman, are there any questions?"

As Dean Herbert Martin fielded the first few questions, it occurred to Lyman that there would almost certainly be no obstacle to his obtaining that set of wheels he had been longing for. He had some money, and there did not appear to be any rule against having a car on campus. Still, he thought he'd better ask, just to be sure.

"Well, yes," the dean was explaining to a graduate of the

Helmut von Moltke Military Academy, "I suppose you can stand at 'parade rest' whenever you wish, but, to repeat, we don't have a morning formation, as such, here at Persons.

"Yes?" he continued, pointing to Lyman.

"Uh, Mr. Martin, Sir..."

"Doctor Martin. Yes?"

"Uh, Doctor Martin, can students own a car?"

"Certainly," the dean assured him. "Parking fees run $299.95 a semester and up. Did you bring a vehicle of your own?"

"No sir, I thought I might buy one in town."

"Fine," responded the dean. "May I suggest Honest Herb's Chevrolet? It's about a mile off campus on Route 52."

"Thank you, sir," Lyman mumbled as he re-took his seat.

"Quite all right," replied the dean.

*****

"Yeah, well, maybe eight hunnit might seem like a lotta dough for a forty-nine Chevy, but it's in real good shape, ya gotta rememba dat."

"Gee, I don't know," Lyman fretted.

Honest Herb sighed and started to remove his mirrored sunglasses for an eye rub. Thinking the better of it, he flicked the sweat from his bald pate instead.

"I tell ya what, kid," he leaned in and informed him on the sly: "I got a coupla Phi Gams comin' in any day now to pick up this baby for the eight hunnit, but they been grab-assin' around tryin' ta get the money up. F'you can show me sem fitty cash, you got it, okay?"

"Done!" Lyman shot back with a triumphant shake of the dealer's hand. As they walked to the office to draw up the papers, Honest Herb quickly kicked shut the door to the closet where he'd stashed his toupee and his tweed suit.

"Kid," he congratulated the young man, "ya may jaself a real deal."

While Lyman's car hardly resembled the sleek, smooth machine Honest Herb had described in the lot, at least it was running, which was more than could be said for the MG on the shoulder, up the road. A well-tanned upperclassman stood glaring into the car's engine as he rubbed his hand agitatedly through the short blond hair he had only recently stopped wearing as a flattop.

"Hi," Lyman called out as he pulled alongside the sports car. "Needa ride back to the dorms?"

"Yeah," enthused the stranded motorist as he hopped into Lyman's sedan, "I sure do. Thanks.

"So, what are ya, a freshman?" he asked Lyman as the car lurched off.

"Howdja know? The name's Lyman Pendergrast Bumpo. The Third. Uh, do you know anything about the frats they got here?"

"I guess!" the passenger snorted. "I happen to be rush chairman of Bravo Phi Delta, the top frat on campus, bar none."

"No kidding? "Gee, then it's really an honor to be givin' you a lift."

"I like the way you put things, Bumpo. Hey, why don't you make it a point to stop by during rush week? Just tell the guys you know me. My name's W. Frederick Caswell, but everyone 'round here calls me 'Fred the Mover' for obvious reasons."

"Is that because you do all right with the ladies?" Lyman queried.

"You have guessed 'er, Lester."

"Lyman," he corrected him.

III

Between parking fees and the sundry repairs needed to keep his car running at least some of the time, Lyman had quickly exhausted the last of his summer earnings. Only by securing work as a dishwasher in the school cafeteria at the not-so-munificent wage of $1.75 per 90-minute shift, did he manage to keep any money coming in at all. And he needed every dime he could lay his hands on, for he had pledged Bravo Phi Delta at the behest of his new friend, Fred the Mover.

It was during the second of his three daily shifts that he saw her. Hot and tired as he felt, Lyman had popped out of the kitchen to grab a glass of iced tea off the cafeteria line. As he removed the drink, he spotted her passing through on the other side. Beyond the immediate droppage of his jaw and the glass, Lyman found himself unable to find any other way to transmit to this beautiful creature the totality and depth of his love.

"So anyway, ya goin' t'the concert?" asked the dumpy girl beside her as they slid their trays beyond where Lyman stood like a frozen pantomime of a youth holding a glass.

"Yeah, I s'pose," she answered, her every word, her every tone, the song of a nightingale.

That night Lyman, after having stewed about the matter for six hours or so, decided to seek the advice of an expert.

"Fred," he blurted out as he rapped anxiously on the Mover's door. "Fred, you gotta help me." Lyman could detect a whispered, inaudible conversation along with the squeak of bedsprings from within the room. Eventually he heard someone get up and pad to the door.

"Lyman?" Fred inquired through the still closed door.

"Yeah, it's me. Listen, Fred, I got a really big, major problem."

"Well," Fred tried to explain, "I'm a little, uh, busy right now. Can this wait 'til tomorrow?"

"Fred, you don't understand! I found the girl I've been looking for all my life. I'm in love and I don't even know her name or what to say to her or *anything*!"

"Awrite, take it easy," Fred grumbled. "I'll meetcha down in the lounge. Gimmie about ten minutes, okay?"

An hour later, Fred plopped down in the chair across from Lyman, lit a cigarette and started his concise, foolproof lesson on The Way These Things Worked.

"What you gotta remember," Fred began, "is that these broads want it just as bad as you do. I'd say go up to her, introduce yourself real politely, then ask her out to dinner anna flick in town. Nothin' to it."

"Yeah?" Lyman asked, his spirits rising quickly. "And then what?"

"Aah, it's simple as pie. Alls you gotta do is get 'em talking. Get 'em talking about anything at all, it doesn't even matter what, because here's the deal: you're gonna slowly work the conversation around to the subject of sex. Before you know it, one thing'll lead to another, and, like I say, these broads want it as bad as we do. Y'get it?"

"Sounds easy," Lyman agreed.

"You bet it is," Fred assured him. "Now where'd you say this hot chick was at?"

"Oh, man, I don't even know that," Lyman moaned.

"I'd say that you got some legwork to do," offered Fred.

"Wait a minute!" Lyman shouted. "Now I remember, she's goin' to the concert next week with some fat broad."

"Well," Fred advised him, "there you are."

*****

The fact that the folksinger's agent had booked him for a five-night stand did not make life easier on Lyman and his already-strained budget. Only by taking on a few extra shifts in the kitchen and doing some mercenary typing could he scrounge up the money for admission to all six concerts, including the matinee.

By the sixth performance, Lyman had grown thoroughly sick of the singer and decided to count himself lucky if he never heard him whine another note. Even worse, she had not showed up yet.

"Jesus," Lyman thought, "what if she changed her mind? I went through all this trouble and expense for nothing."

At the intermission, he ran into one of his new frat brothers, "Animal Crackers" Lyons.

"Hey, Bumpo, how they hangin'?" he hailed Lyman.

"Fine, I guess," the freshman replied absently. He was still scanning the crowd for her.

"Look, Bumpo, let's split this wimpy scene and head out to the lodge," Lyons suggested. "We gotta coupla townies comin' by to take on the brothers. F'you can get us out there now, maybe we won't have to settle for sloppy eighty-seconds or somethin', okay?"

Lyman's eyes widened. Here at last was a solid, ironclad chance to lose his virginity. On the other hand, he had serious doubts about giving up his search. The tickets had cost him a fortune, and, if he didn't manage to spot her here, he didn't know how he'd ever track her down. As it was, he had nearly been fired from the dishwashing crew for spending so much time on the food line, trying, without success, to get another look at her.

"Uhhh...welll...," Lyman started to answer, not certain of what he was going to tell Brother Lyons, when he noticed the fat broad. She was standing outside the ladies' room.

"'Scuse me a second," Lyman muttered as he headed off toward the restrooms.

"Hi," Lyman explained to the fat broad, once he had caught her eye. "My name's Lyman Pendergrast Bumpo III, do you like this music too?"

"I sure do," she chirped. "My name's Angie. Yeah, I really dig it," although she could have said, "I eat corpses," for all

Lyman noticed because at that precise moment, SHE came out of the ladies' room.

"Ya ready?" the fat broad asked her.

"Yeah, let's go."

"Say, wait a minute," Lyman blurted out, "aren't you going to introduce me to your friend?"

"Oh, I guess so," the fat broad sighed, "Whad'ja say ya name was?"

"Lyman," he reminded her.

"Yeah, right. Darlene, this is Lyman. Lyman, that's Darlene, okay?"

"Hi," Lyman beamed. "Ya like the concert?"

Darlene shrugged her shoulders.

"Hey, look, Darlene, can I maybe take you out to dinner and a movie sometime?"

"Maybe," she allowed. As the two girls headed back to their seats, Lyman shouted after her.

"So where can I reach you at?"

"Pickends Hall, we're in the book," the fat broad called back to him as they disappeared into the crowd.

By this time, Brother Lyons had given up waiting and hitched a ride with someone else, not that Lyman was interested in his offer anymore. After all, why should he waste his very first time on some floozy when, in a little while, he'd be making it with Darlene, the lady of his dreams.

"How many roads must a man walk down," he sang happily to himself, "before he is washed to the sea?"

IV

"For God sakes, Martha, will you get a move on?" Lyman Pendergrast Bumpo, Jr. yelled up to his wife, "We'll be late for th'leven o'clock service again."

"I'm not setting foot outside the door until I find that hat," his wife insisted. "You can sit still and be patient."

"Women!" he grumbled as he switched on *Holy Roller Derby* and flopped into his TV chair.

"Stay tuned as Terrible Tillie Tataglia of the Avenging Angels has an appointment with Millie 'the Mangler' Moran of the Grand Inquisitors, after this word from our sponsor," announced the announcer to the elder Bumpo, *et alia*.

"Let's go, everybody, I found my hat," Mrs. Bumpo declared.

"Just when the ladies were comin' on," her husband muttered as he snapped the TV off.

"You're mad at me, I can tell," she observed as they drove to church.

"Well, I guess I am," Mr. Bumpo answered after a pause. "Damn it, Martha, you had no call sendin' the boy two hundred dollars like that."

"Now Lyman," she reminded him, "I seem to remember you were young yourself once. Besides, you read his letter. This is obviously something very important to him."

"Aahh, crap! How many times you think that kid's gonna fall in love over the next four years? And what happened to the god-damn dough he made last summer, huh? Christ, it's only October, and already he's writin' home for money. How're we gonna teach the boy any self-reliance that way?"

"Oh, don't be such a fussbudget," she counseled him.

As she drove on, Mr. Bumpo turned to their eight-year-old son in the back seat.

"Get this straight, young man, if you ever throw your cash away on some dame, it's just gonna be tough beans, y'got that?"

"Who, me?" the youngster answered, "Why would I wanna waste my money on some dumb girl?"

*****

"Well, um, that was some movie, wasn't it?" Lyman asked her as they sat waiting for their food. Darlene shrugged and stared at a distant corner.

"Y'know that part where they hopped into to bed together?" Lyman began again, "I think that was kinda symbolic of something, d'ya know what I mean?" She did not seem to know.

"Um, uh, hey, here's something I bet you never thought about," he went on. "Ever notice how some words can be perfectly ordinary, but they sound real poetical when you say them, like, 'basement steps,' for instance?"

"Huh?"

And so did it go the duration of the evening. The next day, Lyman went over to Fred's dorm to find out what he could possibly have done wrong.

"I dunno, it's hard t'say," Fred offered after Lyman had put that very question to him. "Maybe she's holdin' out for the finer things, in which case, you probably better back off or it'll wind up costin' you some real dough."

"But, Fred, you don't understand, I gotta have this girl! I'll go crazy if I can't."

"All right," sighed the Mobile One, "if you want her so bad, then here's what you need to do. First, instead of a flick, take her to a live show, maybe somethin' like *Carousel*. Yeah, that's supposed to be a good love story, oughta put her in the right mood. I think it's still at the Lyric Stage for another week or so. And then, instead of Baldy's House of Beef, take her to that fancy French joint, you know, the one about two blocks from the theater? *Trezz trezz expahngseeve*, but she'll definitely see you're a guy with lots of class, right?"

"Yeah, I guess so. What then?"

"Well, it's exactly like I said before. Just get her to talkin' about anything. Again, it doesn't matter what, so long as you slowly, gradually work the subject around to 'Topic A.' With that, plus she's bound to be impressed you're spendin' some bucks on her, why you got it made in the shade."

Perhaps there was something to Fred's advice, for Darlene did accept Lyman's invitation, even if she demonstrated a remarkable ability to restrain her enthusiasm.

"Does m'sieu wish to order cocktails?" their waiter sneered. Lyman glanced at the menu and blanched.

"Could I get a Perrier and soda, please?" he asked, and, at that, he probably impressed the waiter over the course of the dinner more than he impressed Darlene, who remained as uncommunicative as ever. Not even his hilarious imitations of the guys on the dishwashing crew got a rise out of her. When she bid him good night, just prior to running into the elevator at Pickends Hall, without so much as a handshake, it marked the longest sentence she had directed his way all evening. Lyman looked at the slip of paper from his fortune croissant and sighed. If only, he thought as he read again the sage advice: "Man who lose key to girlfriend's apartment…no get new key."

The next day at lunch, Fred, who had not yet learned better, sat down across from Lyman.

"Hey, stud, how did it go last night?"

"It didn't," Lyman mumbled.

"What, you mean you struck out?" Fred inquired. "How can such a thing be? Did you do everything I told you?"

"To the letter, and it still didn't work."

"Uh huh, uh huh," proclaimed The Man with the Moves, as he brought his keen analytical mind to bear on the situation. "It just goes to show you, I was right in the first place, wasn't I?"

"What do you mean?" Lyman asked him.

"When I said to forget about that broad. I mean, was I right or, in the alternative, was I right?"

"Fred," Lyman struggled to reiterate, "there's something you're not getting here. I can't forget about her. I absolutely know she's the one for me, and I've *got* to have her. Can't you think of *something*?"

"Jeez, I don't know," Fred replied as he tapped a cigarette on his tray. "I suspect the lady isn't particularly interested in your company."

"Yeah, I guess not, but what can I do about it?"

"Look," Fred tried again, "are you positive you did everything I told you? The show? The fancy restaurant?"

"All of it, and it cost me a fortune."

"So what did she talk about that you couldn't slowly work the conversation around to sex?"

"That's the problem," Lyman sighed. "She wouldn't open up the whole time, no matter what I said."

All this talk about frustration and defeat was getting into an area Fred considered unfamiliar and more than a little demoralizing. In fact, it was giving him a headache.

"I don't know," he summed up, "let me think about it. Maybe I'll figure out something, but, Lyman," he advised the youth, "don't get your hopes up, okay?"

"Yeah, okay," Lyman agreed as he trudged off to yet another stint at the sinks. Surely, he reasoned, surely, Fred the Mover would come up with something to get him off the dime.

*****

Fred, for his part, had several matters of far greater importance than Lyman's social life to occupy his mind, not the least of which was putting the make on that new waitress at the local coffee house. His first few moves had gained him nothing more than a demitasse of espresso. As he stirred in the sugar and plotted his next gambit, the young performer on stage launched into a sentimental ballad:

Stewball was a horse, now,
'Cause he was not a cow,
And he never was meant to
Be pulling a plow.

Well I raced him in Italy
And in Afghanistan;
Though I did not win diddly,
I got a good tan.

So go and bet against Stewball,
All you gamblers so brash.
You'll find it's a new ball-
game when you've lost your cash.

You can bet that bay filly
Or the dapple-gray mare.
If you want to get silly,
Bet the big dancin' bear.

But, if it's money you're hot on
The trail of at all,
Then put all you've got on
The nose of Stewball.

As the patrons snapped their fingers in appreciation, an idea
dawned on the Mover. Making a mental note to follow up on it
once he got back to campus, he called the waitress over for another go-around.

While he was waiting for the latest word to come down from
Fred, Lyman sat in the Bigelow Hall lounge, far from the scru-
tiny of his nosey roommates, upstairs, and composed a sonnet to

the Lady of his Dreams. As he wrote on, he started to feel better and better. By the time he got to the end, he was borderline ecstatic.

"Wow," he complimented himself, "hot stuff!" He held the paper up and read it again.

A Sonnet to My Love by Lyman Pendergrast
Bumpo III

Fair maiden, how can I express my love
To one whose heart of stone is so made out?
Why must I sit inside my dorm and pout,
When you and I could sore like clouds above?
Our love would know no limit or no bounds
If only you were willing just to try
To spend one night in some motel or my
Own room, providing I can get those clowns
Who room with me to stay the hell away.
Then you'd be mine and I'd be yours 'til time
Stands still. Is going all the way a crime?
I don't think so, and that is why I say
That love is something that is meant to be
A special kind of thing 'tween you and me.

"Shakespeare couldn'ta said it better," Lyman assured himself as he considered how to deliver the goods to the One True Love of his Life.

"Maybe I should get this published," he thought. "Wouldn't that impress her?"

"'Ey!" shouted a tall, bespectacled freshman from across the lounge. "Your name Bumpo?"

"Who, me?" asked Lyman, who normally remembered such things.

"Yeah. Your name Bumpo?"

"Uh huh."

"Someone on the pay phone for you, this side."

As he got up to take the call, the alert messenger swooped in and snatched the ten-cent piece Lyman had been sitting on all the while.

"Hello?" Lyman inquired of the mouthpiece.

"Lyman? It's Fred. I think I got this idea that's bound to be sure-fire."

"Oh, really?" Lyman asked casually. He wondered how Fred's suggestion could possibly rival his sonnet.

"Yeah, here's the deal. Y'ever been horseback riding?"

"Once or twice, nothing serious. Why?"

"It's like this, y'see, these broads go ape for ridin' horses on accounta the movement of the horse imitates the old pelvic thrust, y'know what I mean?"

"Right, of course!" Lyman enthused as he tried to figure out what in the hell Fred was talking about.

"So there you are," Fred continued. "She's gallopin' along, gettin' hornier and hornier, and you get her to start talking. What with everything else, you'll have no trouble eventually whippin' the conversation around to sex. Before you know it, you two'll be in the sack."

Fred went on to describe a farm with a stable, a bit beyond the north campus, where Blind Johnny McGregor, crazy old coot that he was, could be persuaded to let a couple of his steeds for an hour or two, "if the feel 'a yair money is rrright."

In the end, Lyman decided that, sorely as he needed the bucks, he would forego the royalties from the publication of his sonnet in favor of getting those words into HER hands right away. He stuffed his creation into an envelope, on which he hurriedly scribbled, "To the Fairest Maid in #307."

As he hiked over to Pickends Hall to deliver the goods, there was a bounce in his step once again, for, between Fred's great scheme and his great poetry, the bitch didn't have a chance.

V

Renee Johnson stopped by the front desk in Pickends Hall.

"Any mail for 301?" she checked with the girl stationed there.

"Nothin' in the mail s'mornin'," the girl responded, "but there's something in your box." She pulled out an envelope with no stamp on it.

"Some guy musta brought this over," she told Renee. "Looks like hot stuff."

Renee peered at the envelope.

"Girl," she scolded, "that ain't no 301."

"Hmmm, it's kinda hard to read that chicken scratch, but, yeah, I'd say that's a 301. Maybe it's for your roommate."

"Say what? That poor fat child ain't been out with a man yet. Who's gonna send her a note like this?"

"Well then," the girl behind the desk suggested, "maybe it's for you."

A few seconds passed while Renee tried to picture anyone she knew, here or back in Detroit, referring to her as "the Fairest Maid" of anything.

"No," she finally agreed, "I guess this fool's writin' to Angie."

*****

Fred's advice seemed to be right on the mark this time. However Darlene may have felt about Lyman, she adored horseback riding. To this point, nobody else except her friend Angie had been remotely interested in going with her to ride. The one occasion when they had gone to the McGregor farm, Blind Johnny had been able to tell from the pitch of Angie's voice that she'd be too heavy for any of his horses, so he had turned the girls away.

"I'm sorra, but I canna let ye rrride," Blind Johnny sighed, trying to break the news to them as gently as he could, "because one 'a ye lassies iss chust too fat."

But when Lyman and Darlene dropped by, the wily horselender quickly judged that neither of them would weigh too much for his steeds. After carefully feeling Lyman's money, he led them over to the stables. Eventually Lyman found himself aboard a small, light gray pony that was plodding well behind the Love of his Life, who had the bad luck, as he saw it, to have been stuck with a much more spirited animal.

"Say, Darlene," he yelled during a brief period when their two horses were only six feet apart, "how'dja like the poem? I write stuff that good all the time."

Darlene stared at him blankly. So many guys had been sending her poems and stuff, it was hard to keep track of them.

"Yeah," she answered, assuming that one of them had to be from this guy.

"Huh? Oh, hey. look," Lyman went on, as her horse reacted to the dig of her heels and began to re-open its considerable lead, "how about if I write you another one, okay?" By the time he'd finished his question she was out of earshot. Still, Lyman figured, her noticeable lack of criticism surely proved sign she was hot for his poetry.

"Now if only I could get her hot for my body too," he mused as he struggled to make his placid mount go a little faster.

Once again Lyman heard the squeak of bedsprings as he went to knock on Fred's door. On one hand, he didn't want to disturb the guy, but then, the whole fiasco with the horses had been Fred's big idea, so Lyman didn't feel too bad about bothering him now. In any case, he was getting desperate for a solution to his problem.

"Fred," he spoke into the key hole after a tentative knock, "it didn't work." The springs continued to squeak. Lyman knocked harder on the door.

"Fred, you in there?"

"YES, I'M IN THERE. NOW GET LOST!"

"Oh, okay," Lyman agreed, "I'll be down in the lounge."

He waited there for three-and-a-half hours, wondering after a while if he shouldn't go back upstairs and check on Fred, in case he'd forgotten. Then he tried to compose another sonnet, but, good as he normally was at it, he found he couldn't get his concentration up. In the end, he decided to head back to Bigelow Hall and hit the sack. Maybe if he went to Viet Nam and got killed, that would show them all.

*****

It was Saturday morning, and Fred had just finished with his pain-in-the-ass advanced chem lab, in which the professor had taxed him with the challenge of producing a beaker of green liquid by combining blue and yellow food coloring in water. He dipped into his shirt pocket for a cigarette and found the pack empty. As he crumpled it, he spotted a brother, H. Johnson Knoff, the Bravo Phi Delta pledgemaster, coming down the hall.

"Hey, Jack," Fred hailed him, "you got a smoke I can use?"

"Call me John," he snapped as he nudged a cigarette from his pack and pointed it at Fred.

"Yeah, sure, whatever, so how's tricks?"

"'Bout the same I s'pose. Hey, what's wrong with your boy these days?"

"Whozat?" Fred inquired.

"You know, Pledge Bumpo. Saw him in the lounge last night, lookin' like he'd lost his best friend."

"Aah, he's hung up over some cold bitch that won't put out."

It was only after he left Knoff's company that Fred began to realize what a heel he must have been. Here was some poor sap battling hopeless odds, and he didn't even have time to help him anymore. Of course, Fred reasoned, the kid ought to throw in the towel. Any rational man would. Hell, after what he'd had put up with, any irrational man would. Still, Fred felt bad about the whole sorry situation. Moreover, a true Bravo Phi Delt would never have left a brother—even a brother pledge—in the lurch. Fred burned with shame for the first time in years.

"Lyman," Fred assured him over the phone, "I tell ya what. Meet me in the lounge at eight tonight, and I'll give ya somethin' that's bound t'work, okay?" He was sure he could come up with an idea by then.

That evening during the suppertime shift, even the horrible noise the disposal made when a piece of crockery fell into its gaping maw did not get on Lyman's nerves the way it usually did. He felt certain that, this time, success lay right around the corner.

"I wonder what she really thought about my sonnet?" he mused as the disposal chewed pensively on a saucer.

*****

"I think it's some pretty hot stuff, don't you?" Angie giggled as her roommate was reading Lyman's piece.

"Hm. I guess. Say, where'd you meet this turkey anyway?" Renee asked her.

"Funny thing," Angie beamed. "I met him at that concert last

October. I was with Darlene—you know, my friend in 307?—
and I thought he'd actually gone for her, but… well, you can see
for yourself who he really wants."

"Yeah, and it's plain to see *what* he really wants. You better
be careful."

"Oh, I'll be careful all right," Angie said, "but I'm definitely
following up on this."

*****

"Okay, here's the plan," enthused the Maker of Moves: "We're
gonna get her to start the conversation by givin' her something to
talk about. Dig?"

"What do you mean?" Lyman asked him.

"Like I say, I got a plan," Fred continued. "Now pay attention.
First, has that blind old fart got a white horse?"

"Well, the one I had last time was kind of a dirty white, more
or less."

"That's close enough. Make sure you ask for that one again."

"But that horse was so slow…"

"What are you, the Lone Ranger?" Fred sneered. "Don't
worry about how fast the damn horse goes, that's not your problem. Now here's what we do. Next Saturday we'll sneak into the
stables at exactly seven PM."

"Why then?"

"Because I found out from a buddy of mine who lives out
that way, the old man always plays his bagpipes, full blast, on
Saturdays at seven sharp. So, what with him bein' blind and
those pipes squealin', he'll never catch us."

"Great!" Lyman responded with a clap of his hands. "Uh,
what is it he's never going to catch us at?"

"Painting, my boy. We're gonna paint the legs of your horse
red!"

"Does that make him go any faster?"

"You're not pickin' up on this too quick, are you?"

"No," Lyman admitted, "I guess not."

"Doncha see? When the chick notices the legs of your horse turned red, she's bound to say somethin' about it, and that'll break the ice. Alls you gotta do then is keep the conversation rolling along and gradually work the topic around to sex. I bet by the time you get back to the stable, she'll be ready for a ride of a different kind, if you catch my drift."

"Right," Lyman agreed, "we'll definitely be goin' back to campus by car."

Fortunately for Lyman and Fred, the old man kept to his schedule. He started to play his pipes at seven o'clock on the dot, for on Saturday night, Blind Johnny prepared his favorite meal: corned beef, ground up and fried with potatoes, then garnished with a poached egg. This had been a popular dish of the McGregor clan for as long as anyone could remember. It was said that, back in the auld days, the women of the clan had taken to playing a special kind of bagpipe whenever they had prepared this recipe, so as to carry the glad tidings to their men in the fields. Those instruments, in fact, are believed to be the very first hash pipes known to Western Man. As Blind Johnny had no wife, he had to supply the traditional piping himself.

In any case, the two lads managed to slip into the stable, do the deed, then slip out, despite the row raised by Rrrufus, the farmer's vigilant watchpig, whose outraged squeals Blind Johnny had been unable to differentiate from his own soulful rendition of *Loch Lomond*.

Darlene, for her part, had already agreed to go riding with Lyman the next afternoon. Had she said so much as one peep about the legs on Lyman's horse, the plan would have gone like clockwork.

VI

Lyman stopped by the desk in the Bigelow Hall lounge.

"Any mail?" he asked the guy behind the desk.

"Hasn't come yet," he replied, "but there's somethin' in your box, might be for you." He pulled out an envelope without a stamp on it.

"Some chick musta brought this over. Looks like hot stuff, man."

Lyman looked at the envelope. "To Lyman from your Fair Maid," it read.

"Yeah, boy!" Lyman smiled as he sniffed the perfumed envelope. "Hot stuff is right!"

Up in his room, he ripped open the envelope and proceeded to read the letter:

My Dearest Lyman,

I have read your wonderful poem over and over again. It's really something!!!

I don't think I'm quite ready yet to go to a motel with you or stay in your room all night, but if you're willing to settle for taking me to the movies, you can meet me at the Student Union tonight at eight. There's going to be a Gummo Marx Festival, which ought to be fun. After that...who knows?

Til tonight, my Sweet Prince.

Love,
Your Fair Maid

Lyman fell backwards onto his bed, his face contorted into a coprophageous grin.

Alll RIGHT!" he gloated. He was rereading the letter when he got interrupted by someone knocking loudly at his door. He leapt up with a start and, quickly removing his hand from inside his pants, yanked the door open instead. It was Jack Knoff.

"Call me John," he growled.

"Pledge Bumpo," he addressed Lyman, "your presence is urged to the extent of being damn near required at the Bravo Phi Delta lodge tonight at oh-eight-hundred hours. Object: extreme inebriation and the testing of your capability to handle same. One word of advice: be there."

"But, Jack, uh, Pledgemaster Knoff, sir," Lyman protested, "I can't make it tonight. Honest, I—"

"You WHAT?" bellowed the chairman of the Hazing Committee, "Are you defying me, PLEDGE?"

"No, honest. C'mon, you gotta give me a break. I got the date of my life lined up tonight. Hey, if you only knew how I been workin' to get this..."

"Very well, Bumpo," replied the pledgemaster calmly, "go on your date if you wish, but I'll remember this when Hell Week starts. Next week." He paused briefly. "Or have you forgotten about Hell Week, PLEDGE?" The spittle flew from his snarling mouth.

"No, sir, I haven't. Look, can't we..."

"Good day, Mr. Bumpo. I hope your date will have been worth it."

*****

Lyman arrived a good twenty minutes early, in case Darlene had decided to come a little early herself, which, considering her letter...

"Hi, Lyman!" a voice rang out from the other side of the lobby. It was the fat broad.

"Oh, uh, hi," Lyman stammered as he tried to remember her name. "How are you?"

To his surprise she caught him in an enthusiastic embrace

that felt as though it must have cracked most of his ribs. He staggered back as soon as she released him.

"Strange girl," he thought as he was gulping for air. "Say, have you seen Darlene around?" he inquired at last, "I'm supposed to meet her here for the festival."

The sparkle abruptly vanished from Angie's eyes, and two large tears began to form.

"What did you say?"

"I'm meeting Darlene here in a few minutes," he explained to her. "We got a hot date."

"Dar*lene*? Lyman, how could you do this to me?" she sobbed. Lyman began to get worried. He had no idea why this crazy girl was trying to make a scene, but he sure didn't need her lousing things up when his date arrived.

"Look, honey, I don't know what your problem is," Lyman explained to her, "but if me and Darlene wanna have an affair, it's none of your business, okay?"

Angie blinked her next tears away and regained her voice. "You stupid little jerk, you're not havin' an affair with Darlene, and you know it! She wouldn't give you the time of day. Yeah, and she sees lotsa other guys she likes way better'n you.

"And you can take your stupid little poem and CRAM IT!" she yelled as she stormed out of the lobby. Lyman looked around helplessly and shrugged his shoulders in bewilderment. Then he stepped outside for a very, very long walk.

*****

Never had Fred the Mover hugged any of the countless women he had known as hard or as fervently as he hugged the commode that morning, the result of his boastful attempt the previous night to consume a whole keg of beer by himself. The notion, he imagined, must have been brought on by all that wine he had polished off beforehand. Either that or perhaps the fifth of gin he and Jack had chug-a-lugged earlier.

"Call me John," moaned Knoff from the floor of the next stall.

Even as he savored the ten-second respite between violent heaves, Fred's throbbing headache had reached the point where he could scarcely tolerate any sound louder than a cockroach belching in the farthest corner of the basement, three stories below.

'FRED, WHAT'LL I DO?" Lyman shouted in a voice that would surely wake the dead, whom Fred so bitterly envied. "SHE JUST WON'T TALK TO ME ABOUT ANYTHING, NO MATTER WHAT I DO! BESIDES, I THINK SHE'S SEEIN' SOME OTHER GUY! WHAT'LL I DO, FRED?"

"Dunno," Fred mumbled into the basin, "paint the whole horse red, uk..."

Lyman let Fred attend to his toilet and swung into action.

The next Sunday found Lyman astride his usual horse, well behind Darlene, who, as ever, barely seemed to notice his presence. Deep down, he didn't think much of this latest scheme, but, then, who was he to doubt a renowned swordsman like Fred the Mover? In any case, Lyman's latest raid on the stable had gone off without a hitch, and now his horse was colored red from the neck on down.

As Darlene's mount paused to nibble at a tree branch, Lyman finally caught up with her. Before he could say a word, she turned and looked at his horse.

"Hey, your horse is all red," she remarked.

"Yeah," said Lyman, "let's fuck!"

MCNAMARA'S GARDEN
by La Donna Mobile

Ms. Mobile, the self-described "Alabama Songbird," was glad to compose this story for us between her many failed auditions.

She has landed but one part on the stage, which was allowed to come about only as a result of some considerable—shall we say—"handkerchief-pankerchief" with her cousin, the show's director. In that production, she played the role of Guacamola, the evil sorceress in the best-forgotten Gilbert and Sullivan operetta, *The Dominatrices* or *The Lass who Loved Leather*, with the Selma, Alabama Players (SAP). And, while her performance could hardly have been termed a critical success, she managed to prepare and subsist on a good deal of nourishing soup with the overripe produce that the audience members chucked at her, each and every evening the show ran. She could have provided for herself even better had some public-spirited citizens not burned the theater to the ground after the show's first week.

When she finally ran out of food, she decided to buckle down and try her hand at storytelling. Here then, is her hand in all its okra-tinged glory.—tcl

I

Shamus McNamara was an old man. If the calendar did not make that sufficiently clear to him, the arthritic state of his joints surely did. It was as much as he could do to grip a pencil, let alone a spade or hoe.

He lived alone. His wife of many years had passed away, or

so she said. His three sons were grown and scattered far from the ramshackle house in the small town where he lived.

Shamus had never made a lot of money, nor had he been particularly frugal with what he did bring in. On top of that, because he always did his food shopping at the little grocery around the corner, instead of the mammoth supermarket down the road, he wound up having to pay more for his groceries than he should have. It was not just for convenience. Even when he had a car and could have easily driven to the supermarket, he declined to do so. After a bizarre incident in the store, years earlier, he vowed he would never go there again.

Back when he was young and single, Shamus had entered the supermarket, trying to the best of his limited ability, to stretch his tiny food budget as far as possible. He was in the produce section, picking out lima beans, on sale @ 10¢ per dozen. As he did so, he got the unmistakable feeling someone was watching him. Finally, when he could stand the suspense no longer, he quickly turned in the direction of where he thought the observer stood. He caught only a glimpse of a figure, seemingly clad in a black dress, ducking into the next aisle over.

"What're they tryin' to do, spot me shoplifting lima beans?" Shamus wondered. He imagined the shadowy figure might have been a newly-hired house dick.

Leaving it at that, he made his way into the coffee aisle, where he bought a bag of the weakest, bitterest, cheapest whole bean coffee in stock. After all, there was no need to throw his money away on the ground stuff when he had a perfectly good hammer at home. Then he felt a prickly sensation in his spine.

"I shoulda been more careful about takin' the pins outa that new shirt," he lectured himself. He spied what he felt sure now was that same black dress. This time he saw it contained an elderly woman, who had been peering at him rather intently, it seemed. As soon as Shamus made eye contact, she fled around a corner.

"Is there something wrong with me?" Shamus wondered. "Do I have a big glob of snot on my nose?" A quick peek in the reflection from a pan dangling in the kitchenware section, revealed that, for a change, he did not.

As he was rummaging through the Expired Bologna Bargain Bin, he once again felt himself being watched. He looked up and, there she was, running off to another aisle.

"What's with that old biddy?" he wondered as he strode toward the next item on his list. He had three more things to buy, and, at each location, he caught the strange woman staring at him, then dashing off.

It did not occur to Shamus that she had done anything but follow him around, but he soon realized, she had been shopping quite a bit herself. As he went to check out at the one open register, he noticed the lady ahead of him with a cart so full she could have fed the Red Chinese army... for a week.

"Well, what the hell," Shamus thought. "I'm stuck here anyway, I might as well get in line and let her get a good gander at me."

He waited behind her, and for a while, she did not even bother to look at him. Then, when the cashier was finally nearing the end of her order, the lady said something to her in a quiet voice, then turned around to address Shamus.

"Pardon me, sir, I must apologize. As you may have noticed, I've been staring at you."

"Yes," Shamus replied, "I noticed."

"You see," she explained, "I don't want to seem rude, but you resemble my son, who died last week. I couldn't help but to stare. You so remind me of him."

"Oh, gee, lady, I'm really sorry to hear that," he told her as she stopped to stifle a sob.

"Do you think I could ask you to do a small favor for a grieving mother?" she asked him as she dabbed at her teary eyes with a hankie.

"Sure I could, lady," Shamus was quick to reply as he felt his own eyes moistening.

"If, as I'm leaving the store, you could wave at me and say, 'Bye, Mom,' it would mean the world to me."

You bet I will," he assured her.

And so, just as she had asked him to, when Shamus saw the woman reach the exit door, he waved to her and called out, "Bye, Mom!"

Meanwhile, the cashier had finished ringing up his few items.

"That'll be $387.59," she announced.

"WHAT?" the surprised shopper inquired . "I only had six lousy items, and I do mean lousy. Where do you get 387.59?"

"Yours," the cashier patiently explained to him, "plus your mom's stuff that she said you're payin' for."

Now, living the life of a mal-vivant in his own not-at-all-golden years, Shamus found himself having to scrape by on Social Security. His infirmities increased relentlessly as he aged until he was spending the biggest part of his income on his health. To help make ends meet, he came up the idea of starting a vegetable garden in his backyard.

Sure, it sounded like a fine plan, but starting it would be an awfully daunting challenge. He himself was incapable of spading the rock-hard soil, and he could hardly afford to hire someone to do it for him. His one hope was to convince one of his sons to do the job.

"Fat chance," he sighed.

*****

He first thought he would ask his second son, Patrick, who lived in New York City—a considerable distance away. Still, he was geographically the closest available offspring, and, for that reason alone, the most logical candidate for the job.

Nothing else made Patrick very suitable for what his father needed to get done. He qualified, hands down, as the laziest of Shamus' three sons. When he was a boy, it had been all his parents could do to make him dry a dish, let alone paint the house, regrout the bathroom tiles or patch the roof.

No, Patrick was neither a roofer nor a grouter. Patrick, so he imagined, was a poet. He had left home as soon as he could and headed for Greenwich Village, to become a "beatnik." If so, then he would surely have been the last of the breed. Still, it remained his most ardent wish to be regarded as a beatnik, simply because he was "so very fond of beets." Patrick was also an idiot.

Before beginning the daunting task of writing to his nincompoop son in New York, Shamus allowed himself the more pleasant distraction of writing to his oldest son, Peter, the most unavailable of them all, not because of distance, but because of the nature of his domicile. Peter, you see, was doing time and lots of it.

He was the brightest of the three McNamara boys, which would not have been saying very much, except he actually was quite sharp. Once, when he and Patrick were teenagers and the family had rented a beach house for their annual vacation, he attempted to impart some of his knowledge, in the all-important field of picking up girls, to his younger brother, who had been nothing but a failure at that endeavor for as long as he had been trying.

"Look," Peter told him, "since we're at the beach, this is a perfect opportunity for you to test out my great trick. It's bound to work, and, best of all, you don't have to say a word, which, in your case, is probably a good thing."

"What am I supposed to do?" Patrick asked him.

"Simplest thing in the world, just stuff a big potato in your swim trunks, then parade up and down the beach. Mom won't notice one potato's missing from the bag, but chicks will notice, believe me."

Patrick obeyed enthusiastically, stuffing the biggest potato in the bushel into his tight Speedo trunks, but the trick did not work at all. In fact, it frequently had the opposite effect on girls he sauntered past.

"I can't understand it," Patrick complained. "I did exactly like you said and nothing—worse than nothing."

His older brother sighed and shook his head. Then he carefully explained: "The potato goes in the front, not the back, ya feeb."

In addition to his brains, Peter possessed a brutal and violent nature that simmered only reluctantly beneath his veneer of debonairity. When he left home to seek his fortune, he took with him the family's ancestral pitchfork.

"This is all I need to make my way in the world, Dad," he said, to his father's enormous relief. Shamus had been deathly afraid the boy was going to ask him for money.

Peter moved to Chicago, where he promptly offered his services as a collection agent to one of the town's most beloved loan sharks.

"I dunno if I wanna take on any new help," groused the shylock. "I got plennya legbreakers workin' for me now, and they ain't doin' squat. I got delinquent accounts up the wazoo."

"Maybe you wouldn't have so many deadbeats on your hands if you let me persuade 'em t'pay up," Peter suggested.

"With what?" asked the guy who was on his way to becoming the loneliest of the loan sharks, "yer winning smile and yer way wit' words?"

"Why yes sir," Peter agreed. "And with this as well," he added as he brought out the pitchfork.

The skeptical loan shark hesitated. Then he gave himself a pop quiz on the subject of what did he have to lose? The correct answer he arrived at was zero, especially matter of Benedetto "Benny The Yegg" Scramboli, his most difficult client. It seemed that nobody had enough nerve to confront Scramboli regarding bad debts or any other topic, for that matter.

"Kid, if you can get me the fifty G's this joker owes me, ya gotcha self a job," the hopeful mortgagee told young McNamara.

"Hello, Mr. Scramboli," Pete McNamara greeted his assigned deadbeat. "I'm here to collect the sixty large that you owe my supervisor."

"The WHAT?" queried Scramboli. "I got forty-five of it, right here under my coat ." He reached inside his jacket and whipped out an automatic.

"Here, ya go, spor—" he had started to say as he pointed the gun right between McNamara's eyes. The gun and the hand that gripped it did not stay there long. Faster than the thug could have imagined, Peter swung the pitchfork he had concealed behind his back and ran it through his attacker's forearm, pinning it to the table that stood between them. Did I forget to mention the table? Well, there was a table. Make note.

"Jesus H. Kee-riste!" Scramboli shouted to commemorate the occasion.

"Now about that seventy grand," Peter went on. "For as long as you do not pay up, I'm coming after you with this pitchfork. If you insist on staying delinquent, you should picture yourself married to a rather large actress, because you'll be getting' the tine daily. Capeesh?" Benny opted for a very, very speedy divorce.

In no time, Pete McNamara became, not only the star performer in his employer's stable, but the most notorious bill collector in the greater Chicago metropolitan area. Nobody wanted to get on McNamara's bad side. Everybody feared "Mac the Fork."

He had managed to steer clear of trouble with the law, first because no one dared to rat him out and second, because no cop wanted to match wits with Pete's pitchfork. On top of that, zealous debt collection was regarded as simply the way business got done in the town and, for that reason, the local authorities largely ignored it.

Peter's troubles began with the sudden depopulation of a gang run by Ollie "Owly" O'Brien. In honor of their chief, the gang members named themselves "The Owls" and greeted one another with what they imagined to be that bird's call. These boys were none too bright to begin with and woefully ignorant about the workings of Mother Nature. Their owl imitations were so wretchedly poor, they became known as The Gang that Couldn't Hoot Straight.

One thing they could do, though, was go missing with alarming regularity. Most of them did so by finding refuge, along with their collections of boulders or concrete blocks, on the floor of Lake Michigan, where, oddly enough, the police had not thought to look for them.

Still somebody needed to act on these suspicious disappearances. In desperation, the chief of police raised his thermostat.

"The heat is on," grumbled Salvatore "The Trombone" Tedesco, who had been behind the vanishings in an effort to corner the local hopscotch action. His solution was to direct the authorities to a suspect who had the crucial qualification of not being Salvatore Tedesco. It was while he was aboard that train of thought that the name of Pete McNamara came to mind.

Now Sal Tedesco, on the bravest day he ever lived, would not have gone within three blocks of McNamara but, then, he didn't need to. He equipped his ablest goon with a pitchfork and instructed him to stick it through the heart of one of the few surviving Owls: Louie "The Briber" O'Toole. Louie, as you might have guessed, was in charge of police payoffs, and he had always done his job quite well. The cops would be none too amused to learn of Mr. O'Toole's demise. Tedesco further instructed the hit man or, rather, the pitch man, to refrain from giving O'Toole the usual burial at sea, but to leave the man's corpse right out on the pavement, in broad daylight, where everybody could see it and the pitchfork that was planted in its chest.

It was only a small matter of time before Pete McNamara was arrested, although his subsequent sentence amounted to anything but a small matter of time.

II

My Dear Son,

Not a day goes by that I do not grieve over your situation. Just know that I believe you when you say you are innocent, and I always will. That said, let me tell you about the troubles I am having in my old age.

Not only do my joints ache like hell, my back has become so sore and stiff, I can hardly lean forward, let alone bend over, without getting this horrible pain.

I am spending so much for medicine, I scarcely have anything left for food. Just the other day, I went to buy a can of dog food, which I hoped might tide me over for a few days. Joe, the guy that owns the store, was behind the counter when I give him the can to ring it up.

"Shamus," he says to me, "I know good and well you ain't got no damn dog. Dog food's for dogs, not people. Put it back."

Well, he got me there, so I had to put it back. The next day, I tried to buy a can of cat food.

"Put it back, Shamus," he tells me, "I know you ain't got no cat neither."

So, the day after that, I come in with a brown paper bag and set it on the counter.

"What's in the bag?" Joe asks me.

"Why don't you pull it out and take a look," I says.

Old Joe, he reaches into the bag and then pulls his hand out real fast. He looks at the stuff all over his fingers and he's sure got no trouble smelling it.

"What the hell?" he asks me.

"Okay, now that I've shown you the proof, will you sell me a couple rolls of toilet paper?"

I do have a plan to put food on the table though. I aim to grow a vegetable garden. The only trouble is, I got no one to turn up that soil so I can get started. I know you'd help me out in a flash, if only you weren't doing 20 to life in Joliet, but you are, so you can't. I am hoping I can get one of your dimwit brothers—God love them, but that's what they are—to give me a hand, but I am not over optimistic.

Well, that's about all I know from here. Dress warm. If they give you an orange jump hat to wear with that orange jumpsuit, make sure you wear it when you're outdoors in the yard. And don't let the screws put the... carpet tacks to you. Write when you can.

        Love,
        Dad

                        *****

No coffeehouse in Greenwich Village or any other part of the city would have anything more to do with Patrick McNamara, neither as a poet nor, eventually, as a customer. Before very long, he became a "street poet." Somehow that sounded slightly more elegant than "street person," which in turn was a little more prestigious than being a bum, which is what he was. But this bum recited poetry. That, he explained to himself, was an important distinction. The packing crate that he called home did not have a numbered street address, as such, so his sparse mail went to General Delivery. That a letter would soon await him was of scant consequence to Patrick as he emerged from his crate for another day of struggling against hope to enlighten the heedless masses.

After gingerly opening the empty violin case in front of him, he climbed upon the footstool he kept and began his daily rant.

Oh, ye of little faith and no
Charity at all, hearken to these words of
Wit spoken through my
Teeth of wisdom.

I bring to you the gripes of wrath,
Moans and whines too long
And large to explain, so instead I
May just list 'em.

And high as a kite on
This twisted list in the twilight
Of no-parking zones, is the thing
That I scarcely dare mention.

Some funky old punk with
A trunkful of junk may try
With the nip in his grip
To bedazzle or frazzle your cat.

But you know it's so, as
Well as I do. He only wants your
Cat for a stew.
I think I am smelling a rat.

Patrick peered into the violin case and saw a quarter, two pennies and three jelly beans.

"What a haul," he chuckled.

*****

"What a waste of a good stamp," Shamus muttered as he mailed the letter to his middle son. Still, he felt he needed to make the effort. Peter remained in the slammer and his youngest, Timothy, was off somewhere in Ireland doing God-knows-what.

"If that chucklehead, Patrick even gets the letter," Shamus figured, "he'll probably find some way to weasel out of the job. Hell, it ain't like it's Hercules' mucking out the stables or nothin'."

As it turns out, Patrick did receive his father's letter, and he replied to it right away, inasmuch as he wanted to give Dad the lowdown what was, like, happening, like, garden digging-wise.

Hey Ho, Daddy-O,

This is your where-it's-at hepcat, Pat, reporting in with the latest dope on vegetable gardens. Is dope actually a vegetable? If it is, then count me in, but I am beginning to get the feeling it is not. Too bad. Too bad you're sad, Old Dad, but scratching dirt that does not even itch is just not my thing.

I wish you a groovy, far-out trip with your garden, even if it is a row I do not wish to hoe. What I will do is, like, inspire you with one of my special gardening poems.

Dig

Rows and rows of food
For the crows, it's
All in a day's work. Can
You dig it? While
Both flower and weed
Upon which Fido peed on
His way to the next
Thing to peon, wilt like
The stilt in the
Heat of the day. As
We're melting away, let's
Think of cool things, say,
Like maybe a
Gallon of Freon. Can
You dig it? While
Others may bet on a
Fast game of Mexican
Sweat, you've no
Need to fret if your soil
Gets wet. Can you
Dig it? I suspected
That you could.

Later,

" P."

"Perfect," Shamus thought as he finished reading the letter, "Looks like I'll have to find out where Young Tim's wandered off to."

III

Dear Dad,

I am sorry to hear that you are in pain and that you are having such difficulty getting your garden started. I know you will manage somehow. Have a little faith.

Life here continues in its dull miserable way. I don't suppose there's going to be any chance for an appeal, say, on the grounds that I flat-out didn't do it? I should watch what I'm writing, though, and so should you, Dad. The prison officials read all our mail, incoming and outgoing, and they know what we're saying. If I were you, I would refrain from referring to the dedicated public servants who watch over us as "sc--ws," unless you are looking for a particularly vigorous cavity search when you visit this Christmas.

Oh, I just had a thought about how you might get some help for your garden. I got a letter from Timmy a couple years ago, all the way from County Mayo. It seems he's been staying with our cousin, Jimmy Fitzgerald. If you can't get Pat to help you, maybe you could try contacting Timmy, care of his cousin. It's just a thought.

Keep well, or, at any rate, don't get any worse.

Love,
Peter

*****

The brains in the family, that Peter, alone among the three boys, inherited, came from their mother's side. Their lack was clearly a gift from the McNamara strain. Shamus, who was not about to be mistaken for a genius in any context you could imagine, still turned out to be smarter than his immediate ancestors.

One only had to go back to Willie McNamara, the boys' great, great-grandfather, who rode out west to seek his fortune as a bounty hunter.

"I'm lookin' fcr a man with a price on his head," he informed the sheriff of the town at whose stop he had been discovered and pitched off the train. "Who d'ye got that needs roundin' up? Sure, I'll bring him in dead'r alive."

"Now, that's mighty sportin' of ya, pardner," laughed the sheriff. "As a matter a' fact, we were just fixin' to put a price on the head of The Brown Paper Hat Kid."

"Ya don't say," Willie replied. "What's this joker look like?"

"Well, for starters, he always wears a brown paper hat, as you mighta guessed. What's more, the guy wears a brown paper shirt and brown paper pants and a brown paper vest. For all I know, he might even be wearin' brown paper drawers."

"Mighty strange," Willie deduced. "So what's he wanted for?"

"Rustlin' of course," the sheriff said.

"I'm right on it."

For reasons he could never fathom, Willie did not get his man, nor was he able to apprehend the notorious Chinese bandit, Hu Flung Pu. His exhaustive search for the infamous bank robbing team of Dick Kurtz and Mike Hunt got him exactly nowhere.

"Y'know," he told the sheriff one day, after years of futile sleuthing, "I'm surprised ya don't have folks dropping dead by the dozens, what with all these dangerous desperados about."

Willie eventually moved back to from whence he came and got down to raising a family. His son, Willie, Jr. had no more brains than the father, although he did have the advantage of indoor plumbing. In spite of that, whenever Willie, Jr. saw a sign that read "Wet Cement," he did.

And his son, Willie McNamara III, was not so much dimwitted as he was plain crazy.

People tended to regard Willie III as merely eccentric for many years—long enough for him to have married and fathered three children, one of whom was Shamus. Not until his children were in their teens did everyone come to agree that Willie needed to reside in a sanitarium.

Shamus' father did possess one talent, though. He was a pretty fair landscape artist, even without the numbers. They gave him all the supplies he needed to continue his painting within the asylum walls, and, before too long, word of his artistry began to get around.

"I believe these paintings demonstrate a clear and creative mind," social worker Petunia Dowd lectured the chief resident psychologist. "Such a gifted individual surely does not belong in a place like this."

"Well, we believe he does," he demurred.

"I should be allowed to interview this man," she insisted. "I'm positive I will find he's as normal as you and I."

"I suppose I can arrange an interview, Ms. Dowd, and we'll certainly take your observations under consideration," the psychologist told her. "But we, not you, will determine whether or not he needs to remain here, and it is still my belief that he does."

"We shall see," Ms. Dowd huffed.

*****

"Now, then, Mr. McNamara, I understand you're quite the *artiste*," Petunia Dowd began her interview with Willie.

"Oh, I don't know. I do dabble a bit in landscapes," Willie admitted, "but I still consider myself an amateur, next to the true masters."

"I see," the social worker noted, "and who do you consider to be the true masters?"

"Well, now that I think about it, I guess I'd have to go all the way back to Claude Lorraine, whose pastoral landscapes affected generations of artists to come. Even those ink wash studies he did of the landscapes he copied in oil are, themselves, works of absolute beauty.

"And then there was Gustave Courbet. He is most interesting because of how he he reacted against the romantics in his work, although it went against the grain of his era. I particularly admire his bold and creative use of earth pigments.

"Of course, all the great landscape painters were not Frenchmen. I would be remiss if I neglected to mention the English artists, Constable and Turner. If you've seen my own work, you may have noticed I painted a copy of Turner's 'The Burning of the Houses of Parliament,' although I'm sure mine does not hold a candle to the original.

"I also like the Impressionists. You know, Monet, Renoir, Pissarro, those guys. They actually painted outdoors, by the way, not in a studio. I admire the way they filled their canvases with light, which is where I part company with that philistine Degas, who used to mock the brightness of their landscapes.

"Lately, I have been studying Cezanne, although it may take me some time to fully digest his style."

"My goodness!" the social worker remarked. "That was a most lucid and informative response, Mr. McNamara. I must say that I am surprised, no, make that aghast, that these…these…oh, dear, one hesitates to call them quacks…these *bureaucrats* insist upon keeping you caged like some sort of wild beast. You may rest assured, Mr. McNamara, that I am going to march right up to those people and give them a piece of my mind!"

"That would be most kind of you," Willie told her.

"It is the least I can do for such a brilliant and erudite individual," she replied. "My good man, you have a wonderful career ahead of you in the art world. I just know you do. Let me bid you good day for now, and tomorrow, I shall return to have a very stern talk with your doctors."

Petunia Dowd had no sooner started down the path toward her car when she was knocked flat on her stomach by a well-thrown rock that Willie McNamara bounced off the back of her head. As she struggled to her hands and knees, trying desperately to focus her eyes, she looked back at Willie, who was smiling and waving to her.

"You won't forget me, now, will you?" he shouted.

IV

Dear Son,

How it pains me to think of your being locked up for something I know you did not do. Even though you are innocent, the prospects for an appeal are dim. That Judge Scramboli really threw the book at you, didn't he? If I could afford to, by God, I'd go out and get you one of them sharp Jew lawyers that never loses a case, but I can't, so we're stuck with that fool of a public defender, who couldn't get the Pope off on a trespassing charge if he had a jury of bishops. Just the other day, the clown was telling me that, since the authorities believe you done in the rest of the Owl Gang (Never mind that they haven't found so much as a body), they are going to stick it to you until you confess. Then, if you do, they'll stick it to you even more, I'm sure.

Your lazy, worthless brother Patrick refuses to help me spade my garden, so I have got exactly nowhere since I last wrote you about it. By the way, thanks for the tip about Timothy's whereabouts. I know he didn't leave home on the best of terms, but maybe enough water has passed over the bridge, so he might be willing to come home and give his old dad a hand. I plan to write him care of my nephew, just like you said.

I also decided to take your other advice and stop calling the screws "screws," but I can't think of what else to call them. Since I am being so reasonable, I hope you can put in a good word for me with the screw who does the cavity searches this Christmas.

Try to stay well and safe. I will write again when I get the chance.

Love,
Dab

*****

Timmy McNamara and his cousin, Jimmy Fitzgerald, were in London, indulging in some window shopping. It was about all they could afford on their vacation from busing tables at the Wimpy's in Castlebar.

"Maybe this wasn't such a hot idea," Timmy had thought, more than once, as he wandered amongst the cluttered tables. The original plan had been, move to Ireland and somehow strike it rich. As it was, he was lucky Jimmy had been able to use his pull as Assistant Head Busboy to get him this job. Time and again, Timmy asked himself how it was a guy like him, with such smart brains, had accomplished so little. He knew for a fact he was smart. Up until his early teens, people had always told him he was a fool, particularly his oldest brother's girlfriend, Griselda, whom he repeatedly called "Grizzly," long after her second-grade classmates had tired of the joke and found some-one else to torment.

She and Peter could hardly spend a minute in the house with-out Timmy finding a way to make a first-class nuisance out of himself.

"Grizzly and Peter, sittin' in a tree..." he began taunting from his perch atop a low branch, completely oblivious to the ambient irony.

"God, Timmy, I'm gettin' tired of saying it, but you really are the biggest fool in the universe," she chided the boy.

"Yeah, well, if I'm such a fool, then how come I ain't been hurt since Junior High?"

"I don't know," she guessed, "because you're still in seventh grade?"

"Seventh grade just happens to be junior high, Brainiac! Ha, what a rank!"

"Fine, Timmy," she conceded. "Then it must be because the Lord finds a way to protect fools."

"Izzat so? We'll just see about that." Then Timmy stormed back into the house for what the couple hoped would be a good long sulk. They had been relaxing in the family's two plastic lawn chairs, talking about one thing and another, when, suddenly, an upstairs window flew open and, with a blood-curdling cry of "Gerommino!" Timmy flung himself out, then onto the yard with a loud, hard thump.

"Owwww! My leg! My leg! My leg!" he pointed out.

"Geez, I think it's broken, I'm gonna get help," Peter said as he dashed off.

"Walked right into that one, didn't you?" Timmy taunted Griselda through clenched teeth.

"I'm sorry, what did I walk into?"

"When you said the Lord protected fools. Well, my leg's broken, and yours ain't. So, who's the fool now, Grizzly, WHO'S THE FOOL NOW?"

Never mind, the lads were on vacation at last, having a bit of a browse. At one point they found themselves inside a very expensive men's haberdashery. Jimmy happened to notice the price tag on a fine-looking pair of shoes. The number on the tag read "£475."

"Occh! Mother 'a Gawd!" Jimmy yelped in amazement. Timmy came over to take a look and was equally astounded.

"May I be of assistance to you gentlemen?" a store clerk inquired, noticing their proximity to such high-commission merchandise.

"It's just these shoes," Jimmy replied "They're awful dear, ain't they?"

The clerk patiently explained the price on that particular item was so high because the shoes came from the rare and extremely dangerous crocodiles of the Nile River The store, he went on, had to pay plenty themselves for such an item, and could ill-afford to sell them for a penny less than the listed price.

Suffice it to say that neither of the lads bought those shoes or any of the other costly items in the store, but, as they left, a sly smile played upon Jimmy's face.

"Y'know," he said to his cousin, "if we was ta take ourselves down ta the River Nile and catch a few of these crocodiles, we could make our fortune, now, couldn't we."

*****

Timmy and his cousin had been gone for a year and a half, when Shamus' letter came back from Castlebar, marked "Moved, no forwarding address." What Shamus did not know, and what their co-workers at the Wimpy's were hard pressed to understand, was that the pair had indeed ventured down to the River Nile.

The thing had been anything but easy. It took every cent they had saved and then some, to get to their destination with the proper crocodile-hunting gear. The many depredations they had suffered from prolonged exposure to the elements were minor compared to those they suffered from prolonged exposure to the crocodiles. Timmy was missing two fingers, while Jimmy was a foot shorter (the right one) after they had been on the job almost two years.

Still, they refused to give up the dream of striking it rich. Sooner or later, they realized, success had to come their way.

One morning, as the lads sat around, practicing up on being morose, they spied a familiar rippling in the river, about ten feet from the shoreline.

"I think it's one of them crocs," Timmy opined.

"Well, then, let's hop to it," Jimmy suggested.

The lads splashed into the river, pen knives at the ready. Sure enough, they discovered the object they had spotted was a croc, and a particularly nasty one at that. The fight was not pretty. Both boys nearly drowned. Timmy wound up with a horrendous gash along the diagonal length of his face, and Jimmy emerged missing a nipple, but come out of the river, they did, with the corpse of their stubborn, but finally subdued opponent. They threw the beast ashore and clambered up to have a look. Eagerly they flipped it over onto its back and stared. Then they both sighed deeply.

"I tell ya what," Jimmy said after a painfully long pause, "if the next one we find turns out ta be barefoot, I say we chuck it and go home."

V

Dear Son,

Well, I must say it was a right nice visit we had this Christmas. I'm sorry about your present. I had bought you a nice new hack saw, but the warden himself confiscated it. That's why you had to settle for the prize inside that box of Cracker Jacks I'd brought along for the trip. Maybe we'll have better luck next year.

I still got no one to spade my garden, though. Not only is Patrick too lazy to help out his old man, I seem to have lost track of Timothy all together. I hope he is okay, but I haven't a clue where he is. On the plus side, my doctor put me on to some new and better pain pills. I know I'll be hurting like the dickens, especially after I'm done, but, I think if I take an extra-big dose of them pills, I might just be able to dig that garden after all. Ah, the wonders of modern medicine!

In a couple of weeks, when the weather has warmed up a bit, I plan to get started. Before you know it, I'll be awash with produce—tomatoes, asparagus, the works. Who knows? Maybe I'll send you a great, big eggplant (with a hack you-know-what inside...heh, heh.).

Love,
Dad

*****

Dear Dad,
For the love of God, don't go digging around in the backyard! There's a good reason why they haven't found those bodies from the Owl Gang. Do you understand what I'm saying? Lay off.

I went along with the whole thing about digging up the yard for a garden because I never thought you'd get around to it. Look, if you really need some extra vegetables, I'll try to send you a few bucks out of the magnificent 25 cents a day I earn here doing laundry. Then you can go to the store and buy some, okay? Just LAY OFF THE BACK YARD. Get it?

Love,
Peter

*****

"You people got your assignments straight?" Agent Luis Cruz of the FBI quizzed the cops with him in the van. Three of them were carrying automatic weapons while three others had shovels. Additionally, there were a couple of picks and a crowbar stashed in the back.

"We're gonna pull around the corner and hit this guy at exactly 0600 hours. Just enough light so we can see what were doin', but early enough so we'll prob'ly catch the son of a bitch asleep. Okay? Let's go."

Shamus McNamara was actually awake and putting on a pot of coffee, when the the task force burst through the front door.

"Freess, *Pendejo*! FBI!" Cruz shouted as he leveled his pistol at Shamus' head. "I din't bring you clowns along just to stand around and gawk," he snapped at his men, all of whom had frozen stiff upon their chief's command, with their machine guns (or shovels) pointed at the suspect. "Now get to work!"

"Wh-what the hell's goin' on here?" Shamus queried.

"Yeah, pops, as if you didn't know."

*****

Dear Dad,

I'm sorry that I had to deceive you and that I ended up sounding so hard in my last letter. I'm also sorry that the FBI people scared you so bad you had to go change your pants. Most of all, I'm sorry I caused you to lose faith in me, if only for a moment.

Well, Dad, the FBI came, the FBI went, and in between, they dug up your back yard, didn't they? It was the only way I could think of to help you get the job done.

Good luck with the garden. If you're going to plant tomatoes, I suggest you don't do any more than two or three rows, because they'll grow like nobody's business. As for asparagus, remember, it will take two years before you have a crop. And about those "special" eggplants, if you send me one, I'll probably donate it to the commissary and let them whip up a batch of Hacksaw Parmagiana.

Love,
Peter

YET ANOTHER VAMPIRE TALE
By Beauregard Augustus Diehl

B eau Gus Diehl was only too happy to contribute this tale to our collection. If you ask us, he seemed a little too happy, but never mind. His socks matched, and that was the important thing. We were equally happy, we suppose, to accept it.

When we went down south to pick up the goods, Beau Gus acted ever the gracious host, as he gave us the "gardener's tour" of his portobellum mansion.

"Is this place as haunted as it seems to be?" we asked him in a moment of mild panic.

"Why yes it is, by the evil spirit of Mr. Mortimer Gage."

As if to make the place even more sinister, befitting the tale that is to follow, we noticed a sheet atop the secretary in the parlor that bore the letters "KKK" on top.

"What's this?" we wondered aloud.

"Oh that," he hastily explained, "uh, er, ah, those're the opening words to a song called 'Beautiful Katy.' Surely you've heard of it."

Surely, we had. Even so, we are glad to report, there are no references to "Beautiful Katy" in the pages to follow.—tcl

Millions of years ago, give or take an eon, the villagers of Veendouw, situated in the lowermost corner of the Upper Goulash Palatinate, had many matters to vex them. For one thing there was the constant bother of trying to remember whether it was the turn of the Catholics, the Protestants or the Muslims to overrun and forcibly convert them. For another, there were the periodic visitations of the carnivorous seventeen-hour locusts. On top of that, the shops almost always ran out of dog food, forcing most of the residents to dine instead on cats. And as if all that were not enough to stand the white hair on end (as the peasants liked—nay, craved—to say), there was a vampire. Actually, this terror was known by a number of names in that region. Some called him the creature, others the viper, still others the gangster of blood, while some people just called him Maurice, but they all meant that fellow who poked holes in your neck and sucked out the blood.

The local landfill was a landfill in name only. What it really consisted of were piles and piles of desiccated corpses, with but a sprinkling of sod on top to mask the horror of what lay beneath. And still the viper continued to claim victims. At one point, his collection of claim tickets became so immense, he needed a footlocker to hold them (and some of the victims' feet, of course).

But as terrifying as this monster's work had been, it was considered bad luck to speak of him. The minstrels of the town took pains (typically inflicted by the magistrate with thumbscrews) to avoid the subject, preferring to drone on and on in such ballads as this.

Nobody groused about the great joust
To be held on the fourth of July,
A date in the year that stood without peer,
Though nobody seemed to know why.

Now every knight who came there to fight
Was bold and of fine pedigree.
With lance or with blade, was quite unafraid
To take on somebody like me,

To win the fair hand of a lady most grand,

The king's very favorite niece.
A damsel named Nellie, whose clothes weren't so smelly
Nor spattered much with grime and grease.

The gold in her teeth stood out like a wreath
In a field of the purest white snow.
'Neath her nose, downy hair was but sparsely there,
And, where others would sweat, she did glow.

But winning her favor was a challenge far graver
Than facing a few balladeers.
To carry the day in a meaningful way,
A knight must defeat all his peers.

There was Vlad the Impaler and Pat Spens, the sailor
And Gallidan Pallidan Jones.
There was Simon the Pieman, a crafty and sly man,
Enchanted by witches and crones.

There was Louie Catorss and his dubious horse,
Named Francis, who some claimed could talk,
While Eric the Red said he'd not be caught dead
On such a nag, rather, he'd walk.

Well under the spell of the fair and sweet Nell
Did each of them vie for attention.
They'd fight or they'd grovel or sleep in a hovel
Or do things too nasty to mention

If she would but linger while pointing her finger
Somewhere in their given direction,
Their joy and their glee would run wild and free,
And below, they would spring ...up and dance.

You boys know the score and a little bit more
Nell said to the knights with a wink.
But this is much more than playing at war.
The winner must show he can think.

Pick me, yelled a knight, whose pants were so tight,
His face always looked red with wrath.
It's been many a day or a year, anyway,
Since the last time I suffered a bath.

My words came out crisp, and I sure didn't lisp,
Explained the king's niece loud and clear.
Howe'er bad you stink, I said you must think,
So clean out the wax from your ear.

Your challenge so grand, I have in my hand.
The thing that it is, you must guess.
I'll give you a clue, or perhaps even two.
I scarcely could do any less.

Your brains you must trigger as you struggle to figure
The thing that this object might be.
But then, mark ye well, I am just here to tell,
The prize that you win shall be me.

The object I hold is smaller than gold
And dearer than one grain of sand.
It's bigger by half than a hyena's laugh
And louder than all the king's land.

Divide it by four and you'll have seven more,
Which is well over twice what you need.

Increase it by two, and you'll find even you
Can't possibly stay up to speed.

The knights were quite hushed, and each of them blushed
At the feebleness of his own mind.
Some prayed to God, while some hemmed and hawed,
And one of them claimed to be blind.

Then out from the back of that befuddled pack,
Strode a knight oh so handsome and fair.
From his head to his feet, he looked natty and neat
Much more so than anyone there.

Pardon, fair maid, though I be sore afraid
That my guess shall soon prove to be wrong,
Said the knight to the lass as her stare turned to glass,
And inside her head, rang a gong.

I was never too smart, I'll admit to that part,
Said the handsome young knight, calm and cool.
It's true that I stayed, ever since the third grade,
As far as I could from a school.

So here comes my guess, in a moment or less
As soon as my wits I can jog.
The thing that you hold, if I may be so bold,
Is a fat, slimy, wart-covered frog.

With a long noisy sigh and a blink of her eye
Fair Nellie beheld him and said,
Though your guess was quite rough, it is nigh close enough,
Now let us both dash off to bed!

The unhappy village of Veendouw happened to be the seat of Gdjingafoos County, the least popular borough in all the Upper Goulash Palatinate. And, though that one hamlet had been cursed with the presence of the vampire, the surrounding villages feared the spillover.

"When that creature runs out of Veendovians for to suck from the blood, he will surely come after us," warned the village elders. This included the elder of the village of Pnoot, where poor Phrau Gfortska and her eager young son, Igor dwelt.

The two dwelt in a hovel alone because Señor Gfortska was no longer among the living. It happened one day at the brewery where he worked as a vermin skimmer.

At the end of that tragic day, a few of his colleagues came by to break the sad news to his wife.

"A thousand pardons, madame," their spokesman said. "Might you be the widow Gfortska?"

"Well, I am Phrau Gfortska, but what do you mean by this 'widow' business?"

"I am afraid your husband is dead," the gentleman explained. "He fell into a vat of beer and drowned."

"Ach, the poor man, he never had a chance," lamented the widow.

"Oh, I don't know," said the spokesman, "he managed climb out two times to pee before he finally went under."

"Igor, you must be wary and eat your wax beans," Phrau Gfortska warned her son, a few years later, "else the viper will come and suck your blood."

"What's wax got to do with it?" inquired the youth, for whom the prospect of wax beans was almost as dreadful as that of desiccation.

"Eat your supper," she commanded him, "then get to your chores."

"I'd rather go play in the dungeon with dragons," he sulked.

"Do not duck the issue," his mother replied, "for it is half past midnight: time to drive the cattle into the forest."

Dutifully, Igor assembled their small herd and began the long hike into the forest, where the cattle could gorge themselves on nightshade and loco weed. It was not without some degree of trepidation that he placed one foot in front of the other. Even though the fiend had not yet seen fit to pay them a visit, there was a first time for everything. As if to remind himself of just that very thing, he recalled the popular minstrel ballad that was, if not all the rage, then surely most of it:

The life of the party, whose laughter rang hearty,
(He invented the fake rubber puke),
Was the loudspoken man with a grin on his pan,
And everyone knew him as Luke.

The well and high born, most able to scorn
The great need to toil for cash,
Would call on our man when it was their plan
To host for their friends a big bash.

One morning the Earl of Spit-on-the-Curl
Decided to step up and pay
For a bachelor party. (His oldest son, Artie,
Had plans to be married next day.)

Eftsoons and gadzooks, amongst all of the Lukes,
The one in the Bible is dead.
So I'll summon the other, and I don't mean his mother,
Thought the Earl, who, for once, used his head.

Though the Earl had decided that all he invited
Should have a time happy and gay,

There was not a fat chance that a cent in advance
His Lordship was willing to pay.

Cried Luke with dismay, that is usually okay,
While prising his wallet apart,
But today I'm as broke as the nethermost spoke
Of a wheel on an overturned cart.

To his Jill-of-all-trade, a winsome young maid,
Elizabeth, shapely of leg,
Luke said aloud I am never too proud
To seek or to grovel or beg.

If you have but a clue as to what I should do,
Pray, speak, but don't try to be funny.
Said Liz, I'm afraid all the plans that we've made
Require the outlay of money.

You can see for yourself, all that's left on the shelf
Is a tired old yellow balloon
And the script of a farce that's a bother to parse
'Cause it's written in Ancient Walloon.

Said Luke with a sigh, as much as I try,
I know I shall yet rue this day.
How can I festoon with just a balloon
And the script of this god-awful play?

He moaned, It's no use, for surely my goose
Is cooked to a near-blackened turn.
If I cannot come through, then what will I do
When my services all start to spurn?

Then Elizabeth said, in no small state of dread,
For her boss's foul temper was mighty,
Perhaps then this play could yet save the day,
A tale that is silly and flighty.

And written, no doubt, by a fat, stupid lout
To whom cutting off heads might be droll,
Stormed her boss in a rage, ripping out every page
And tossing each one in a bowl.

But first he took care to make sure that there
Was nothing left to understand.
With each page he gripped, he tore and he ripped
E're the paper would fall from his hand.

So! As he spat, he said, Let them read that,
As right out the window he tossed
The fragmented bits of the wiles and wits
Of a poor writer's effort, now lost.

Oh dear, said the girl, it appears that the Earl
Was standing right square on the spot
Where the trash you did chuck had the very bad luck
To get itself where he had got.

Aha! Luke proclaimed, an invention most famed
I believe I've this moment devised.
Listen now, Betty, we'll call it confetti,
A festive refinement most prized.

Yippee and yahoo, I'm talkin' to you,
Yelled Luke to the Earl in the street.

I call this confetti, and I'm sure that you're ready
To tell me it cannot be beat.

Hip hip huzzah, or, better yet, BAH,
His Lordship replied in a huff.
I shall chop off your head until you are dead.
I believe that is payment enough

For the act that you've done out here 'neath the sun
Of this otherwise fine, balmy day.
The insult so brash you purveyed with your trash
Is something for which you will pay.

Hey, Swimsuit, Liz called, while her boss stood appalled;
From below, snapped that ill-tempered churl:
From London to Lido, I'm often called Speedo,
But, my real name, to you's, Mister Earl.

My boss did not mention, to get your attention,
Was all he was striving to do,
Said she to the Earl of Spit-on-the-Curl,
But you stopped us before we were through.

Cast your glance here, up top, and I'll make your eyes pop
With the wonderful thing that we chose.
Note how I'm slipping—we call this stuff stripping—
Piece by piece out from all of my clothes.

Said the man in the street, I'm not sure this would meet
Up to even the morals of France.
Though I'm forced to admit, somehow, bit by bit,
There is something astir in my pants.

Elizabeth said, Are you living or dead,
You great, silly sleepy poltroon?
If you'll stop being a sap, then soon on your lap
I shall dance by the light of the moon.

The thing they invented, then grandly presented
As the new entertainment deluxe
Was not shredded paper but a neat little caper
That always will rake in the bucks.

So caught up in the ballad was Igor, he failed to notice one of the cows had strayed into the deepest, darkest part of the woods. At a loss to find it, he climbed a tree and dug a hole so he could search high and low. No sooner had he finished those tasks, when he heard a most terrible moan of distress from behind him. Sick as he was with worry, Igor dashed off in the direction of the noise. He saw the corpse of his missing cow, drained of all blood, with two holes in its neck. Next he heard a fiendish laugh, briefly interrupted by an enormously loud belch. This could be no one but the viper.

As the boy fled in panic from the woods, his herd left far behind him, he regained enough presence of mind to realize the blood-sucking monster had branched out from Veendouw at last, and was coming soon to a hamlet near you. And, though they had no guns in his village, it was still a long cherished tradition to kill the bearer of bad news. That was something Igor had no wish to be. When he stumbled, in his headlong flight, upon a vegetable garden, he paused for a moment to pick three beans before continuing his desperate race for home.

"So?" asked Phrau Gfortska, "where are the cows?"

"B-beans!" Igor blurted out. "I traded them for magic beans! See?"

"I might have known this would happen sooner or later," she sighed.

*****

"Have you seen Old Man Pffofaff?" inquired the village barber of his customer, "He usually comes in for a light trim and blood-letting every two weeks, like the workings of a clock."

"Now that you've mentioned it, nay," answered the customer. "What is more, I saw a pile of town criers at his doorstep, still awaiting their tip."

"How peculiar," the barber remarked, "especially since Old Man Pffofaff has never in his life ventured outside of Pnoot."

"Maybe," said the customer in an ominous tone, "maybe he did not venture at all."

"You're done," announced the barber.

"What do I owe you?"

"Let's see...shave and a haircut...two bites."

"This time try not to slobber so much," the customer griped as he held a leg of mutton up for the barber's hungry attention.

"What's the occasion?" the butcher asked the candlestick maker, as the baker handed him a piece of cake and strapped a funny hat onto his head.

"Why, we're throwing a search party," the candlestick maker told him, "for Old Man Pffofaff."

"At last!" the baker proclaimed. "The entertainment has arrived. Pray give us a song."

The Knave of Hearts, yes, he did steal those tarts,
Of which, there can be little doubt.
While both you and I may have asked ourselves why,
The answer is what I found out.

It seems that no task'll e'er daunt this rascal,
If it involves some sort of crime.
To go and then snatch a right tasty batch
Of tarts is a deed quite sublime.

But that surely is not to say that he got
His fill of malfeasance galore.
His first little theft decidedly left
Him longing to do a lot more.

His crimes were so grand they traversed the land,
From murder on down to jaywalking.
They say that a few people both saw and knew,
But none of them felt much like talking.

A mob of the just then did what they must.
Some say 'twere some sharp poison darts
They all threw around that soon brought him down,
The doughty but doomed Knave of Hearts.

As he lay down a-dying and discourse was trying,
He spoke but what little he could.
The main reason why I changed into that guy
Was because I've been misunderstood.

From that, my mad rage then got to the stage
Where this bad behavior oft' starts.
When I gave my name, it was always the same:
Did I hear you say, "Knave of Farts?"

So grant me some peace with death's sweet release,
Though now a new vision yet starts,
There, carved on my stone, just these words alone:

Here lies the bold Knave of Farts.

The townspeople expressed their gratitude to the barefoot minstrel by throwing a large quantity of boots and shoes at him. But the time had come time to hunt for Old Man Pffofaff. First they looked here, then they looked there. As a last desperate resort, they looked everywhere, yet the old geezer persistently refused to turn up.

"I know," said the barber. "Let's try his house."

A delegation of search partiers knocked on his door, but got no answer. Next they rang his bell and ran, having left the requisite burning bag on his porch. There was still no response.

"I guess we need to go inside," one of the group concluded.

They came in through the bathroom window and looked around. At first the place seemed normal, but uncharacteristically quiet, for the old man was the champion snorer of Gdjingafoos County. Then, at the bottom of the laundry chute, the men discovered the body of Old Man Pffofaff. The pallidity of his skin could mean only one thing: this guy was *really* old. As they were toting the corpse out to the city dump for the traditional "open-air" burial, the fellow who was carrying the arms noticed a peculiarity he had not seen earlier

"Gadzooks!" he cried out as he dropped his end of the body.

"Gadzooks don't feed the vultures," griped the fellow who had been carrying the legs.

"No, look! Come and see, all of you," the first man called out to his comrades. He pointed to the two small holes in the corpse's neck. In a moment they all knew that the viper had come to town at last.

"How can that possibly be?" one of the nosier villagers demanded of the narrator. "I don't see this 'viper' anywhere. He isn't up the street! He isn't down the street! He isn't high up in the sky, he isn't on the ground! We'll tell you, me, myself and

I, he's nowhere to be found! Heeheeheehee...there is no viper, DO YOU HEAR ME? Blubblubblubblub, if I can't see the viper, then: THERE IS NO VIPER! Hahahahaha!"

"What's with him?" asked the candlestick maker.

"You know what they say," the baker replied, "out of sight, out of mind."

*****

"Igor! Where is your garlic?" Phrau Gfortska shouted with alarm, when she saw that her son had removed the talisman from around his neck.

"Aw, Mom, it's too stinky," the boy complained as he buffed the manure he had generously spread on his shoes to a bright, glossy shine. "Now I'm going out to spray polish on our garden."

"Not without your talisman, you're not!" his mother insisted. "I don't care how much you hate the smell, it is the only thing that protects us against that blood-sucking creature from Veendouw."

Igor did not dare to talk back to his mother. To do so would have meant getting his mouth washed out with soup. True, most mothers used soap on their smart-mouthed offspring, but so go-dawfully vile was Phrau Gfortska's mulligatawny that the use of soap for that disciplinary purpose would have been regarded by her son as a mere slap on the wrist.

And thus did the days pass, one after another, as Igor and his mother continued to fear the viper. But the passing days terrified them nowhere nearly as much as the passing nights.

One windy night, the two of them heard a scratching at their window, which they felt certain was the Veendovian menace, coming for them at last. It was only a wayward branch from a tree. They quickly remedied that problem by burning down the tree (and their hut, nearby, in the process, then rebuilding it, a bit farther from any other trees in the yard).

Months later, they once again heard a scratching noise at their window. This time, it was a raccoon, which Igor promptly dispatched with the business end of a rake.

And, a few weeks after that, they detected more scratching at the very same window. It was the town drunk, Pfred the Quadruped, so named because his habitual guzzling frequently rendered him unable to stand upright. At that, Pfred had been scratching, not their window, but his own head. Even so, Igor promptly brought the business end of his trusty rake to bear on the latest pretender.

"Thank God he never lived to be victimized by that bloodsucking fiend," Phrau Gfortska observed while frenetically crossing herself.

Though they continued to wear their garlic necklaces, they neglected to realize that, with age and exposure, the garlic within was losing more and more of its potency. After a while, but unbeknownst to them, it had become so weak, it would be of no further use as an instrument of vampire prevention.

One very dark night, while Phrau Gfortska and her son slumbered peacefully in their beds, they awoke with a start to hear an ominous scratching at their back window. The offending tree had been reduced to a pile of ashes. The raccoon was carrion, and so was Pfred. There was, then, no other possible explanation for the noise.

"Dear God in Heaven, it's him!" Phrau Gfortska cried out.

"Do you really think so, Mom? I mean we've been rubbing our talismans like crazy, and the guy's still there."

"You mean he may not be the viper?"

"NO!" thundered the sinister figure from outside as he drew a white cloth from under his cloak (to stifle their screams?). "It so happens I AM the Veendouw Viper, and I have come to VIPE YOUR VEENDOUWS!"

OUR MAN IN THE STREET
by Tucker Doubt

T he successful submission of this shaggy dog story to our anthology represents Tucker's first foray into the world of the Published Author. We do not mean to imply that Mr. Doubt is without talent. Rather, he has been without luck, more than anything else. So many of his creative projects, he complained, have been just this close to fruition, but, in every instance, the cigar that dangled ever-so-close to his lips was cruelly yanked away.

He cobbled together a number of television pilots that almost made the grade, but not quite. Among them were "The Twilight Sector;" "Homer Pile, USDA;" "Have Brass Knuckles, Will Travel," and, later, a sassy comedy about a tavern in New York City's Kingsbridge neighborhood: "Bronx Cheers."

Bringing his self-proclaimed musical talent to the fore, Tucker penned a number of near-miss Broadway smashes, including *Make Out with Me, Kate; South Atlantic; My Average Lady* and, more recently, the tale of Juan Peron's ambitious wife, *Mrs. Peron.*

"I don't know why any of those shows failed to catch on," Tucker told us as we were trying to read the story he had submitted, "for I am a tunesmith extraordinaire."

"Surely," we demurred, "there must be some flaw in your composition, if none of them made it to Broadway."

"Oh no, I've got the goods all right," he corrected us. "Just listen, and I'll play you yet another one of my songs that never got picked up, for reasons I'll never be able to figure out." He sat down before his piano and proceeded to play a melody that, in short order, had tears streaming from, not just one, but both or, rather, all of our eyes.

"That was the most beautiful song we have ever heard in our lives," we observed when he had finished. "What did you name it?"

"*I Love You so Fucking Much, I Can't Shit.*"

Let us hope that you will love the story he has provided us, at least enough to want a cup of coffee.—tcl

I

It was hardly an original idea, even for the 1950's, but it was still a popular one, and that's what counted. For a five-minute segment every weekday morning, the TV talk show would cut away to "Our Man in the Street." Then Gilbert Thurlow Partay, the show's roving reporter, would have the opportunity to interview those passersby who cared to engage him in conversation, about whatever happened to be on their minds. It was a job Gil loved, not only for the comfortable living he earned from a 25-minute work week, but for the sheer joy he derived from the lively conversations he struck up, all in the public eye, with him in the spotlight.

Of course the spotlight was never essential to Gil's happiness. He was a gregarious soul, happy to interact with people whenever he got the chance, on the clock or off. One night, for example, he had spotted a concerned-looking nun standing outside his favorite bar as he prepared to enter.

"Pardon me, Sister, I couldn't help noticing. You appear to be lost. Can I be of any help?" Gil asked her.

"No, thank you," the nun answered. "I'm not lost at all. I'm just studying this place where all the sinning happens. I want to figure out why so many people seem eager to fall into Satan's grasp."

"Come, now, Sister, with all due respect, I think you're making more out of this than there really is," Gil told her. "I'm sure if you were to come inside with me and take a look around, you'd see it's quite a respectable place."

"Do you really think I should?"

Once they were inside, Gil began to give her the tour.

"Now, over there is a fellow playing the piano. Nothing racy, just pleasant melodies meant to help the customers relax after a hard day at work. And back behind those swinging doors is the kitchen. You can actually get a halfway decent meal here, if you know what to order. And over here, of course, is the bar—"

"Oh," she proclaimed, "that's where all the sinning goes on, isn't it?"

"Not at all, Sister," Gil assured her. "Honestly, I don't see the harm in taking a little drink or two, every now and then. It helps you to relax, and, if you don't overdo it, you're not really harming anybody, including yourself. Say, maybe you should give it a try. Why don't you let me buy you a drink?"

"I don't know..."

"There's nothing to worry about," Gil added, "Just consider it a learning experience."

"I suppose, if you put it that way," she finally agreed.

"Now order any drink from this list, and I'll have the waiter bring it to you," Gil offered as he seated her at a nearby table.

"Hmmm," she said after a thorough perusal of the list, "I guess I'll have the double mar..tin...eye."

"Scotch rocks and a 'double mar...tin...eye'," Gil told the waiter.

"Hey, Joe," the waiter relayed to the bartender, "scotch rocks and a 'double mar...tin...eye'."

"Oh, Christ," moaned the barkeep, "is that nun back again?"

Most people Gil interviewed during his TV segment wanted to talk about politics, local, national or global, sometimes, even interplanetary. And if they gravitated to Gil's microphone, it was a fair bet they had a rant ready to launch.

"This whole business of flourinating our water? It's a Commie plot," a street pundit would explain to Gil and his listeners. "First, they flourinate our water, the next thing you know, they'll be gunning for our soda pop. Wake up, America!"

Some of the interviewees broke out in song, while others would recite poetry. Well, actually only one guy, whom Gil sought out, again and again. This odd fellow happened to be an obscure Czech poet named Glub Dzmc, whose collected works, *The Lost Notebooks of Glub Dzmc*, the editor inserted his $0.02 into this narrative to say, can be found in the appendix. On any given day, Glub was good for a poem, and Gil was always happy to hand over the mike and let him hold forth. On this particular day, the poet was in a mood to recite one of his shorter pieces:

Hypotheticalspalooza

suppose the bats, the
ones in your belfry, went
on strike today. no more hanging
right side up, they say, or
working during the
day and an end
to guano production quotas. could
you function or get an injunction or follow somebody
else's compunction? or would
you cave or rant or rave or take
the extremest of unction?
would you run far
away and hide for a day, or would
prudence prevent a repeat of the

1

lark was nowhere to be heard.
that's the last word.

"That was our poet laureate of the park bench, Glub Dizmik," Gil said into his microphone, "always good for a few words of wisdom. It seems today's words were fewer than usual, so we may have time for one more interview."

Gil did not locate the next interviewee; he located Gil.

"Hey buddy," a scrofulous man of no fixed address hailed him, "you got a smoke?"

"Sure, pal, here ya go," Gil replied as he tossed the guy two half-smokes he had recently purchased from a street vendor. "That oughta do the trick."

"Huh?" the stranger effused.

"Now that I've done you a favor, suppose you do one for me."

"Whaddya mean?" the guy asked.

"Well, I'm Our Man in the Street, and I'm looking for people who have something to say. How about it?"

"Ya wanna hear a knock-knock joke?" the stranger asked him.

"Sure," Gil responded with a wink to the camera, "let's hear it."

"Knock knock," the guy began.

"Who's there?" Gil chimed in, right on cue.

"Argo."

"Argo who?"

"Arrrrr, go fuck yourself!"

In no time at all, three goons from the FCC swooped down on Gil, snatched away his microphone, and beat him to a pulp. A few minutes later, three more FCC goons barged into the office of the network president, slapped him around for a while and left him with a bill for $15,000,000. That's million, with an "m."

"Mr. Partay," the network president managed to sputter through his newly-swollen lips and three missing teeth, "this is all your fault. Not only should you consider yourself fired, right here and now, but you should know for the truest fact in the world that you will never—that's right, folks—work in this town again. Now get out."

II

Life, Gil T. Partay realized, was not going to be the same, and for a good long while. No more night clubs or day spas; fancy clothes, wild women, wild clothes or fancy women. No more going to the most expensive deli in town and ordering his favorite lunch: a cherries jubilee sandwich (on toast, natch) with a side of caviar. But, however much time it was going to take, whatever he had to do to make it happen, Gil would return his life to the exact same happy place it had been before that awful day—so help him.

First came the all-important matter of finding another job— any job—that would enable him to take care of the very, very basic necessities while he embarked upon his quest. Soon enough, that is to say, before the unemployment checks ran out, he procured work with the Majestic Eagle Nourishment Provision Consortium, d/b/a Stinky's Carry-Out, as a dishwasher.

Every minute he could spare from his six-day-a-week job, he

spent eating, sleeping and going to the bathroom. Oh yes, and re-
searching all the knock-knock jokes known to man. He combed
through every joke book he could borrow, buy or steal. He sought
out strangers and his sharply dwindling number of friends to ply
him with knock-knock jokes. And, whenever he thought he had
heard them all, he would run across a new one.

Throughout his exhaustive search, he met Sam and Janet
Evening; he encountered Sarah Doctor in the House; he was ordered to amster the damn phone, and he experienced the eupho-
ria of not hearing them say banana again.

He took voluminous notes. Even using the shorthand of list-
ing the jokes merely by their punchlines, he accumulated so
many notebooks, he needed to invest in a bookshelf, and a rather
large one at that. And still the hunt went on. This endeavor took
him twenty years, give or take three minutes.

III

Beatrice was not without a few flaws. She was morbidly
obese, which at least served to mask the undeniable fact that she
still would have been hideous, were she a size 2. Her complexion
was a fright and her interest in sanitation approached a level of
nil. She couldn't be bothered to shave any part of her skin. To top
it off, she had a foul disposition and an IQ of 63. Beatrice's lone
endearing trait was that she happened to be the only child of the
now-unbelievably-wealthy network president who had fired Gil
Partay, years ago. The network had learned its lesson well, then
had gone on to greater and greater success, to the point where
even the mail room boys were rolling in it.

Life would be a dream (sh-boom, sh-boom), the TV executive
thought, if only he could find someone, *anyone*, to marry his
daughter and—hope against hope—provide him with a couple
of reasonably viable grandchildren to whom he could pass on his

wealth and position. As if that task were not daunting enough, factor in that Beatrice hated men with almost as great a passion as she loved chocolate cake.

Time and time again, her dad, through the use of large bribes, had tried to "fix her up," at least with a first date, which invariably triggered a furniture-busting, glass-smashing tantrum that only Sara Lee could abate.

After having learned so many of them, Gil was able to steal a little time from the pursuit of knock-knock jokes to use in the pursuit of Beatrice, the network president's daughter. At length, he learned where she liked to do her drinking (The Bull & Femme) and what her favorite drink was.

"So tell me," Gil grilled the young lady's chauffer, "how do I go about getting on the lovely Beatrice's good side?"

"What good side?" the lackey replied. "Besides which, she don't particularly like men. In fact, she spits on 'em if they even try to talk to her."

"We'll just see about that," Gil muttered.

*****

"My dear lady," Gil implored Beatrice as he planted himself onto the barstool next to her at the Bull & Femme, "might this poor, unworthy soul have the everlasting and undeniable honor to buy you a boilermaker?"

"Get lost, Shakespeare...PTOO!" Beatrice snapped/spat at him.

"Ah, my sweetness, if only you would re-"

"PTOO!"

"consider and unlock"

"PTOO!"

"the iron gate to your heart,"

"PTOO!"

"Is this guy givin' you trouble, Bea?" growled the muscular, tough-looking bartender, as she threw her dishrag aside and picked up a bottle.

"Just leaving," Gil informed her.

*****

"The usual," Beatrice grunted as she plopped herself down onto the nearest empty barstool.

"Allow me, lovely lady," said the mysterious stranger, dressed in a yellow rain slicker and wearing Groucho Marx glasses.

"PTOO!" Beatrice hinted.

"Saay," interjected the bartendrix as she began fondling another empty bottle, "don't I know you from somewhere?"

"Just leaving," Gil volunteered.

*****

"It's from the table over there in the corner," the waitress told Beatrice as she gave her the gift-wrapped package.

"I can't see who's at that table," Beatrice pointed out, "so how can they see me?"

"I dunno, I just work here," the waitress explained.

Nevertheless, a gift was a gift, and Beatrice did so enjoy opening them. This one turned out to be a box of saltines.

"Now what the hell am I spoz'd to do with a box of crackers?" she wondered for a moment. "I know. I'll eat them," she decided. "I ain't et for over a half an hour."

Just as she was shoving the last of the saltines into her mouth, Beatrice sensed that same clown standing behind her.

"I'll bet a cool, refreshing boilermaker would really hit the spot about now," Gil murmured into her (conch) shell-like ear.

"PFF! PFF!" Beatrice answered in a noticeably unsuccessful attempt to spit on him. "Damn!" she observed, "I'm all outa spit."

"So marry me instead," Gil suggested.

"What the hell," she agreed.

IV

"Now let me get this straight," the network president questioned Gil, "you actually wish to marry Beatrice. Are you serious?"

"I am serious as all hell," Gil assured him.

"And, though I made it as crystal clear as a thing can be made that I never wanted to lay eyes on you again, here you are."

"Yes, here I am, offering to marry your daughter."

"What's the catch? There must be a catch, other than my being richer than God."

"Well, there is one, tiny little thing," Gil admitted. "I want to get back into television, on this network..."

"Out of the question!" the great man thundered.

"You know," Gil observed as he began to pull on a pair of galoshes, "I believe I'm starting to get cold feet."

"Well, now that you mention it, I imagine we could find you something. How are you at sorting mail?"

"No, no," Gil was quick to correct him, "the question is, how am I at interviewing people, live, on the street?"

"At WHAT?" the president demurred.

"You heard me."

"Ab," he replied, "by which I mean, 'ab,' which is to say so that there will not be so much as one iota of doubt in your mind whatsoever: AB...solutely not!"

"Now I think I feel a touch of frostbite coming on."

"Look, be reasonable, will you?" his possibly future father-in-law begged him. "You know what a calamity your last live interview was, and, believe you me, buster, the stakes have gotten a lot higher since then.

"That fifteen-million-dollar fine the station had to pay might of seemed like a real whopper back then, but it was chicken feed compared to what those guys'd sock us with if such a thing happened today. It'd run to twenty times that much, at least. And if it ever did happen again, they promised me that they would personally nail me to a cross. Every holy roller in the country would demand a boycott of our network and our sponsors, and, just incidentally, after your unfortunate incident, the only way we managed to sell any advertising at all for our shows, even to this day, was to stick a clause in the contract that gives our sponsors back a whole year's revenue if that word ever gets broadcast again. Are you beginning to get the picture?"

"What you do not seem to grasp," Gil explained to him, "is that I have done my homework since I was fired. I've learned from my mistakes, and I've learned how not to repeat them. And as for those damn knock-knock jokes, I defy anyone to run one past me I have not heard at least twenty times."

"You know, now that I think about it," the president allowed, "I guess we could put your interviews on videotape, and then we could edit out any obscenities. Yeah, that's the ticket."

"Ah, ah," Gil corrected the president, "no videotape. Totally live."

"But we're taking such a risk..."

"Trust me," Gil assured him, "there's no risk whatsoever."

"I don't know..."

"You *were* counting on grandchildren, weren't you?"

*****

"What'll it be, Mac?" queried the counterman at the If You Have to Ask Deli.

"Cherries jubilee on rye with a side of Russkie fish eggs," Gil called out, for the first time in many, many years.

V

"That whole Russian Revolution business? It was a Commie plot, mark my words," proclaimed the interviewee in Gil's first Our Man in the Street segment in twenty years.

Ah, Gil thought, it was good to be back. The weekend before the re-launch of his career, he had experienced a slight pang of doubt: slight, but significant enough to make him pour over his notebooks full of knock-knock jokes, one last time. There was hardly any need. He had them down cold. Even the distraction of his recent marriage to Beatrice and their nightmarish—to sugarcoat it—honeymoon could not make him forget even one of those jokes.

"You can do this," he reminded himself for the 3,562nd time.

Gil conducted a few more brief interviews with passersby, but, as he went on, his enthusiasm for the project began to wane. Sure, he enjoyed being back in the biz, but he really wasn't proving anything substantial, either to himself or to his employer. There was one interview he desperately wanted to conduct and, so far, he had not seen hair nor hide of his subject, who might be dead, for all Gil knew.

By now, he was intentionally sidestepping people until he could spot a familiar face. And then he saw it: not *the* familiar face, but a very familiar face nonetheless. There was no escaping a confrontation as the strange poet, Glub Dzmc, made a beeline for Gil and his microphone. Nothing would do, Gil realized, but to let the man have at it. The interviewist aimed the mike at him, but, all the while, continued to scan the street for the one guy he really wanted to see, as brother Dzmc held forth.

Gambit for an Ivory Queen

i never met
the one eyed texas
ranger, an incomplete stranger, before
he started to pour out his heart or
some other part into a bottle of beer. never
fear, i snorted in disbelief, just for a bit of
cosmic relief on the unforgiving
chessboard, where kings and prawns
try to rook the bishop out of all his hard
earned cash. and on alternate squares, the
white knights in pairs say they're coming to
pick up the trash. wrap
it up says the man in the seer
sucker suit, whose microphone
faces my mouth. i don't have all day.
why not go away and take a vacation
down south? that does sound
like fun, but i've only begun to

"That was our old friend, Glub Dizmik, folks, with more of
that poetic wisdom that never gets old or understood," Gil informed his listeners as he strode away from the poet as quickly
as he could. "Now I wonder if there might be one more colorful
person out here who can leave our viewers with a few final words
of wisdom...somewhere....out here...I wonder if..."

And then Gil spotted him: the knock-knock joke guy, picking
through an outdoor ashtray in search of a decent sized butt.

"Hello there," Gil greeted him, "do you remember me?"

"Get lost," the guy recommended.

"Come on, now, that's not what you said the last time we

spoke," Gil reminded him.

"Ya wanna sandwich?"

"No thanks, I just had breakfast."

"I mean a knuckle sandwich. They're good any time 'a day."

"Where is all this hostility coming from?" Gil asked him. "The last time, you told me a joke, remember?"

"Oh, what, so you want me to tell you a joke? Okay, how 'bout a knock-knock joke?"

"YEAH, how about a knock-knock joke?" Gil instantly agreed.

"Knock knock," he began.

"All right, wise guy, who's there?"

"Emily."

Emily? *Emily?* A wave of panic washed over Gil. Of the countless thousands who had knocked at the door throughout his research, not a one had been named Emily. But Gil's studies had not been completely for naught. Over the years, he had learned enough about how these jokes worked to figure, with bedazzling rapidity, there was nothing in all creation this joker could do to make a dirty line out of a name like 'Emily.'

"Emily who?" he asked with a knowing smile.

"Arrrr, go fuck yourself!"

THE TIZZ BOTTLE
By van Winkle Ripley

O ur man, van, sent us this last of the shaggy dog stories
from his spacious ranch, just prior to boarding the place
up and moving "back east, where I belong."

Once upon a time, van had been a wildly successful Wall
Street day trader, but then he tired of the whole phony New York
"scene." He let his imagination wander to a simpler place where
he could live on the land, in peace and quiet amongst good, honest folks.

Before he knew it, van had cashed in his chips and purchased
a huge ranch out in the middle of the Big Sky country.

"This is the life," he said to himself as he settled in to his new
digs. Three days later, he felt himself starting to go stir crazy. It
was December and a great deal of snow had fallen, with more
expected. Even without the snow, there was not another building
of any kind around as far as the eye could see.

"What have I gotten myself into?" he wondered. Just then, he
heard someone pounding at his front door. Eager for any sort of
human contact, he ran to the door and opened it, even though he
knew in his heart of hearts, it was not going to be the Chinese-
food delivery.

"Howdy, neighbor," boomed an enormously large, muscular,
but jovial man. "I'm yore next-door neighbor, Big Buck. I live
about forty-five mile away, over them there mountains, across
the river. I come to invite you to my annual Christmas party."

"Why, that's mighty...um...neighborly of you, Mr. Buck," van
told him.

"Yessiree Bob," Buck went on, "Big Buck's big bash is the

highlight of the social season 'round these parts."

"A real shindig, huh?"

"Boy, I'll tell you what, you best bring yore appetite, 'cause ol' Buck's gonna lay out a spread the like of which you ain't never seed afore. And I shore hope you can hold yore liquor, 'cause they's gonna be plenty of liquor to hold. Or, if that don't get you crazy enough, I got me about fifteen, twenty pounds of high-grade merry joo wanna."

"Say, this sounds like it's going to be a real orgy," van surmised. "Any chance I'll get lucky?"

"You mean is they gonna be any sex? Hells bells, I guaran-damn-tee it!" Buck thundered. "They's always plenty a' non-stop humpin' at Big Buck's big bash, no maybes about it! Of course, with all that wild action goin'on, seems like they's a big fistfight just about every year."

"I've been in a few fights," van answered. "I think I can handle myself, if it comes down to that."

"That's the kind of talk ol' Buck likes to hear! Tell ya what, son, since yore new to these parts, I'll come by and getcha so's ya don't get lost or nothin'."

Came the night of Big Buck's big bash, Buck showed up, as he said he would, and drove the newcomer over to his place. "Gosh, I hope I wore the right clothes," van worried as they walked through the door, "I have no idea what the other people are wearing."

"What other people? It's just you and me, little buddy."

But enough about van. Let's discuss the story he has provided. If there exists in this short, transitory vale of tears a worse Shaggy Dog story than this one, nobody has apprised us of it. Nor are we certain we would ever wish anyone to do so. Keep in mind that what follows will be the ruthlessly edited, drastically slimmed down version of *The Tizz Bottle*.Even so, we feel we

should leave you with this wise old Latin saying: *Cave canem-*
-tcl.

PROLOGUE

Once upon a time in the none-too-distant future, there came
to pass or, rather, will soon come to pass, one Captain Ralph
Armstrong, who had made his way into the Camp Snorkel
Officers' Club latrine. As I said, he had come to pass.

Though he hadn't expected to linger, he began to wish he had
brought along something to read. A quick survey of the floor
revealed what looked to be a magazine in the next stall over.
Ralph strained after the object as best he could without too great
an affront to his dignity, and eventually managed to clamp his
fingertips around a corner of it.

"Wonder if there's any skin in this one?" he thought as he
dragged the magazine (I was right! It *was* a magazine!) across
the floor and into his stall. He picked it up, gave it a few quick
shakes, then thumbed through the pages. As it turned out, those
pages dedicated to the subject of skin had already been excised
by some archivist or archivists unknown.

"Nuts," muttered the disgruntled captain. He flipped through
the remaining portion, hoping to find something else of interest.
He glanced for a second at the next feature, *The Day Big Tex Got
the "Drop" on Two-Gun Gonzalez, the Terror of the Plains,* but
then continued on until he got to the end, where the classified
ads were. He scanned the first page of ads as he debated whether
to pick up on Two-Gun Gonzalez or just clear out. The first ad
he looked at stated: "Hate-filled misanthrope, wishes to be left
alone. No smokers, please" Then he turned to the general section
in the very back, where his eye caught a potentially interesting
phrase in another ad. "$50,000,000," it said. He quickly focused
on the full text, which read:

WANTED: HIGHLY INTREPID INDIVIDUAL
TO FETCH ME A TIZZ BOTTLE. VETERAN PFD.
$50,000,000 REWARD PLUS EXPENSES.
SEND RESUME TO BOX 7473

Ralph wrote the address down on the next available square and put it in his pocket.

"Aah," he thought as he washed his hands and socks (Remember we are only visiting the future. It is not for us to judge the customs of the people who must live there.), "it's a goddam waste of time." Then he thought about how long he had been stuck as a captain in this miserable swamp and how dim his prospects for advancement seemed to be. Next he thought about his hitch, which would be up in another eight days. His resume was in the mail that afternoon.

SEMIPRO LOGUE

With a desultory toss, Mr. Joshua W. Hay threw a last handful of money in the air and sighed wearily as the coins and bills fell onto his head.

"I don't know what it is, Throckmorton," he confided to his butler, "but I find more and more that being filthy stinking rich isn't all it's cracked up to be."

"Indeed, sir," the faithful servant replied as he vacuumed up the cash. "Uh, sir, if you don't mind..."

"Eh? Oh, yes, of course," the tycoon sighed. He stood on his head while the butler grabbed him by the ankles and, with a few vigorous shakes, dislodged the krugerrands that had gone down his collar. It was an ordeal the old man hated like lima beans. He wondered as he sat exhaustedly on the floor, how other men of wealth managed to get through it day after day.

"I wish I was a young man again. I mighta been poor, but I

had plenty of get-up and not an inconsiderable amount of go. I'd of chased after it myself, believe you me!"

"Are you referring to that bottle, sir?" inquired Throckmorton, who had endured this many times before with the master.

"I sure as hell am!" he snapped. Throckmorton took a look into the study. Sure enough, the bottle was gone.

"I shouldn't let it trouble you, sir. After all, there's plenty of gin in the pantry. I'll go and get some more."

"Imagine my relief."

I

As usual, Captain Ralph Armstrong could hear the band practicing through the wall while he waited in the orderly room. It was, so his commanding officer had often said "a great and everlasting honor for Camp Snorkel" to be the headquarters of The Jarheads of Note Jazz and Light Infantry Ensemble. That the band's rehearsal space had been situated right against their offices, at the behest of the camp commandant, General Stuart B. "Stubby" Toze, only underscored the everlasting aspect of that honor.

"Better you than me," General Toze had explained to them.

Ralph continued to check over his discharge papers. As he did, he could make out the unmistakable voice of the band-master, Sgt. Chuck "Birdland" LaDow, counseling one of his musicians.

"I tole yuh to improvise, Pommeroy! Y'call dat improvisin'?"

"Sir, no sir!" yelped the unhappy trombonist.

"Now when I tell yuh ta improvise, MAGGOT, jus' how duh hell are yuh gonna DO IT?"

"By the numbers?"

"I can't hear you, SLIME!"

"BY THE NUMBERS, SIR!"

The band once again had at the Halls of Montezuma, following which a clerk opened the office door and spoke to Ralph: "Major Sanders will see you now."

"COME RIGHT IN, ARMSTRONG!" the major greeted him. "HAVE A SEAT!"

"Sir, the music, uh, THE...MUSIC...HAS...STOPPED!" the clerk pointed out.

"OH GOOD!" the commanding officer effused as he removed his earplugs. "SAY, ARMSTRONG, WHAT'S THIS I HEAR ABOUT YOU GETTING OUT?"

"Sir, you don't have to shout," the clerk reminded him. "The band is taking a break."

"And high time too," muttered the major, "NOT THAT WE AREN'T INDEED HONORED TO BE SITUATED SO NEAR SUCH A FINE AND DISTINGUISHED OUTFIT!

"NOW THEN, ARMSTRONG," he proceeded, "WHY'RE YOU LEAVING US? AREN'T WE FEEDING YOU ENOUGH?"

"It's a long story, sir."

"SO I GATHER, ARMSTRONG, SO I GATHER!"

*****

"I trust you've had time to study the material," inquired Ralph's possible patron.

"Yes, sir, every last holograph."

"And you believe you could recognize the bottle on sight?"

"Absolutely."

"Fine, fine," the old-timer called out, whereupon the gentleman got up and whacked it with his cane.

"Cuckoo," responded the antique clock, duly chastened.

"Now then," the tycoon continued, peering keenly in Ralph's

general direction, "you should bear in mind there are only three Tizz Bottles extant in the entire known universe, and any one you

II

go after will be extremely difficult to retrieve.

"The first of these bottles brought to my attention was lost somewhere in the Hootintoot territory of Nkwhmiland in south-east central Africa. I would be remiss, young man, if I failed to point out that the people of this territory are hostile to a fault. When the monstrously cruel dictator, Udu Balootu, was deposed some years ago, his long-time enemies, the Hootintoots, insisted upon escorting him south to their province for 'asylum,' where-upon the terrified despot fled north as far and as fast as he could. I believe they finally found him dead from apoplexy, still looking over his shoulder, somewhere in Murmansk.

"The second of these bottles, I learned, is buried some-where within the icy wasteland of Antarctica in what is now the Albanian Interests Sector. It was left there centuries ago by don Hidalgo de la Vaca, the famous 'wrong-way conquistador,' amongst other trinkets he had hoped to fob off on the Turks in exchange for vast quantities of their tobacco. A word of warn-ing: woolen knickers are what you would call dee rigoor in this region, and an ambulatory knowledge of your Albanian irregular verbs would be useful in the extreme, which is where you would be.

"Sgt. Vassily Ghespinkov of the then-Soviet navy discov-ered the last known Tizz Bottle while on a tour of the famous Novgorod Junkyards and Cultural Gardens. Unfortunately, Sgt. Ghespinkov developed a sentimental attachment to the thing. Thus, when he volunteered for his country's space program and went to the Moon shortly thereafter, he took the bottle with him.

Upon the crew's successful arrival onto the Moon, after the rest of them had passed out from too much freeze-dried vodka, this fellow Ghespinkov went bouncing off, bottle in hand, for points unknown. Neither he nor it were ever seen again.

"So tell me, Mr. Armbruster,"

"Armstrong," Ralph corrected him.

"Yes, well, whomsoever. In any case, I need to know, young man, what is your decision?"

"I'll take the job!" Ralph blurted out before he could adequately entertain his doubts.

"Excellent," his new employer beamed. "And which of those bottles do you plan to get me?"

"Gee, I hadn't really given that much thought."

"Oh, go get the one in Africa, why don't you," the old man suggested. "It costs a fortune to outfit an expedition to the South Pole, and of the Moon we shall not even speak."

"Yeah, sure, fine," Ralph boldly agreed, jumping up three times, slapping the back of his head twice and finally depositing a glob of spit on his patron's left shoe. Again, remember: neither our time nor our place to pass judgment.

*****

"I'm half starved," Ralph said to his guide, Jungle George Cazootey, as they drove along the outskirts of the Nkwhmiland Game Preserve. "Pull in here."

The guide turned sharply and brought the jeep to a halt in front of Farmer Tpulu's Little Red Bar 'n' Grill. HOLD THE THISTLES, HOLD THE LEECHES, WE DON'T COOK ENDANGERED SPECIES, read the comforting sign by the door.

"I'll have a couple of your foot-long twigdogs and a side of mulch," Ralph told the waiter after a careful study of the menu.

"And to drink?" the waiter inquired as he began tattooing the order onto his chest.

"Mineral water, heavy on the minerals. And make sure you fill my glass to titular capacity."

"I'll have the monkey's paw," declared the guide. "Does that come with the three wishes?"

"Of course," the waiter affirmed. "And what would dose wishes be?"

"I want the mixed grubs, a plate of refried coffee beans and skip the third wish."

"Real hot-dom good," beamed the waiter in admiration of Cazooty's savvy order.

"Yeah, sure, I hearda that bottle," the guide told Ralph between gulps of his food. The way he wielded his chisel and spatula, you would think he had not eaten since Halloween. "M'brother, Rudy, went out searchin' for it a while back. Found the sumbitch too."

"He DID? Well what did he do with it?"

"Damn if I know."

"He didn't tell you?"

"Not exactly. Y'see, before he could hustle it outa there, the Hootintoots caught ahold of him. Alls I know is where he'd gone to before they got him. Can't say for sure about your bottle."

"I don't suppose he lived to tell the tale," Ralph asked him.

"Well, they discovered hacked up pieces of his remains all over the province. Y'call that livin'?"

"I guess not."

"Good guess. I can tell you're a sharp cookie all right."

They finished eating a little while later. As they backed out of the parking lot, the jeep narrowly missed a rusty pinball machine by the side of the road.

"Be careful," Ralph cautioned. "We're on a game preserve."

"Think I don't know that?"

Eventually they left the preserve and picked up the main highway that would take them east, into the land of the dreaded Hootintoot warriors and the Tizz Bottle they held captive.

They were not long enroute before they spotted half a dozen turban-headed individuals seated determinately in the middle of the street, passively resisting the flow of all traffic, of which Ralph's jeep had been the lone example that day.

"Uh-oh," muttered Cazootey as he peered through his 3D glasses, "looks like Injuns alright."

"What do you think we should do?"

"I think we better try to set up a parlay. You stay here with the jeep. I'll wander on up the road and see if I can't talk tofu with these jokers."

"Excusing me, sir, and what is the nature of your trespass?" queried the tallest of the Indians.

"Well, it's like this, buddy," Jungle Geo. explained, "we're headin' out to visit the Hootintoot. Now I don't see as to how that's any concern of yours."

"Excusing me another time, but nobody shall pass along this road without giving an account of his wretched miserable life to the almighty Guru Rammalammadingdong, which I am having the honor to be. Also a contribution of all your worldly goods is considered essential for achieving the enlightened opening of your third nostril."

"Sounds good t'me," agreed the guide. "Lemmie go back and tell the boss.

"Hop in," Cazootey shouted to Ralph as he gunned the engine. "They asked us if we'd be so kind as to run their asses over."

As the guru and his gurupies lept up and scattered, the intrepid bottlesnatchers drove on. Soon the open road gave way to a forbidding jungle.

In the interest of maintaining the tight, economical style of

this narrative, I will but gloss over such inconsequential inci-
dents as the boa constrictor that fell from an overhanging branch
and proceeded to squeeze Ralph's toothpaste from the top of the
tube; the charging sloth (I mean this is some very, very hostile
territory we're talking about.) that chased the pair down an embankment, then stole their supplies; or the gaggle of rhinoceri
that had seen fit to kill and eat their jeep. In any event, they soon
encountered one Jean-Pierre LeDuc, formerly of the Foreign
Legion. Upon ascertaining to his satisfaction they had no association with the Legion or his missing status therefrom, he
happily agreed to give the two explorers a lift.

"You know, of course, *messieurs*, we are entering some *dan-
gereaux* territory."

"Tell me about it," grumbled George in and of the Jungle.

"As you can plainly see, we've lost our supplies," Ralph informed their new host.

"Including ze toothpaste, eh, *mon ami*?"

"Especially the toothpaste."

As they drove along, the Frenchman elaborated on the chain
of events that had brought him to this place.

"Who gives a rat's ass?" the guide volunteered as they stopped
by an unattended corn crib, but Ralph, who had returned from
raiding same, was all ears.

In his youth, their driver expostulated, he had been a successful *billet-tireur* in the prestigious Gare de l'Ourst of Paris.
In a mere two metric days on the job, he had been promoted to
the rank of marquis and awarded the *croix d'horreur* for perfect attendance. His future looked as rosy as a riveter's, but then
the migraines started. As the headaches grew worse and worse,
his efficiency diminished on the job until, one day, the exasperated stationmaster sent him packing. He dutifully unpacked and
re-packed every suitcase in the station, yet not even that would
not make the headaches go away. Eventually he sought medical

help.

"I 'ave a theory about such maladies," his doctor offered, after every conceivable medication had failed to effect a cure. "Only zc castration will mak' zem go away."

"*Sacre bleu!*" the young man concurred.

After the surgery, the doctor counseled him. "You 'ave a very difficult adjustment to make, *mon ami*. Perhaps you will nevair be able to look your frands in ze eye again, *n'est-ce pas*? It would be best to leave Paris, change your name, and, where possible, join ze Foreign Legion," all of which the patient did. He shipped out of Paris without so much as a suitcase and, later, enlisted in the Foreign Legion under the name of Jûles Cesar.

"Your life in zis place will be exceedingly miserable for what will seem an eternity," the first sergeant assured "Jûles" and his fellow recruits. "Now go get your uniforms."

When his turn at the quartermaster's window came, Jûles smiled pleasantly at the scowling figure on the other side.

"Shaddup!" barked the quartermaster. "In zees place, I mak' ze talk, while you mak' ze listen, *capish*?" The veteran outfitter studied the recruit for a few seconds, then began ordering up his clothes.

"Boots, size nine," he shouted to the clerks behind him.

"Zat is amazing," Jûles observed, "'ow do you know such a thing?"

"I 'ave said shaddup, *n'est-ce pas*?" growled the quartermaster. "Eet so happens I 'ave done zis job for most of my life. By now, I can know what size a man must wear simply by taking one look at him. For example, you tak' ze size seven hat, eh?"

"Exactly!" agreed the recruit.

"Just so, now shaddup! Hose, size nine," he went on, turning once again to the clerks in the back. "Undairpants, size 36—"

"Aha!" Jûles exclaimed. "I 'ave got you zis time, *mon vieux*. I wear only ze size 32 undairpants,"

"No, no, ze right size for you is 36."

"But I wear size 32 all ze time," Jûles protested.

"Ah, but you should not," the quartermaster insisted. "To do so will give you ze migraines."

Shortly after the Frenchman had finished with his tale of woe and Jungle George had awakened, there remained little more to talk about, chiefly because they had been attacked and (again) stripped of their jeep, this time by a cohort of warriors. Insofar as they had to run at top speed for several hours, so as to avoid the slings and arrows of outraged Hootintoot, there was but scant room for conversation in any case. Only by diving into the murky waters of Lake Mpoto were they able to save themselves, as the inhabitants had a silly, superstitious fear of crocodiles. Luck seems to have been with them (the explorers, not the crocodiles), as they were able to press on for another three days. But their pursuers had been gradually catching up. Soon, they were only yards away. It was then that Ralph had the bad fortune to trip over an exposed root. His guide, faithful to the end, was trying to help him up when the warriors caught up with and grabbed them. LeDuc escaped into the dense jungle, safe among the cobras and kraits, but Armstrong and Cazootey were screwed. In short order, the warriors had bound the two and begun dragging them off to the headquarters of the dreaded Hootintoots.

"What do you think they'll do to us?" Ralph asked the guide, talking out of the side of his mouth so that the natives could not possibly hear him.

"What?" he replied, using the same subterfuge.

"I said what do you think they'll do to us?" Ralph repeated on the sly.

"Nothin' good, I imagine."

At that point, one of the tribesmen shouted something unintelligible to them, although, judging from the way he brandished his knife, there seemed to be a local ordinance against communicating out of the side of one's mouth. Upon their arrival at the village, the captives were secured to any of several extremely tall wooden posts.

"This looks like a real high-stakes game we're playing," Jungle George fretted.

"Silence!' barked the man who would serve as their interpreter. Just then the chief came out, placed an inflated whoopee cushion on his throne and sat down. The tribe fell silent. After a short speech that seemed to be directed at the captives, he nodded to the interpreter.

"Chief say you must pay for trespass in our lands. Chief say you lucky he knee- jerk liberal. He grant you one last wish before we put you to death.

"You say first," the translator commanded, indicating Jungle George.

"I'd like to hear my favorite song, one last time. You people got an orchestra?"

"Of course we do! What do you think we are, savages?"

"Well, then." Cazootey told the go-between, "I'd like to hear that classic old American folk song, 'Achy Breaky Heart.' You boys know that one?"

"And why would we not?" He snapped his fingers twice, and several of the tribesmen began to appear with their instruments. Ralph's eyes bugged out in terror. .

"Before we sing The Achy Breaky Heart," the speaker said, turning to Ralph, "tell me your wish."

"*Kill me first* !"

Two days after the then-alive, then-Captain Armstrong had spotted the ad that would launch him in pursuit of the Tizz Bottle, The Jarheads of Note had an engagement to play the Camp Snorkel Officers' Club, as they usually did when no one else on Earth had a use for their services. During a break, Trombonist

Second-Class Kermit E. Pommeroy ducked into the latrine and then into the third stall from the window, where he noticed a magazine wedged between the partition and the back wall.

"Might be some skin in this rag," he thought as he pulled it out of its place. "Rats," he griped once he realized there was no skin within. Still, he figured, the less time he had to spend under the baleful glare of that bastard, LaDow, the happier he'd be. He flipped though the pages, looking for something interesting to read. "Hey, what's this?" he thought as his eye fell upon the next page.

THE DAY BIG TEX GOT THE "DROP" ON TWO-GUN GONZALEZ, THE TERROR OF THE PLAINS
By Winthrop "Gabby" Farnsworth III

Nobody around these parts ever did learn his right name. When we called him at all, we just called him Big Tex. He wasn't the kind of hombre you'd want to fool around with. Why, the last guy to give him an exploding cigar is buried somewhere out on Galosh Hill. 'Course the joker died of pneumonia at the ripe old age of 94, but, still, Big Tex was not a man to mess with, much beyond the odd exploding cigar and the like.

Well, you try and tell that to one Aurilio Domingo Gonzalez y Corona-Sanchez, better known as Two-Gun Gonzalez, the Terror of the Plains. The name pretty much much explains what business he was in, and, believe you me, he didn't much care with whom he tangled. That might be why he was known as the Terror of the Plains or, as the Mexicans liked to call him, *El*

Terroristo de los Ordinarios.

It seems Big Tex had finished riding shotgun for the local posse comatose and decided to make camp along the south bend of the Rio Loco. It was not a particularly good place to choose for a campsite because, at that very same time, Two- Gun Gonzalez (The Terror of the Plains) was riding around the area, looking for somebody to terrorize.

Soon the fearsome bandit came to the sleepy little town of Los Nadies, which, he realized, he had not terrorized, even so much as one time. He galloped into town (as did his horse) amidst a cloud of dust. In the time it took the dust to settle, he had stampeded all the animals (including the mayor's wife's parakeet), outraged all the women, shot the town full of holes and made off with 85,000 pesos, or $1.42 American.

"This will never do," he concluded after riding out with his faithful cloud of dust. "To get my hands on some big money, I must find a gringo and rob him of his diamond- studded spurs."

Meanwhile, back at the camp, Tex was feeding his horse, Paint. Little did Two-Gun Gonzalez know as he rode ever closer to the campsite, that Big Tex had left his diamond-studded spurs with the local blacksmith to get a few of the loose stones pounded back into shape.

"That is all right," Gonzalez would have said had he known what was not in store for him, "I am a desperado, first and foremost, whether my reward is a diamond-studded spur or a scrawny chicken."

"I ate the scrawny chicken last night," Big Tex was explaining to his horse at the moment.

No sooner had Tex settled into his mantra when he heard the sound of hoofbeats behind him, which he chose to ignore, and a voice saying to him: "Psst, 'ey, *Señor*, steek them op," which he chose to heed in deference to the caliber of the ordnance aimed at him. Once Two-Gun had gotten beyond the first step of getting his victim to stick them up, the operation began to go sour. Not only was Big Tex out of jewelry and chickens, he had not been paid for well over a month.

"Hell," he interjected, "I ain't been paid *well* yet."

Be that as it may, the whole affair was turning into a real bust for Two-Gun Gonzalez, who, after all, had a reputation to maintain. Then he caught sight of the cowboy's horse relieving itself and got an inspiration.

"*Señor,*" he mentioned to his captive audience, "do you see your 'orse dropeeng? Pick it op and eat it."

"What? Me, Big Tex, eat horse droppins?" Tex inquired. "Why, I'd—" The bandit cocked his six-gun. "Yeah, well, I can sorta relate to that," the Texan continued as he reached for a small morsel of the droppings.

The gringo's humiliation was proving so hilarious, the outlaw could hardly contain himself. He laughed harder and harder until tears began streaming from his eyes. Soon the tears were mixed with dust, a generous handful of which Big Tex had thrown in his face. The next thing he knew, the six-gun he was holding got knocked out of his hand and one of an entirely different flavor was lodged inside his heretofore wide-open mouth.

"¿M?" queried the bandit.

"All right, ponder, I gotcha covered," Big Tex explained. "Now, you see the rest 'a them there droppins? Well, finish 'em off."

"What?" screamed the outraged outlaw. "Me, Two-Gun Gonzalez, the Terror of the Plains, eat 'orse droppeengs? *Señor,* you must be joking." Big Tex drew back the hammer on his forty-five. "Chure, man, why didn't you say so?" agreed the Terror with a sick smile.

That evening, a long, lanky, mighty sour looking cowboy rode into the tiny village of Los Nadies. He was leading another horse behind him.

"This cannot be," whispered the mayor to the sheriff. "It

looks like the horse of Two-Gun Gonzalez."

"You mean the Terror of the Plains?" whispered the sheriff.

"I mean the very self-same," replied the mayor. They deputized some poor soul to talk to the mysterious stranger with the horse of Two-gun Gonzalez, the Terror of the Plains.

"Psst, *Señor*," the frightened deputy whispered, boldly peeking out over the boarded-up saloon doors.

"Somebody call me?" Big Tex wondered aloud. "*Si, Señor*. 'Ave you met by chance Two-Gun Gonzalez, the Terror of the Plains?"

"Yup."

"*¡Madre de Dios!* And yet you live to tell the tale," marveled the deputy. "Yup." "Tell me, *Señor*, what happened when you met him?"

"We had lunch."

"Hey, Pommeroy!" a voice yelled into the latrine, "Getcher ass out here. We gotta start the next set."

Kermit "wiped out," as they would say in those days, and left the stall, tucking the magazine under his chain-mail tank top for future perusal.

*****

Without missing a beat the trombonist picked up where the piano left off, embellishing the original melody with a lively bit of syncopation that soon had the people rubbing their stomachs and slapping their faces.

"Wow," thought Kermit E. Pommeroy, then but a sophomore at Rizzo Remedial High, "that's how I want to sound someday." Meanwhile, in the afterlife, Rizzo was urging Attila, "Trust me on this, Bubula, the earring goes on the *right* ear. And that pink spandex jumpsuit? It's you, baby, it's you!" Turning aside, he muttered, "I'm gonna make Attila the Hun look like a faggot if it's the last thing I do."

Being too poor to afford a trombone of his own, young Kermit bought a slide whistle instead at the local $8.95 & $9.95. He practiced for the better part of a year until he could reel off such traditional favorites as "The Twist Again Like We Did Last Summer Dirge" and "Pavanne for a Whole Lotta Shakin' Goin' On." Thusly emboldened, he auditioned for a spot in the school's duck-walking band.

Kermit explained to Mr. Frötingschlosch, the band leader, that he had perforce been practicing trombonery on a slide whistle, due to his limited means. "Old Frothingslosh," as the kids liked to call him, was a fellow who believed every child...or...well... almost every child should be heartily encouraged to play an instrument. He personally had drawn inspiration from the legend of his great, great, great, great grandfather, the legendary washboardist, Otto Frötingschlosch, whose mastery of his instrument even in the dark days of the Third Reich, had earned him the affectionate nickname, *Der Gauleiter von Schwing*. Thus would the kindly old teacher have been glad to provide Kermit with one of the school's many fine trombones. Unfortunately, the only ones in stock were...ah...missing their mouthpieces, stolen, no doubt by some naughty students. *Ja*, that must be what happened.

Eventually, Kermit would learn enough about the trombone to secure a berth on the Jarheads of Note.

"I don't know," fussed the lieutenant after Kermit's audition. "He's not very good, is he?"

"Hell, sir," the recruiting sergeant reminded him, "there's a war goin' on!" (Sorry, folks, nobody said the future would be all pickles and cream). "We're hurtin' for certain."

"Very well, sergeant, issue this man a trombone and dispatch him to footwear camp." Thus was licked the mucilage of Kermit's fate.

As he suffered through his hitch, he realized more each day

what a mistake he had made. Finally he reached the moment when he had this in common with the late Captain Armstrong: his hitch would soon be up. As he lay on his waterbunk (heavy on the ice cubes—We Build MEN at Camp Snorkel), patiently awaiting the start of the next chapter, several critics, who insist on counting themselves as legionnaires, or something like that, advised with the voice of no more than one, that here would be an ideal time to tell the reader more about Kermit so as to provide a better understanding of his character as the story "progresses."

Very well: he had a third nipple, which, while often mistaken for a mole, would ultimately prove to be every bit as useful as the other two.

*****

"Frankly, Throckmorton, I'm worried. We should have heard from this Armbruster fellow by now."

"It's Armstrong, I believe, sir."

"Well, nevertheless, it's high-enough time I got some word about what the hell's going on over there. Why, he could be dead, for all we know."

"Perhaps you might wish to consider another of the candidates," the butler suggested.

"Other candidates?" snapped the tycoon. "If you'da been a little more proficient as a snoop, like you're supposed to be, you might of noticed no one else applied for the job."

"They must have regarded your offer as a jest. In any case, you could always run another advertisement."

"WHAT? At $68.75 a word? Are you crazy, Throckmorton? Why, I'd ak, ak, ak, ak...."

Only seconds after Throckmorton had finished administrating the sedative, he heard a knock at the door.

"Who could that be?" he wondered as he placed the gun and

remaining darts back in the cupboard. When he pulled the door open, nobody was there. He did notice on the doormat the severed head of a hippopotamus, in whose mouth lay a nightlight and a set of dog tags. Throckmorton, who had read every volume in the Tarzan series many times over, quickly deduced the meaning of this anonymous gift.

"Sir, we've received a message from the dreaded Hootintoots of Nkwhmiland. It says, 'Your friend Captain Armstrong sleeps with the hippos.'"

"Far out," the old man sighed.

*****

WELCOME* TO PHILADELPHIA
THE CITY OF GRUDGING BROTHERLY TOLERANCE
This does not apply to trombone players

Kermit stared idly at the sign in the bus terminal as he waited for his baggage to arrive on what he hoped would be the next bus. It was, he felt reasonably sure, good to be home after four long years. Still there seemed to be something uglier than usual in the atmosphere, though he couldn't quite put his finger on it.

"Then take ya mittens off, ya stoop!" shouted a derelict mind-reader.

At last Kermit became at one with his luggage, after which he hailed a cab.

"Where to, Ace?" inquired the robot driving module.

"The Palazzo di Roma," Kermit replied. His mother worked there as a waitress or, rather, a nourishment transport engineer, as such people would come to be called.

As they drove along, he studied the notice posted behind the driver's seat: a silhouetted image of a trombone with red diagonal line drawn through it.

Once inside the restaurant, Kermit saw that the old oil painting of The Withholding of Spumoni from Saint Stephen had been replaced with a much larger picture of the evil emperor Nero sliding away on the trombone while Rome burned.

"Hi, Mom, guess who's back?" enthused Kermit, as soon as he spotted his mother.

"I dunno, who's back?"

"Why, it's me, your son, the trombone player."

"Yaaaaaagh!" she was quick to reply, "I have no son, least of all one who plays the *trombone* f'Christ sake! Y'HEAR THAT, FOLKS? I HAVE NO SON!"

"Hey, Mom, what's the idea, don't you remember me?"

"Get lost, you," she told Kermit. "I din't raise no tromboners, and that's that!"

Things might have looked bleak for Kermit had he not run into his old friend from high school, Barney Bogda.

"Hey, Pommeroy, ya simp, where ya been hidin' the last coupla years? Ain't seen ya 'round for a while, not thatcha missed much." Kermit reminded his friend that he had enlisted to join the Jarheads of Note shortly after graduation.

"Oh, yeah, that's right," Barney recalled. "You was inta that kind of stuff. Hey, if you're lookin' fa work, I got a uncle who's big in the musicians union, y'know?"

"You think he could get me a jig?"

"A what?"

"A jig. You know, like, a date to play at some club or something?"

"Oh, right. Yeah, sure, he could find you sumpn."

"Hey, great!" Kermit responded to the first good news he'd heard all day.

"So what's your instrument?" Barney asked. "I forgot what it was you did."

"The, um, trombone."

"Ah, ha, ha, ha, ha, ha! Y'know, Pommeroy, that's what I always liked aboutcha, ya got a great sensa huma! Now, come on, what do you play, really?"

That night a dejected Kermit E. Pommeroy sat on his bed in a grubby transient hotel room, wandering what he was going to do next. He began unpacking his bags. As he pulled out his Class-A military jumpers, a tattered magazine fell from them and landed on the bed. He sat down and started to flip through it, beginning with the classified ads in the back.

"Hey, what's this?" he mused. If, at that moment, an expert lip reader had been able to see Kermit through the grimy hotel window as he ran his finger across the page, that observer might have been able to make out the words WANTED...HIGHLY...IN...TREP...PID...INDIVIDUAL...

III

WELCOME TO LITTLE AMERICA
LAND OF THE FREEZE
AND HOME OF THE BRRRRRRAVE

Proclaimed the sign Kermit saw as he deplaned in that zone of Antarctica administered by the United States. Inside the terminal, festooned with banners advertising the various rent-a-dogsled services, he made his way to customs.

"Any icicles, snowballs or tinsel from foreign sources?" intoned the customizer.

"Nary a one," Kermit assured him.

"Fine, you're free to depart. Next flight to civilization'll be at 1500 hours."

"But I'm not departing," Kermit explained, "I'm arriving."

The agent leveled a hard stare at him. "Mister," he asked,

"how much do you know about penguins?"

"Enough," Kermit mumbled, not wishing to go into his past experience with those birds, and with good reason.

It happened during the summer after high school, as he cruised up the Vine Street Expressway in his van, that he noticed a truck pulled off to the side of the road. A stocky man stood beside it, frantically waving to passers-by.

"Hey," Kermit realized, "I'm a passer-by, maybe I should wave back."

As he released the steering wheel to return the man's wildly enthusiastic two- handed waving, his vehicle chose that opportunity to drift onto to the same shoulder and nuzzle against a light pole.

"Thank God you've stopped!" the trucker greeted Kermit as he rushed over to the van.

"Yeah," Kermit agreed, "I guess I have."

He looked closely at the truck driver. On his coveralls an embroidered logo spelled out "Orwell's Animal Farms." More significantly, he seemed to be chewing on a cigar.

"So what brings you to these parts?" Kermit asked, hoping to get some clue as to the cigar.

"Look, I'm in a jam, and I'm thinkin' maybe I can getcha to help me out." He pulled a five hundred dollar bill from his wallet. "Here," the trucker instructed, "you take this money, okay? Now there's a dozen penguins in my truck that I gotta take to the zoo, and I mean pronto. I'm sure they can fit in that van of yours, so how about it?"

"Sure, Mister, I'll be glad to it."

After a good amount of time, effort and expense, the trucker finally got his rig working and was on his way to the zoo. As he waited at a light a few blocks from his destination, he saw Kermit walk across the intersection with the dozen penguins waddling in single file behind him.

"Hey!" the driver hollered, "Ya goof, where ya goin' with them penguins?"

"Who me?" Kermit wondered aloud.

"No, ya nitwit, I mean Saint Mother Theresa! Who the hell ya think I mean?"

Kermit glanced around but was unable to spot anyone in the crowd who could even begin to pass for this Mother Theresa dame the guy was yelling at. Then it dawned on him.

"Oh, I get it, you're being ironical, right? I bet you really meant me the whole time."

"Listen ya little twerp," the trucker continued, "where the hell ya think you're goin' wit' my penguins? I tol' ya to take 'em to the zoo!"

"Oh, I did," Kermit assured him, "but we had enough left over from the dough you gave me, I thought I'd take 'em to a movie too."

"Well," allowed the customs official, "maybe you do and maybe you don't. Now what's this about wanting to go over to the Albanian Sector? If you plan to visit that pretickulla area, you'll have to go see The Man."

A few minutes later, Kermit found himself entering the office of Albanian Permissions and Lassitudes.

"Excuse me." he called to the people behind the counter. "I'm here to see The Man."

"The Person," corrected the severe woman, turning to Kermit. "Just take a seat on that bench, Sonny, and I'll let you know when I'm ready for you."

*****

"I tell you, Throckmorton, I flat-out don't like it."

"Indeed, sir." replied the butler. "Nobody ever said you did."

"I should have my head examined, sending that pipsqueak

off to the South Pole like that. He'll never find it, I just know he will."

"He appeared a pleasant enough chap, quite enthusiastic, I'd say."

"Yeah? Well that and $38.50 will get you on the subway."

"And it's not," his faithful servant reminded him, "as though you failed to give him a thorough briefing. Surely, he's had the presence of mind to memorise those guidebooks. I'd say, with a bit of luck, he should be setting things up with the local authorities down there, as we speak."

"I don't know, I have my doubts."

"Well then," Throckmorton suggested, a malevolent gleam shining throughout his eye, "perhaps you might care to run another advertisement."

With a final confident look at his phrasebook, Kermit strode purposefully up to the Albanian customs desk.

ESHT TOKE NGRITE SHQIPERSE
HYRJA NDALOHET

effused the sign above the Albanian consular desk. The guards glowered and anxiously fingered their anti-tank pistols.

"Welcome to planet Earth. May I have the pleasure to burn down your goat pens?" Kermit greeted them in fluent Albanese.

*****

"Hexcuse me," said the stranger to the elderly man, who had been so busy poring over his E-Z KwikFind Vendetta Checklist, he hadn't noticed the other's presence. "Are you mindink if we jointly occupy this table?"

"I suppose not," the man grumbled, although there were

plenty of empty tables on the terrace of the Olde King Zog
that morning. "I am no sure I recognize you face," he told the
stranger, checking his list once more to make sure.

"Oh, I am from north of here," the newcomer admitted. "My
four bears came from Montenegro."

"Funny, you don't look Montenegroid to me."

"Hexplain to me, pliz," he continued as the visitor pulled up
a chair, "what brinks you to my table of all places in Tirana to
be sittink down?"

"Is because yours is farthest table from that drunken braggart
over there. Perhaps if he see I am already engage in conwersa-
tion, he will cease beink soch a bother."

"Oh, him?" the old man snorted, indicating the unkempt figure in the far corner, "That is Mahomet Ali, our former champion. You are right to think him an insufferable braggart, but if
you think you are so easily rid of him, you are sadly mistaken."

Sure enough, as soon as the aforementioned figure had managed to get his glass refilled, he was upon the two of them "like
flies to sandpaper," as the locals say, which is why they take
so few of them alive. Right away Mahomet started in with the
braggadocio.

"I am the least insignificant! I am the least repolsive!

"Jost look," he exhorted them as he placed his medal on the
table.

FIRST PLACE, FREESTYLE GOAT WRESTLING

"You see this? I am win at Olympics. I am so proud of gold
medal, I take it home and have it bronzed."

"Go away, Mahomet," the old man sighed, "we don't want to
hear about it."

"So! You grow tired of my heroics, yes? How quickly they
forgat! Well then, my ingrate frands, if soch is beink the case,

I tell you instead of my hadventures in the land of the South Poles."

"What a relief! This one I have hear only twalve time."

"When I am win gold medal," began Mahomet, "I am private in the army. I figure this is goot time to esk for duty over the sea, so I request transfer to anywhere out of Albania. 'Sure, Mahomet,' they say, 'we get around to it forst of things.' Four year later, I am still in same post, no transfer, no nothink. But here is cominle again Olympic Games, aha! Efter I win second gold medal, I figure I am soch big hero, they will do what I want, yes?

"This time, sad to say, there is problem. Goat cheat and take bite from me on behind quarters. Then goat drop dead. Doctor say is due to food poisonings, so I am disqualify. 'For shame, Mahomet!' everyone say. Now, I am figure, I never get transfer, pfooey.

"But then is big surprise. Keptain order me into his office. 'Mahomet,' he tell to me, 'I have glad tidinks. You are transfer out from here.' 'Hoxadoodledoo!' I am shout. 'Not so fest,' keptain say, 'where you are beink sent is to South Poles.' 'Even is better,' I hexplain to him. 'Always I hev want to see Cracow and Breslau. Also I honderstend the pipple there are very moch intelligent.' 'No, no,' the keptain correct me, 'no Cracow, no Breslau, no intelligent. I am speakink of South Poles where is all the snow and hice.'

"I am stay there many year with no moch to do but freeze buns. For to make slaughter of time, I am lorn Heenglish.

"Then, one day, we get visitor from Unitned Stets, where they are also lornink Heenglish. While he is waiting by his thombs in preventative detention, I decide to go by and try out mine wocabulary. I am remember certain of phrases from my textbook.

"'Goot morrow, gentile man, hev you, by chence, ever see the Catskill Mountains?'

"'I am never even see them kill mice,' he say. I decide to give textbook to trashmens.

"Later I lorn he come all the way down here to look for some kind bottle. What is more, the silly pfool agree to pay me two hondred *fjereza*, kesh on top of the barrel for to assist him. 'Fine and dandies,' I hexplain to him, 'but also you are needink hextra two hondred for to bribe chief of sector to lat you go free.' 'No problems,' he say. I tell him, 'Tomorrow I will talk to chief. Not to worry, for I will appeal to his better natures.' The naxt day, I am go to see chief of sector, the very forst of things.

"'Greetinks, Offendi,' I salute him. 'Death to the Turk.'

"'Yes,' he reply, 'and death to the Greek as well.'

"'Very moch so, and death to the Bulgur too,' I am remind him.

"'Death to the Serb and death to the Croat!' the chief continue with but an instant to wipe from his lips the foam. 'Death to his sheep and death to his goat!'

"'Death to the Christian, Muslim and Jew!'

"'And death to the Godless atheist too!'

"'Death to America, that is for sure!'

"'And death to the Malay of Kuala Lumpur!'

"'Death to the Chinese doble-crosser!'

"'And death to the blacks who live in Mombossa!'

"'Death to the Lap and the Lett and the Sikh!'

"'Death to the Swiss or the Swede, take your pick. But enough of soch plasantries,' say the chief. 'For what reason are you comink to distorb me?'

"'I am forgat.'

"Next day, I remember why I am distorb chief. Perhaps, I figure it out, he will no demand two hondred *fjereza* efter all. Here is chence to make big killink, yes?

"'Chief,' I esk him, 'can you look in other directions while I halp Hamerican prisoner escape? I pay you one hondred *fjereza*, eskink no question.' 'Three hondred and you've got some deal,' chief decide. You see? I know I am no hef to pay him two hon-dred all of the times!

"Lat me make you believe, is very difficult lookink for this bottle. For two year we roam around icy land of waste while polar bear many time try to make from us breakfast. 'If you see polar goat, lat me know,' I tell to Hamerican, 'and I wrestle, two fall from three, but polar bear? No means! You can wrestle yourself if you want. Otherwise we ron like hell.'

"Later and sooner, I am trip over lid of old iron chest. Soon efterwards, I am fall on my face. 'Nobody make to fall Mahomet Ali yet live to pay the price!' I tell to this chest, givink it all the while a hit from mine ex. Again and again I am beatnik this chest so as to halp it lorn never to make pfool with the likes of me. By the time I have lost ex from handle, top of chest is so beat and batter, I am able to open. Is nothing inside but lots of jonks and some writink no mortal man can honderstend, and I honderstend all lenguage but for Greek. One time I tell this to the Hamerican, and he say, 'The feathers of a horse.'

"'No, is true,' I hinsist, 'jost name any lenguage excepting the Greek, and I speak it for you.'

"'All right, how about Japanese?' he say.

"'Ha! Is Greek to me!'

"'It look like spinach,' the crazy Hamerican say.

"'What look like spinach?' I esk him.

"'This writinks,' he tell me.

"'No spinach,' I am counter dice to him, 'is only very old pen and hink.'

"'No,no, I am meanink this words,' the Hamerican say: *'Jugetes y Porquerias por los Turcos y Otros Estranjeros*, that is spinach! In here is bottle at last, of this I am sure!'

"Speakink of bottle," Mahomet beckoned to the waiter, "pliz to bring another bottle of fine Albanian Oozo for me and my two sleepy frands."

IV

It remained the work of an additional eighteen months, ten of which he spent in the American sector, getting debriefed (often by his thumbs as the authorities tried in vain to shake him from his story) for Kermit to make it back to the U.S. of A., T.B. intact.

The return trip took a while, inasmuch as Kermit had to go by boat. AntarcticAire, the lone airline in the area, had just had its assets frozen, possibly due to a court order. Still, the lengthy ocean voyage did not lack its compensations. For one thing, it gave him a chance to practice up on his chucking, even if it did leave him a little green at the gills.

"It's not easy being green," Kermit proclaimed after a particularly wrenching heave.

For another, he met and fell in love with Miss Elvisina Fabietz, who, like Kermit, was a lady (No, that part's not like Kermit.) with a musical background (Actually, that part's not much like him either. Forget we ever said anything, okay?).

Miss Fabietz, though trained in and subsequently hired to teach remedial reading, retained a never-ending passion for choral music. In short order, she managed to land a position on the faculty of the Mt. Mallowmar School for the Severely Bewildered. She soon realized the school and especially the students seemed to have a serious morale problem. It did not take her long to figure out why: there were almost no extra-curricular activities for the children and, can you imagine, no choir whatsoever!

"See here, Mr. Warden," she complained to the warden, "the reason you have so much trouble with these children is that they have no creative activities to occupy their minds."

"Occupy their minds? Are you kidding, Miss Fabietz? Wetting their pants uses just about all the concentration they possess. And you want creative activities? What did you have in mind anyway?"

"Well, I thought I might start up a choir."

"Fine," agreed the harelipped headmaster with a disdainful nort, "go right ahead and organize a choir. I'm sure it will provide you with a real learning experience."

Undaunted by her supervisor's outlook, she posted a notice on the cafeteria bulletin board, announcing a meeting for all boys and girls interested in starting a choir, at 4 PM sharp in the gym. Nobody showed up.

"My dear, one thing you must understand about these children," advised a colleague when Elvisina complained about the students' lack of enthusiasm, "is they are incapable of seeing beyond immediate gratification. If you want them to come to your meeting, you need to offer some kind of a reward."

The next day an identical notice appeared on the bulletin board, this time with the following addendum: CANDY AND SODA POP WILL BE SERVED. Every student in the school showed up. Not only that, but, to the amazement of doubters everywhere, they soon coalesced into a very capable choral group.

"I'm amazed," volunteered Warden, "and I do my doubting right here in the office." There was only one problem.

"Yes, Mr. Warden, what can I do for you?" Elvisina inquired in answer to his summons.

"Well, Miss Fabietz, as pleased as I'm sure we all are with your glee club, there, I'm afraid you need to disband it. The kids are growing too fat and their teeth are starting to rot from that junk you keep giving them."

"But, Mr. Warden," she protested, "how can I get those children to come to practice if I can't give them rewards?"

"You can't. That's why I'm telling you to scrap the whole idea."

Never one to give up easily, the plucky instructrix again sought the advice of her more experienced colleague.

"You know," she suggested to Elvisina, "nothing says you have to feed them candy and pop all the time. I'm sure they'd be just as happy if you provided fruit instead of candy and maybe switched to diet soda.

Miss Fabietz considered that an excellent idea, and, sure enough, that's how things turned out. The kids were content with diet soda and fresh fruit. What's more, they continued to develop and improve until they were able to sing in public to greater and greater acclaim. By the time Miss Fabietz had treated herself to this cruise, the Moron Tab 'n Apple Choir was known throughout the land and parts of the sea as well.

But then, we were discussing Kermit, who was in the process of falling in love with the very same Miss Fabietz, which, of course, he did.

"Just as soon as I get my reward money, I'll return to make you an honest woman," he assured her.

"But Kermit, I am an honest woman," she pointed out.

"Well then," he pointed in, "I'll make you another."

"Oh, Kermit, no one's ever offered to clone me."

Almost before he knew it, Kermit had arrived in America, gone through customs and found himself at his sponsor's door. The Tizz Bottle, like the situation, was firmly in hand.

"Well, well," observed the venerable Throckmorton, "it would seem you've met with success after all."

"You bet I have!" Kermit beamed.

"The master shall be delighted to see you, I should imagine." And so he was, upon seeing Kermit had finally returned, his mission accomplished.

"At last, my very own Tizz Bottle," the old man gloated. "Boy, ya done good. Put 'er there!"

As Kermit reached out to shake the man's hand, he let fall the Tizz bottle he had tightly clutched for the past several hours.

"Hasten, Jason, bring the basin," passed through

Throckmorton's head as he watched the Tizz Bottle shatter into a hundred pieces.

"Whoops," Kermit philosophized.

V

His initial impulse had been to fire Kermit on the spot or, at least, to strangle him very near the spot. Only his quick realization that advertising rates had shot up an appalling 85% in the last two years prevented him from doing so. Silently cursing the Print Advertisers' Guild, (By then, virtually everybody had become sufficiently organized to obtain special legislation permitting price-fixing, which, of course, remained illegal. In fact the sole individual left not exempt from the anti-trust laws was a fish peddler and small-time operator, Pasquale "the Ice Pick" Bogiagaloupe, a proud Sicilian who fancied himself the last of the old "Duck's Ass Pete's." Bogiagaloupe's dedication to the sacred principle of *omega*, he believed, forbade him to reveal even his Social Insecurity number to anyone, much less the *federali*. As a result, the entire staff of the F.T.C., now with nothing else to do, hounded him unmercifully. They constantly hung around his fish wagon, checking to make sure he competed with sufficient vigor against himself. Thus did the unfortunate fishmonger feel compelled to wear shirts that itched and flog himself, several times a day and always after a big sale.), the old man again commissioned Kermit to have another go at a Tizz bottle. This time there seemed little choice but to fetch the one on the moon.

"On the *moon*, Kermit?" Elvisina despaired as their food arrived.

"Combinaisha fly lice?" inquired the waiter, a co-owner of the restaurant with a Ph.D. from the Wharton School of Business.

"Over here. Yep, that's where I'm going," Kermit explained to the two of them.

"I've decided what I want," Elvisina concluded. "I'll have two of your Quemoy- style pork chops."

"Velly good, I bling light away," responded the waiter. "Chop, chop, chop-chop!" he barked to the kitchen.

"But Kermit," Elvisina continued, "you could get lost up there."

"That'd be a switch. Most of the girls I've ever met told me I could get lost right here."

"Be serious," she said.

"You mean space travel isn't plenty serious?"

"Well, I guess it is," she guessed, "but the notion of some crazy old man paying you so much money just to fetch some stupid bottle does seem pretty unbelievable."

"Huh! You'll believe it soon enough when I come back to collect all that toast."

"Speaking of which, you haven't even touched your combination fried rice. What's the matter, dextrose?"

"Aah," he grumbled as he took one more stab at removing the lid, "I can't get these damn tumblers to click."

*****

"I'm sort of what you'd refer to as a jack of all trades, except my name ain't Jack, if you catch my dribble."

"Yeah, I get where you're coming from," Kermit remarked, noticing the decals on his cabinmate's luggage.

"Actually, my name's Phil. Phil T. Snapp. I'm in hypodermics. Here's my card." He handed his business card to Kermit. It read:

PHIL T. SNAPP—SHOTS OF ALL KINDS

"For some reason lotsa guys phone me wantin' to see pictures of naked girls, but I do all right just the same.

"This your first trip to the moon?" he asked Kermit.

"Uh, yeah."

"You'll love it up there. Colder'n a landlady's heart, though."

"Well, I'm used to being cold," Kermit allowed, "but I'm not going for a vacation exactly."

"Oh, a business trip, eh? What's your line?"

"Bottles, you might say."

"Yeah," Phil advised him, "well, Mr.....uh..."

"Pommeroy. Kermit E. Pommeroy."

"Right. I tell ya, E., I'm not too sure how well you're gonna do huckstering bottles on the moon, but if you want someone who knows the lay of the craters, I'm your boy."

"Gee,, I dunno..."

"Look," Phil explained, "I'm not some damn Albanian goat wrestler or nothin' like that. I got experience, plus I come from a long line of hardy adventurous types. Take my dad, Waldo W. Snapp."

"Oh?" Kermit inquired, driving as he so often did straight to the heart of the matter, "And what does the W stand for?"

"Waldo. My granddad didn't have much imagination. But, gettin' back to my dad, a sailor in his day. You talk about hair raising escapades! You want hair-raising escapades?"

"My hair's fine the way it is."

"I'll tell ya, once some sharks went after him."

"Great Whites?" Kermit asked.

"Nah, loan. Sometimes Dad fell behind on the house note, but that was all right, y'see, 'cause he was a sailor and used to hardships.

"Another time he was on a freighter that got attacked by the Japs."

"You mean, like at Pearl Harbor?" Kermit asked. "Wasn't that a little before his day?"

"What Pearl Harbor? This happened at Montauk Point. A buncha princesses got word some third-year med schoolers were on board as summer help. My dad got a broken hand and a fractured butt outa the ensuing stampede, but it hardly phased him, on accounta he was a sailor and used to such hardships."

"Fascinatin'" Kermit sighed.

"Then there was the time he mustered out in Stockholm and went to catch a plane back to the U.S. on some old shot-to-hell four-engine prop job.

"Well, the way my dad tells it, they're cruisin' along at 25,000 feet when there's this sputterin' sound, and smoke starts billowing outa the end starboard engine. So the pilot says over the intercom, 'Don't worry about a thing, folks, we'll reach New York, just fine. Only thing is, we'll have to drop our altitude somewhat, and that'll add about an hour to our flying time. Other than that, though, everything's A-OK.'

"Anyway, the pilot forgets to shut off the intercom, 'cause the next thing comes over the squawk box is him tellin' the co-pilot, 'You watch 'er a minute, Ed. I'm going to check if our tail ain't on fire.'

"Right away the stewardess yanks open the cockpit door, switches off the intercom, and reads the guy the riot act for scarin' the passengers half to death. I guess when she left outa there, he musta hit the switch again, thinkin' he was cuttin' the sound off, 'cause the speakers were back on when he says, 'Boy, I'd sure like to bury my beak twixt them thighs!'

"Naturally the stew does an about-face and charges toward the cockpit, but, this time, the old guy sittin' beside to my dad grabs her by the arm and says, 'There's no need to rush, Miss. Remember, he said he'd check the airplane's tail first.'

"By the time they finally get the squawk box cut off, one of the port engines is smokin' pretty bad, so they cut it back on again.

"'Don't worry, folks,' the pilot says, 'we'll fly just fine on the two engines we have left, long as I jettison the cargo and drop down another couple thousand feet. That'll probably add an additional hour.'

"'Another hour?' moans the guy on the other side of my dad; 'They must think we're made out of time.'

"They get farther along a ways, and then the other starboard engine blows. Everybody must've been scared as hell, but the pilot's right on the ball with the old intercom.

"'Don't panic,' he says, 'I can still fly this baby to New York, but I'm gonna have to drop 'er down a whole lot more and cruise real slow. All in all, we'll probably be another coupla hours late touchin' down.

"'Christ!' my dad's seatmate grumbles. 'If we lose the next engine, we could be up here all night!'

"But my dad, he stayed cool, calm and collated through the whole ordeal. What with him bein' a sailor, hardships like that were old hat."

"Very interesting," Kermit mumbled; "Now I think I better hit the—"

"Then there was the time my dad sailed on that Italian liner, the *A.M.B. Mussolini*. They gave him a can of red-white-and-green-stripe enamel and told him to paint the colors on top 'a the smokestacks. Well, he was finishin' up the last one, when the guys in the engine room decide it's time to go on strike, bringin' the ship to a sudden and abrupt halt. Anyway, this causes my dad to lose his balance, so he falls sixty feet, right smack onto the steel-plated deck".

"I guess that was the end of him," Kermit deduced.

"What, are ya not payin' attention? I told you he was a sailor, so he was used to hard ships. Now Lemmie tell ya 'bout my sister, Ginger—"

"That's okay, you've got the job."

*****

"So," Phil wondered as they wandered along in their lunar
vestments, "where d'ya plan to start digging around' for this
bottle anyway?"

"Well, I'd guess one of the early settlement areas makes
sense, but, really, it could be anywhere."

For the next eight months the two of them searched, going up
one crater and down another, stopping by every shelter module
they found to make further inquiries and finding nary a clue.

Eventually their quest led them to what had to be the last
module this side of *Luna Incognita*. Even the exterior, though of
a design identical to all the other lunar shelters, looked especially
shabby. Inside it was nothing more than a saloon.

"That's all right," Phil surmised, "I need to wet my
whistle."

"You brought along a whistle?"

Right away, Kermit began digging into the pretzel paste that
served both as a handy snack for the patrons and a caulk for the
many fissures that resulted from the indoor furniture being exposed to the extreme cold, whenever the door opened.

"You should try some of this paste, it's really tasty," Kermit
advised his partner.

"No thanks, I never did care for chink food.

"I tell ya what, though, my lips are chapped like hell," Phil
went on. "I sure could use a little lip balm."

"Here ya go, matey, have a smoke on Old Bill," interrupted
the guy on Phil's left as he handed him a cigarette.

"Don't mind if I do," he smiled. He took two deep drags and
was attempting a third when the cigarette blew up in his face.
Old Bill slapped his thigh and laughed until tears began running
down his cheeks.

"Why, you miserable old fart, I oughta—"

"Now hold on there, Sonny," he chuckled. "You're the one came in here lookin' for the lip bomb, right? Now why don't you do me a favor and buy me a drink?"

"Aah, go eat your shoes.

"So tell me, E.," Phil went on turning to Kermit, "what're ya gonna do if this bottle don't show up nowheres? I mean, what if it broke or somethin?"

"I'd rather not think about that," Kermit sighed without so much as the slightest pause in the furrowing of his brow. "Maybe it's hopeless, but I just can't go back empty-handed. I gotta find that bottle."

"A bottle, you say?" the bartender spoke up. "I got several dozen of 'em right behind me in case you hadn't noticed. So what kind of bottle might you gents be in the market for?"

"A full one," Phil requested, "preferably with some halfway decent scotch in it."

"Well, I happen to have a liter of two-year-old Korean stuff, if you're willin' to pay the premium."

"Sure, why not the very best," Phil decided. After they had gotten themselves a little more mellow, about two-thirds the way through the bottle, Old Bill attempted to try his luck again.

"Say, cap'n," he addressed Phil, "I'm awful sorry I give ya that loaded cigarette. Now, just to show there's no hard feelin's, hows about stakin' this thirsty old man to a drink.?"

"What the hell," Phil replied. "What're ya drinkin', Old Timer?"

"Vodka'll do just fine."

"Sure. Make it a double," he told the bartender.

"Why, thankee, there, comrade, that's mighty big 'a ya."

"Excuse me," Kermit asked the stranger, "what was that you called my friend?"

"Comrade," the barkeep confirmed. "Old Bill's a Commie, ain't that right, Bill?"

"Damn right," he answered. "I'm the last 'a' the old cosmo-nauts. My name's Ghespinkov, Vassily Ghespinkov, Sgt. First Class, ret., but, like I always say, you can call me Old Bill."

*****

"Do I still have that bottle?" Hell yes I got that bottle. Been savin' it for when I get some 'a the *good* stuff ta put in it."

"Well now," Kermit began negotiating, "let me ask you, what's more important, some lousy bottle or four, no, make that five cases of the *good* stuff?"

"Ya lookin' ta swap, sonny?"

"You might say that."

"I don't know," Bill hedged, "I had that bottle an awful long time—ever since I joined the space program. Y'know, I only signed up ta get outa bein' sent ta Afghanistan."

"Where's that at?" Kermit inquired. "I never hearda the place."

"Y'mean there's no more Afghanistan? I knew we'd take over that God- forsaken country someday!"

"Oh, I know where you're talkin' about," Phil spoke up. "Yeah, what used ta be Afghanistan sorta got absorbed."

"Like I was sayin'," Bill gloated.

"By the Eurasian Islamic Republic."

"Exactly," Bill went on, by "the Eurasian Islamic WHAT? Do the Russian people know about this?"

"You mean the Russians in the Grand Duchy of Moscow or some 'a them others?" Phil asked him.

"What? What others? Aah, forget it. Let's talk turkey."

"Isn't that what they used to call the Trans-Caucasian Empire before it grew and all?" Kermit asked.

"Damn! Nobody tells me nothin' no more," Bill complained.

"Yeah," Phil empathized, "Up here, I imagine ya don't get ta read the papers much."

"The hell I don't! I ain't missed an issue of *Pravda* since I got here. 'Course I'd been wonderin' why the last several batches was postmarked Pyongyang. Anyway, let's get down ta business. You boys were talkin' five cases, right?"

"Yes indeed," Kermit beamed, "of the finest vodka money can buy."

"Vodka?" snorted the cosmonaut. "Hell, I gargle with vodka. When it comes ta sippin' liquor, I want me some rocket fuel, and I don't mean no watered-down, cheap, contracted out ta the lowest bidder guvvamint junk. No, siree, it's gotta be the *good* stuff or it's no deal."

"Jeez, that could cost a fortune on the black market," Phil pointed out, "plus which, we could get busted if they caught us with so much as a canister."

"Take it or leave it."

*****

"Trudie, darling, will you be a dear and check the mail for me?"

"Sure, Miss Fabietz," chirped the mezzo-soprano, who had been bucking for a full sopranoship.

It had been well over six weeks since Elvisina had last heard from Kermit, although, in truth, she wasn't really sure she wanted to read his next letter. All the others she had received that year had brought nothing but bad news, from his arrest for possession of black market rocket fuel to the five-year prison sentence, to his discovery that the old codger who knew the whereabouts of the bottle had died without leaving so much as a clue.

"All that aggravation for nothing," she sighed.

On the positive side, Kermit's parole hearing came up in another eight months. Furthermore, her career at Mt. Mallowmar had progressed very well indeed. Time and again she had turned down offers to direct choirs of reputedly normal children out of devotion to her less-gifted charges. On top of that, she maintained a firm belief that she would be the one to succeed that son-of-a-bitch Warden as soon as he shuffled off to the Great Beyond. (She felt sure the Great Beyond School of Functional Literacy would be offering him their top spot any day now). If only she could convince Kermit of the virtues of a good, steady job. Then the two of them could settle into a tolerable level of misery ever after.

When Trudie returned with the week's mail, there was still no letter from Kermit, who was occupied at the time with yet another work detail. Even worse, his cellblock had drawn field duty for the week, which, while the assignment provided some slight change of scenery, it promised harder work over a much longer lunar day. To compensate for the greatly reduced gravity, the prisoners had to wear a ball and chain on each of their wrists and ankles.

Thusly encumbered, they were transported to a moderate sized junkyard, not far from the Unexplored Territory. Since this was not Official Government-Sponsored Debris, but, rather "the throwings and leavings of persons or even more persons unknown," as their Activities Monitor had explained, the stuff had to be hauled away. And so Kermit and his cellmates were put to work.

After four hours of back-bothering labor, Kermit happened to spot a shabby, somewhat military jacket laying atop a pile of beer cans and vodka bottles. A name tape over the top left-hand pocket bore the inscription: ß Ѓ3спков. Hardly did he have time to sketch a conclusion about what that signified, when he saw one Chucky "Chain Saw" Grubb carrying a bottle—*the* bottle— over to the trash compactor.

"Wait, Mr. Chain Saw, sir," Kermit called out to the convict.

"You can't take that over there."

"Oh yeah?" queried the killer as a glint of anticipation replaced the glaze of resigned boredom in his eyes, "And who's gonna stop me, huh?"

"Why, uh, nobody, sir, least of all me," Kermit was (damn) quick to react. "It just seems to me that a man of such spectacular criminal accomplishments as yourself oughtn't to be hauling trash like some two-bit punk."

"You're damn right!" agreed the erstwhile sawyer.

"And that's why I thought I'd offer to carry your share of the garbage for you. Whatever you need hauled, point it out, and I'll be glad to add it to my load," Kermit elaborated, "starting with this worthless old bottle here..."

*****

"Our present temperature's 108 degrees," the weather report went on, "with ten- mile-an-hour winds from the northeast, giving us a current wind-chill factor of 103."

"Throckmorton, where the hell are my earmuffs?"

"None arrived in the mail, sir," replied the loyal retainer, "but there is a letter from your Mr. Pommeroy."

"That little twerp? I thought he'd fallen off the edge of the Earth."

"Of the moon, sir," the butler reminded him.

"Wherever," snapped the old retainee. "In any case, you might's well read it to me. I can always use a little more bad news to darken up my day."

"Actually, it's some rather good news," Throckmorton observed after a cursory scan. "It appears Mr. Pommeroy will arrive shortly with the bottle you sent him after."

"And what's more," the weatherman chimed in, "the air quality index will reach a pleasant 219 with gamma radiation the major factor; all in all, as fine a day as we've seen in a long while."

"Oh how wonderful!" Elvisina exclaimed upon reading much the same news from Kermit. She ought to send a response to him, she figured, right away. She hurried off to the music room, where she imagined she had left her writing paper. As she rummaged around, she took care not to bump into she school's carpenter, the former blues clavichordist, "Blind Nectarine" Jackson, who was busily planing his sawhorse while a knotty plank lay atop a student desk beside him.

"I'm sorry to bother you, Mr. Jackson, but I need to look around for my good stationery."

"I see," said the blind man, as he picked up his hammer and saw.

"The master will be here momentarily," Throckmorton informed Kermit, who stood, some months later, at the doorway, Tizz Bottle again firmly in hand.

"Young man," wheezed Kermit's exhausted employer upon finally managing to hobble downstairs, "if you so much as get a look on your face to suggest you might on some future date even consider the outside possibility of shaking hands with me, *I'll have you shot*! Now march over here and set that bottle down on the table."

"Yes, sir, right away, sir," Kermit gulped as he strode down the corridor and halfway across the little throw rug, which then shot up in the air as it flipped Kermit off his feet. Neither he nor the bottle experienced what your space probe types like to call the "soft landing." As it was, Kermit was quite fortunate not to have cut himself, what with all that broken glass around.

VI

Kermit gripped the strap tightly as the train sped out of a

bend and came to its usual screeching halt. A drunk hanging onto the next strap lurched against him and left the fragrant aura of his brief visit burning in Kermit's nostrils. The final two passengers to board the subway at this stop had been a middle-aged couple in formal wear, (which, at this point in the future meant that he sported a tank top made to look like a tuxedo shirtfront, while her miniskirt was painted to match her nails). She wound up with the strap on the other side of the drunk, while her husband had been pushed to his hands and knees and sat on by two other passengers.

"Your mother would pick tonight, wouldn't she?" the husband groused into the cracked linoleum.

"What do you mean my mother would pick tonight?" his wife shot back. "I'm sure she had no idea the taxis would be on strike".

"Yeah? Well she damn well should've remembered the chauffeur had the night off. Now look at what we have to put up with to get there."

"You don't have to remind me, Horace," she told him as the drunk lurched in her direction long enough to make his presence very well known. "I haven't ridden one of these nasty, smelly things in years."

"Lady," volunteered the drunk as the sway of the car brought them together again, "we missed ya!"

Eventually the train reached 145th Street—Kermit's stop, if the directions he'd been given were anything to go by. As he emerged from the station, a sizeable attack rat charged him with fresh meat on its mind. Fortunately for Kermit, the rat got broadsided by a speeding truck and severely inconvenienced as a result.

"¡Su madre!" the angry driver wagged his finger and politely chastised the rodent, whereupon the rat made for the truck and went after the driver instead, oblivious to the man's machete blows, which became ever feebler until they ceased altogether.

Harlem, must remember, had long since lost the happy, carefree atmosphere of the late 1960s.

Actually, Kermit managed to arrive at the address in the ad without becoming anybody's fresh meat.

"Aren't people wonderful?" he postulated as he rang the bell, "Rats too," he added, looking nervously from side to side.

"Whachoo want, BOY?" demanded the scowling figure that had suddenly appeared in the doorway.

"Oh, ah, nothing. I mean nothing much," Kermit answered as he climbed back down from the transom of the door across the hall. "I'm the guy who answered your ad."

"Well, in that case, come right on in, baby. Like the ad says, if Africa's your plan, then Safarry Larry Jones is your man. That's me. Y'see, Mr. Jones is an expert on accounta I can, like, rap wit' the brothers over there an' all, hear what I'm sayin'?"

"Does that include the dreaded Hootintoots?"

"Oh, yeah, Hootintoots, Gypsies, Devil Disciples, whatever they be, long as they got soul, y'know what I mean?"

"I better tell you up front," Kermit explained as he led his host into the vestibule, "it could get mighty dangerous over there." That very moment, a grenade exploded down the hall, followed by two bursts of machine gun fire. "Yipe!" Kermit added as he once again demonstrated his proficiency in the standing high jump.

"Take it easy, baby, you much too uptight," Safarry Larry advised him.

"How can you relax with that stuff going on?"

"Aw, that's nothin," Jones explained. "Tell ya what, just to take your mind offa thangs, lemmie tellya a riddle, okay? Now listen up: my mama had a kid, and it wasn't my brother, and it wasn't my sister. Now you tell me, who was it?"

"I give up," Kermit admitted, after attempting to think of anything other than the gunfire in the corridor.

"It was *me*, man! Y'get it?"

"Oh, yeah, that was pretty sharp I guess," Kermit agreed. While the gag did not exactly leave him rolling in the hallways, it was enough to get him relaxed him to a sufficient degree where he could talk business. Soon, the two of them were able to work out the details, and Safarry Larry Jones had signed on to guide Kermit to the very last of the Tizz Bottles.

"Heaven help us all," proclaimed Stevie Wonder and the old man, very much out of sync.

Kermit, for his part, was grateful for any kind of assistance. Despite his previous luck in discovering the other Tizz Bottles, he was not optimistic about his prospects of finding this one in the wildest part of Africa. He had no reason to consider himself the Great Pink Hunter. The first time he had tried his hand at that activity, he and his pal, Barney Bogda had decided to go hunting for bear, back when bear pelts were all the rage for tea cozies. They had not traveled even halfway to their chosen site when they encountered a sign on the road that read "Bear Left," so they turned around and went home. On another occasion, he and Barney had somehow managed to bag a deer: a fourteen-point stag. Having done so, though, neither of them were quite sure what to do with the carcass, except they had some vague idea you were supposed to tie it to the front of your car. As they dragged the animal through the woods by its hind legs, the lads found they had to stop time after time to disentangle the antlers from the underbrush. Eventually, an older, more experienced hunter saw them and offered some helpful advice.

"Look here," he told them, "you boys wouldn't have no trouble at all if you'd just pull him by his antlers, 'stead of his hind legs like you've been doing."

They took the man's advice and, sure enough, had no more trouble dragging the deer.

"Except we're gettin' farther and farther away from the car," Kermit pointed out after a while.

But perhaps his most disastrous experience occurred when he and Barney decided to join a hunting party at a place known as the Old Log Inn, where neither of them had ever been. Barney managed to find the place all right, but Kermit got lost in the effort. He had no idea what part of the directions he had misread, but, after he had gone the distance he should have to get there— and then some—he found himself utterly alone on a dark stretch of road in a desolate area. As he imagined he was stifling the urge to panic, he crept slowly along the road, prepared to brake at any sign of civilization. Finally, he came upon a car parked on the shoulder. Somebody was evidently inside because the vehicle kept rocking on its springs and the windows were steamed up. Eager as he was to get some bearings, Kermit leapt out of his van and ran to the driver's side window. He knocked on the window several times, to no avail. Nor did the car cease rocking. Kermit tried knocking even harder and faster, in the hopes of making contact, which, after a little while, he did.

The next day, Kermit finally arrived at the Old Log Inn, very much the worse for wear. Both his eyes were blacked, he had a fat lip plus sundry bruises and contusions about his face.

"Geez, what happened to you?" Barney asked.

"I'm still not sure myself. What I remember is, I'm tryin' to get directions from this guy in a car. When he rolled down his window, it looked like he was on top of some girl. Anyway, I ask him, 'How far is the Old Log Inn?' Then, with no warning, all hell breaks loose."

Elvisina, for her part, was displeased as punch to learn about Kermit's latest commission.

"Kermit E. Pommeroy, are you out of your mind?" she quizzed him. "You've just wasted four years of your life—and mine—traipsing around on the moon, and now you intend to run off to Africa for Lord knows how much longer."

"Well, at least it's on the same planet."

"Oh, peachy!" she stormed. "And I suppose we can meet for brunch on the Azores any old time we get the notion."

"Gee, I don't know, I'm liable to be incommunicado for a while."

"Incommunicado? I'll show you incommunicado, you little gleep!"

"Aw, similar down, willya," Kermit assured her. "I won't be gone all that long. I'll bet this job'll be a piece of soup."

She scowled and said nothing.

"Aw, don't be so glum, chum," Kermit suggested. "Tell you what, just to cheer you up. I got a real hilarious riddle, okay?"

She glared at him.

"So okay, now here goes. My mother had a kid, right? And it wasn't my brother and it wasn't my sister, so who was it?"

She folded her arms and turned away from him.

"Whatcha give up already? It was some black dude in New York."

*****

"Well," Kermit observed from his perch, "there goes the jeep," which had, in fact gone, not from the depredations of man or beast, but of the neutral gear.

"Yeah?" countered his trusty guide as the jeep's swift trip downhill abruptly halted when it reached two unyielding boulders, "that's cool. We'll find that bottle any damn way, you hear me?"

"I don't know, maybe we should go back and get a—"

"Look, man, Mr. Safawrence Lawrence Jones ain't gonna let no missin' jeeps cramp his style. 'F I say we gone find it, then we gone find it, ain't that right, bro'?"

The bro, who had just come onto the scene, stared at the two explorers and then shouted some unintelligible words, whereupon several others like him emerged from the underbrush. Kermit indulged in a loud gulp, for, if these gentlemen were not the dreaded Hootintoot, they hardly seemed to be on the verge of inviting them to a frozen soymilk social either.

"'S'happenin', baby?" Safarry Larry inquired of the original tribesman as he elevated his hand with the thumb and pinkie tucked in, in preparation to give the fellow a high-three.

Thwarted by his inability to communicate what was happening, even if he had understood the question, the warrior resorted to sign language: in this case, a spear through Safarry Larry's midsection. If the thrust of the message, so to speak, was lost on the guide (he never did say), it was surely not lost on Kermit. These *were* the dreaded Hootintoot, and he had better get going, preferably in a hurry.

As he did, the warriors pursued him over much the same trail the late Ralph Armstrong and his retinue had chosen, up to and including the crocodile-infested waters of Lake Mpoto. Like his predecessor, Kermit plunged into the water, but, this time, two of his pursuers, who had been within inches of grabbing him, were induced by their momentum to join in the dip.

A crocodile can live on pond scum only so long, and these beasts were not about to be denied again. As the crocs surfaced, the two tribesmen had grabbed Kermit and thrown him ashore to be taken into captivity, but they had not yet figured out how to throw each other ashore. The ensuing carnage did not particularly amuse the remaining Hootintoots, and their failure to dispatch Kermit right then and there can only be attributed to their anticipation of the punishment their mighty chief, wise in the ways of cruelty, would mete out.

As they figured he might be, the chief was furious when he learned of the incident at Lake Mpoto. Whatever it was he was saying, it sounded awfully menacing to Kermit. Soon the interpreter took his turn and dispelled all doubt.

"That's right, chief say he plenty perturbed! You in great, deep trouble now, Mr. White Foreign Devil. Chief say *death*! Death.... *too good* for you! Chief say torture! Torture...*too good* for you!"

A moan of disappointment arose from the assembled tribesmen, but one scornful look from the chief and the audience was awed. They saw his face grow stern and cold, they saw his muscles strain, and they knew that Casey wouldn't let that ball go by again.

The chief solemnly intoned a few more words, whereupon the whole tribe quickly got to work building a set of rafters unto which they could cheer. The interpreter leered at Kermit and, with a triumphant crossing of his eyes, proclaimed: "Chief say, for punishment... you must wear the talisman of shame!"

Kermit, who had only stopped shaking long enough to wonder what that entailed, soon had his answer as two brightly-festooned witch interns emerged from the Big Hut carrying between them a rope, tied at both ends to the neck of the talisman of shame Kermit had been condemned to wear. It was the last Tizz bottle in the universe.

VII

"All right, sonny, you just freeze right there!" the old man snapped.

"I'll do my best, but could you, like, maybe lower the thermostat or something?"

"Well then, stand still, goddammit! Carlos, get over here and take ahold of that bottle."

Carlos, the strongest member of the Flying Juaztecas Acrobatic Light Moving and Hauling Troupe, strode purposefully over to Kermit and relieved him of the object.

"Fine, fine," the tycoon encouraged him. "Now carefully, for goodness sake, bring it here and place it right in that slot. He pointed to an empty space in a disparate row of bottles.

"Which is as it should be," he added. "I'm a very disparate man."

In any case, the bottle sat ensconced in its proper place, much to the relief of all concerned.

"You know, I hate to sound nosy or anything," Kermit said as his patron wrote out a check for the reward, which, by this time, would amount to enough for a healthy down-payment on Elvisina's engagement ring, "but I've always wondered why you wanted a Tizz Bottle in the first place."

"Stick around," the old man advised him, "and you'll see history in the making."

"Your instrument, sir," Throckmorton said as he handed the master a small rubber mallet.

"Excellent, excellent," he beamed. "Now then, are we all ready? Good, here goes…"

And striking each bottle in its turn, he sang, "My coun-tree tizz of thee…"

APPENDIX
THE LOST NOTEBOOKS OF GLUB DZMC

INTRODUCTION

Just who was the strange and difficult poet, Glub Dzmc, and, more importantly, why in the world did anyone bother to find his lost notebooks? I do not feel qualified to give an answer to either question, yet I do.

Let me begin by sharing with you the vast dearth of information I have about the man himself. You may rest assured that, what I do lack in knowledge, I will compensate for through frequent consultation with the child of Necessity.

Glub Dzmc (And, by the way, he pronounced his last name, "Dizmic," although I am not sure anybody else did.), was a man who always considered himself somewhat of a bohemian. This may have to do with the fact that he was born in Czechoslovakia, either before, after or during the Not So Great Depression.

Although, as a student, he refused to accept or attain mediocrity, Glub inexplicably dropped out of school in what he insisted on calling "the 41st grade," citing irreconcilable differences and the dog having eaten too much of his homework. Faced with a barren life of ease and comfort, he enlisted instead in the Czech Navy, in search of, not just a job, but a misadventure.

It was during his all-too-brief stint as a naval, that Glub learned a number of sea shantys, too many of which have found their way into this compendium. Fortunately, he soon disappeared, before he could learn any more of them. And while his jumping of the ship may be seen by some as Czechoslovakia's loss, others would view it as poetry's gain.

As a result of his desertion, Glub found himself a penniless, yet wanted, man. He quickly decided the best thing to do was to make a clean start in the land of opportunity: Siberia. One advantage to having chosen such a place to call home is that, when you perturb the local authorities, they are going to be hard pressed to find someplace worse to exile you to. When Glub did run afoul of the local leash law, (He always used to maintain the collar chafed his neck too much.), the powers that were had little choice but to banish him to Newark, NJ.

His life in this country was unremarkable but, in his later years, reasonably comfortable. That was after he managed to land for himself a sinecure cleaning toilets in the Akron, Ohio, Transcontinental Bus Terminal. It was in the process of removing the endless graffiti from the tiles that Glub became re-acquainted with and more proficient in, by his own rather liberal standards, the art of Haiku. Before that stroke of good fortune, though, Glub found the struggle to keep body and soul together to be a desperate one indeed. At its nadir, he was employed as an advertising copywriter for the B. Walter Horton Agency. He wrote what many would consider to be far too much ad copy during his brief tenure there, and much, much too much of it has found its way into this book. It should be noted that none of the clients on whose behalf Glub wrote those ads is in business today, but that may have less to do with the quality of their product than with how it was huckstered. Mercifully, "Bud" Dzmc (as he preferred to be called at the agency) was handed his walking papers, once his bosses realized that he was not, in fact, the janitor, as they had supposed him to be for many months.

His next attempt to make a living saw him take a job with the E-Z Shake and Bake Ice Cream Parlor and Bakery, where he worked in the Pie Containment Department of the organization. It was during his weeks in the place they called "Pie Pan Alley," that he began to gain some renown as a "piano banger." When the department manager finally found out who had been thumping his baby grand with a baseball bat, Glub was sent packing. His stint in the meat packing plant didn't work out either. Nevertheless, it was around this time that he began to fancy himself a smithy of tunes. You can see the results of that flight of fantasy in the second chapter of this thankfully slim volume.

*****

Let us at last abandon the miserable history of Glub's adventures in the workaday world and dwell, instead on how his supposedly "lost" notebooks came to be found. By the end of his secret life as a poet, Glub had compiled a considerable body of work, edited by Miss Fensterwalder's third graders in lieu of having to rewrite their many missing book reports, into a series of, either meager books or fat pamphlets. As you might expect, nobody at all in any of the great publishing houses of Chillicothe, Ohio, evinced the slightest degree of interest in lining their birdcages with those pages, let alone publishing them. All seemed as it should be when an enterprising outfit in the heart of Dixie decided they were going to compete with the wildly successful purveyors of caramelized popcorn and peanuts. So as to cause maximum customer confusion to their advantage, they named their product RedNeck Jax. They further decided to make the stuff available only in the jumbo, economy 465-oz. box. Now it just remained for them to find a prize to stick inside the box that was, if such a thing could be possible, even feebler than the prizes of their competitor. In a moment of what can best be described as 1% inspiration and 99% perspiration, the new confectioners on the block decided to use the Lost Notebooks as a featured prize. Truth be to tell, one batch of carmelite junk is pretty much like another, and the American consumer can always be counted on to go for the biggest possible size of anything at all. We are left to surmise that the reason the upstart company went out of business with the speed of a nosebleed is because of the quality of the prize in their box. It was only a matter of time (not nearly enough, I'd say) before some discerning collector, who is now in something like the Witness Protection Program, bought up the few boxes of RedNeck Jax that had not yet been consigned to landfills. The next thing you know, The Lost Notebooks of Glub Dzmc had been found. Oh, joy.

*****

High on the list of the many things that the finders of Glub's notebooks puzzled over was the question of what possessed him to write the way he did. Most of his work is in the form of what we might, with the greatest of charity, call "free verse." Other works, though, actually show some semblance of discipline as to rhyme and meter. The facility for these things that he demonstrated in his sonnets, song lyrics and other such pieces can only be attributed to his more "savant" moments, if you get what I mean. As for the free verse stuff, Glub made no secret of being an ardent fan of E.E. Cummings and quoted his poems at great length and with even greater fervor. Actually, he was quoting archy the cockroach all that time, but no one in his very limited circle of friends had the slightest ability to tell the difference. Never mind, in either case, it explains Glub's disdain for the upper case. The roots of his disdain for class, decorum, sanity, syntax, intellectual honesty, mouthwash and toilet paper are a little harder to trace. Please do not imagine for a moment that I am going to make the slightest effort to do so.

If the poems you see in this collection seem a little difficult to figure out, you should bear in mind that they have been painstakingly selected (meaning that having to read any of this stuff is inherently painful) from a seemingly endless array of pieces that hardly make any sense at all. Consider this among the works that got left out. And it's one of the better rejects:

i shrink the bubbles in
my pipe to
better see the grainy
waves of
amber in the garden of
earthly dirt. do
not stop to
snort the flowers on
your way to the old
bathroom floor. give
me all
my sevens. go
fish.

Questionable as the quality of his poetry may be, we must admit he covered a wide range of subjects, and more than a few predicates. In these pages, you will find poems about.....let's see....well, about....no, not really about that either. Nevertheless, in these pages, you will find poems. Let's just leave it at that.

*****

Some things come naturally to us and some things do not. And if a thing like...say...oh, I don't know, poetry perhaps, is going to come to someone naturally, it is probably due to the fortune of genetic immutation. At some point in Glub Dzmc's ancestry, then, there had to be a poet in the woodpile. A lengthy investigation of over 200 seconds into the Dzmc family tree revealed Glub's poetic great-great-great-great-great-great uncle, Decius Brutus Dzmc. There are some who might say they detect strong similarities between Glub's verse and that of his ancestor. For example, the works of both poets contain a rather large number of sexual and scatological references, but nowhere will you find the four-letter words most commonly associated with those activities. Is it because, at heart, they were both men of decency and propriety? Of course not. Their omission of these words is almost certainly due to the fact that, in their native Czechoslovoon, such concepts are expressed, not as simple four-letter words, but, rather, as lurid and disgusting sound effects. Insofar as the spelling of those sounds was considered to be a near impossibility, most Czech authors and poets simply clog danced around them. Presumably, the same habit carried over to the hamfisted attempts by Glub and his far-removed uncle to write English. Still, I have no reason to doubt that the two had some similarities in their styles. You know what they say: "Like great-great- great-great-great-great uncle, like great-great-great-great-great-grand nephew."

Here is what we know about Decius Brutus Dzmc. "B.D..," as his dyslexic neighbors called him, was a wandering minstrel, whose frequent and hurried wanderings were not without reason. At one point in his colorful, rakish life, he had so perturbed the Sheriff of Nottingham with his bad behavior and worse verse, that he managed to bump Robin Hood to #2 on "Ye Ten Moft Wanted" list. Whenever he found himself unable to persuade a nubile young lady to join him in a romp, (as was frequently the case) or even a desiccated old hag (just as frequently), he was known to take outrageous liberties with whatever erotic sculpture he could find. In fact, so often did he take those liberties with a nude statue of Venus in the Nottingham town square it became the first object ever to be named, "the statue of liberty." The hallowed tradition of cutting off the Venus's arms actually began then and there, when the exasperated townspeople hacked the arms off their statue, so as to give Decius less of a purchase when he went to do his thing. That appears to have stymied him for a day or two, until the sight of two dogs in the act of ex-

tending their lineage inspired him to take advantage of the very
callipygic nature of the statue. It may have been because of the
elder Dzmc's shenanigans that the first statutory rape laws were
put on the books.

When he wasn't busy offending the villagers by having his
way with marble, he composed ballads so that he could annoy
the blind as well. We are fortunate, I suppose, that a number of
his ballads have been preserved at the end this collection under
the misbegotten assumption that the reader will not have had
enough by then.

As for me, I have had enough already, and we have not even
gotten going.—tcl

SECTION I
THE LOST NOTEBOOKS OF GLUB DZMC

Young Master Dzmc's 1st Haiku

earwax for a nosh,
ok? quit the jive, dummy,
boogers are the thing.

An Acromegalic Tale

i am only
here to tell
you, oh, yeah, and to pick up a
boobtube guide for the fall, about
the most
legendary guy of
them all, by whom
i mean railroadin'
randy, the fanciest dancer
since mohandas k. gandy. he could
tap out a rhythm or tap out a
keg. either way, it was strictly o.
k. by him, so they said at the
all right chorale in the days
when the skies were
ablaze from the leftover
burps of lucifer's twerps
in disguise with the counterfeit
zircons. then hailstones and
gallstones and millstones and all
stones gathered moss at the rock fest
to fester anew, while the racket of
rockets shooting off to
the moon was enough to make all of
the eels that had merely been
teal, turn a bright naval tincture
of blue. go
get
'em, randy.

The Hornet's Knees

in all the time twixt
now & then, then
back again, i have
found not even
one of what it was i
hide-and-go-sought, back
in the hazy, lazy, crazy day
when alchemy was but
a misdemeanor. there was
a chance, flank'd by sister mary
margaret and the guy who rode
the Hbomb to the ground, that
someone might have stepped
into the lucky remnants of herr
trigger's last repast. scrape-
along, cassidy, if you must. your
boot, i do not think, will
get much cleaner. it always
comes down to a
choice of when to cut the
bait or fish for compliments too
stupid to believe. a lie they
say is white or gray, but
rarely is it simple. a soothful
saying, now that's another
thing, when you come right down to
it or climb right up, depending on
your totem pole position. it makes
no sense to
put the squeeze on me to please. better just to
go and squeeze a pimple.

Tiddily Blinks

so little's
expected of a half
eaten pear, left
out there in the rain to
transfix the insane in
a mock state of
shock, yet
the shelves are
a-chock with overwrought
iron in the hardware
departments from here
to bangkok. in
such a condition, on
such a fool's mission to
the suburbs surrounding
perdition, you hardly
can win. win
one for the
ripper, said coach
jack to his dillers, all
of them killers on a cold
serial track. some
fans came to root, and
others to heckle the
stalwart marauders of
murderer's row, while
spuds on the couch and yams, oh
so dry, on the love seat, watched
the crime of the decade

unfold with the wash. hip, some
cried out, and, you know, that same thing
again, not to mention
hooray. now give us
our money back.

Landscape #1

the chirping of
seagulls overhead in, where
else, the
sky, lends elevated
music to the heaps upon
heaps of old tires, mostly
from tricycles left too long in
the sun. here did there
stand a once-stately
Porto san, long since knocked
down for a chance to enhance
the view from the ditch. the
busy mosquitoes, each
with a stake in the office
stagnant pool, await with
bait on their breath, their
turn to suck
blood from a turnip.

Ablative Moments

up in the pulpit, the
wooly bullies rant,
but do not rave about their favorite
pants with the red
racing stripes and the
flap in
the back. down in
the valley, by which i
mean the
valley so lowdown and
rotten, it
remains to be seen who
will stay long
enough to string up the last
bean midst
tall tales of chile con
carn, while spanish
flypaper hangs mostly forgotten 'til
some fool remembered why
the cows had come
home to their split
level barn. off in the
distance too close to
be measured, a bobble
head icon gives warning of
famine and boredom and
itch, causing the fools to
spend all their
cardboard in the happy

delusion they were once
filthy rich. atop the
toboggans of life on
the fast track to
the short stack,
ganja-fed
ninjas go hurtlin' for
certain, only to crash with
a painful rehash of what one
time had been the world's first
iron curtain.

Miasma Vice

officer clancy, nobody
fancy, is nonetheless sniffing around. i
don't know what just might of happened
here, but out is how it'll
get found. i don't miss a clue
and i don't miss a
cue and i don't miss the
snow and
the ice. just know that i'm
gonna be square on your
case, ace, just like stink
on rice. i'm on the
clock, and i've just begun. like
my long lost sock, you
can hide, but you
cannot run. now
before I accept your
pay for looking
away, i need
you to say, what're
you up to? (tens
and twenties, please, and maybe a
fifty or two.). it's the
very least i
can do.

Glub's Haiku

Child-Proof Caps

help, I cannot get
into my urgent pain pills.
please find a child.

Bargain Days

it's twofer tuesday
at the neighborhood saloon.
be still, spinning room.

Showtime

gala broadway show
awaits my ticket purchase.
equity loan done.

Meter Maids

failed cop candidates,
they scour parking places,
praying for revenge.

Golf Score

no eraser found
on the scoring pencil, so
we lie right up front.

Protest

what slanty-eyed nip
decided that seventeen
is all we can use?

No Request is Too Extreme

the gobs of the greasy, yet
grimy gopher guts,
even the green ones,
are not all
that great, if you ask
me, which of
course nobody ever did. surely you
knew the shape i was in,
ever since my spoon had run
off with the dish. had i
grabbed the big end of
a hen's pulley bone and
blew all the
candles away, while sighting
up high in the twinkling
sky, that great magic
star, as i stood
ankle-deep in the road amidst
apples, then the peace
on this earth that only can
come with a set of new
tires would be my next wish. and
if that one were
taken or somehow forsaken,
i'd wish to opt out of the
picture of bulldogs
playing table-stakes poker, not gin.
let's go to paris and drink 'til
we're plastered, said i to the

mugwump in drag. but i don't hinky
dinky or parley the view, he
protested to no one at all. as it happened, you
see, at that very
same moment, it
transpired that i
wasn't in.

Yes We Have No Bananas in Our Pockets or
Are We Just Sad to See You?

the very first word
of a thought too
absurd to be seen by the
buck nekkid eye is reason
enough to count all
your stuff or yourself
among all of the millions who
have tried to
hide,
while
others coyly smirk behind
ornate electric fans. only the
few, the proud and the
addlepated get to see how
the movie comes out in the end. the rest of
the throng in polka-dot thongs just get to
roll in the aisles. not all who
perform get the big standing o or
even the big standing p. some of the most
bestirring of lines were shouted into
the din of clattering wind-up teeth on
the bottom shelf of a third
rate garage. there is no
beeswax like the show
beeswax, they rose up and
chorused as one. been
there, done that,
moved on.

Luck be a Tramp

fame and/or fortune
lurk, ever mindful in
their mindless way while
the ambitious come
around only to
garner their foolhardy laurels and
the spoils of rotting meat. like
flies to wonton, boys, said old
hop sing to his help, so
let's get this
stuff covered up, lest the board
of health lose
its collective kool™.
just hold
the phone, did i say
lurk back there?
well i only meant it as a
figurine of speech.
fortune, you surely
must know, does
not lurk, but, rather, goes off to blow
on some other guy's die. nor,
in her rightful
mind, does dame fame, whose
rendition of whistle
while you lurk fell into the
eternal blackness of the singleton, never
to see the light of day again and
again, world w/o end, right on. so

let us go a-looming then
over some soft shoulder or
watched pot holder.
whatever makes you older.

The One About
the Traveling Salesman with Only One Shoe
On Each Foot

it is sunday or
at least it used to be, so they tell me,
november thirty
something
in the year of our Lord,
and like some
damn thing or another,
the afternoon fog,
ever soupine in its greenpea mountain majesty,
has once again rolled
through our lives without
ever being detected, deflected or even relegated to some
other place and time
where such things are properly viewed
with terror
and alarm.
and renaissance painters come,
and renaissance painters go,
talking about women who tour or maybe
just the barns
on which they have emblazoned chew
mailpouch, Lord, i don't know.
come, jack, the old man said
to his ten of spades, but then he was
nearsighted, so they tell me, and
difficult to figure out;
come, jack my queen, he

insisted, pulling all the while
at the leash.
let us get a new leash on life, you
and i,
and a flea collar as well.
do you remember that priest, i asked,
the one in the traffic
circle?
they say he yielded, so they say, then too
there once
was a monk
in siberia whose
life just grew drearier and
drearier 'til he
leapt from
his cell with a hell
of a yell and eloped with a mother
superior.
and renaissance painters come,
and renaissance painters go,
talking about the last
time they think they
got fortunate.

Card Scents

pick a card, any
card, it ain't all that hard, said the
greeting card sharper with
the prestidigit fidgets. don't show
me the one you
selected or all of the many you somehow
neglected. to distract your
attention and other such items too
shameful to mention, i'll show you a limerick,
using only my mouth or, rather, a limerick
sampler: not much sense,
but the variety's ampler. there
once was a man from peru
whose poetry never would scan. said
he with a grin as he wiped off
his chin, it's just
when ah itches, ah scratches. was it the
ace of clubs? i thought not, taa
daa!

Yakkity Tuba: An Instrumental Rant

on a night that
was no different from
another, except it
was the day, i asked the magic
cue ball, why it was
that fuzzy wuz-
zy was a bearer of glad tidings when
fuzzy wuzzy had but a
comb over. i was
sad because i had
no hair, spake the Oreo of
delphi, until i met a
man with
hardly any feet, for it
is said, both wide
and far, that those who
cannot do
the funky chicken, teach. you
know, i'd like
to teach the world to
sneeze in 4
part harmony. i'd like to bake
a birthday cake and save
it all for me. i'd like a set of
big white teeth
not sinking in my
hand. i'd like to
be the leader of a
turkish pokla band.

Landscape #2

2 peas in
a pod on the sod in
the uppermost chunk of a contiguous
state lie in wait. nearby a scarecrow
scares nobody but
himself, while the eye
of an elephant is mistaken
at once
for an ear of sweet
corn in the light
of the beautiful morn. then
oceans away, in a
landlocked lagoon, a colonel in
charge of all swampwater taffy, sits
on a thumbtack and wonders at
length why he came to be born.

Who Killed the Dead Sea Scrolls and Why

beware the wrath
of grapes the old dame
warned us in stanzas too
long in
both story and song to
tattoo on a
buttock or even a chest. it's sure
not my place, since the
rent went unpaid, to
contradict or even contra
dance like the ants were
still on
the move in my pants, but,
with all due respect and
some more that's not due 'til the
end of the month, i think that the little
red hen said it best.
be not a jerk chicken, she
scolded the cock on the
walk of the hollywood fame. no
phony baloney on
yank doodle's pony can hope
to get into this game. oh, some
people will, if they fill
up my till, said the crooked
shoe clerk with a wink. and please
do not squeal that
you got a raw deal. compared
to your feet, it does

not even stink. i think it
just wrong you're
bought off for
a song, said the recently traded fly
catcher, concealed in a mask
and a cap. better bought off
than sold off, replied the
tycoon, born with a quicksilver
spoon in the light of the pale bargain
hunter's new moon, and it's
better yet
not to shoot crap.

Clap Hands, Here Comes Chuck

my throbbing ankle
suggests that i limp for a
while, due to a rolling bowling
ball of all
things. why didn't you warn or
call, i asked the rented
narrator. i told you
to duck, did i not, he replied. if
you won't even listen, for there
are none so deaf as them
who will not hear, then it's all of your tough
luck and none of my own. i wondered aloud, but still
in my head, what would illiterate
zorro do? why, he'd go right along,
carving 'x' in the seats of the evil ones'
pants, as though nothing had happened or
had even a chance. i'd be a dancin' fool today,
if only i could dance.

One-Eye Jack's Disenchanted Mantra

long ago in a far
weep from what we know to
be so, i sought the meaning of
it all during the
best years of my
parakeet's life. then and
only then did i come
to see the fact of
the matter, as a matter of fact. and,
if i am not sadly
mistaken, though surely i am, you
were there at the afore
mentioned jamboree, thumping
your own
slappy bass, like you really had something to
sell or tell or yell or even
to reveal the many
things you do not know.
chapter two, this
is where the scions
of the laundromat tell
me where it's at. and as
if in gratitude or remorse, i
boil a horse in water
too tepid to drink. there
were times, the old coot
said, we had to eat our shoes, the
penny loafers, that is, for
only a fool in the

the night would eat a goochy with
nary
a drop of ale in
sight. know
this as ye know the bylaws
of differential
calculus and your
days shall ever run from
sun to setting sun.

Tinkerbelle at 87

what i once took in stride, I now
take no pride in counting along
with my change. the most
odd happenstants to come
down the pike, in this life
or the next, are much
too complex to
arrange. but why, asked i, askance at
last and lost,
because that's
where the money's at, said both
the actor and the fat minnesotan, referring of course to the bank. just a
bit too comforting
to know yet, how
much better would it be
were i a famous
chocolateer, like maybe willy wank. shave and
a hair styling, 349 bits.

Glub's Dirty Limerick

there once was a man,
never mind
what kind of a
man. let's just say he knew
how to get things
done, OKAY? far
be it for me to
describe his height or what
might have been
his very first and
last
hoorah, from brazil,
who swallowed
quite impulsively, might
i add, without so
much as a chew, let
alone the twenty-
one or so required of
every good
eater within hearing range
of an etiquette reader, a birth control pill.
he fell,
as we all
must fall, especially the
bigger, whose fall
was all the harder from
grace, to the ground
and wallowed around,
and got,

as you might
suppose in a play-pretend world,
where all who eat the
porridge get a just
dessert and dogs go to heaven above, a big dry cleaning
bill.

Somewhere Between a Rock and a Parker
House Roll

as i was
fleeing from st. ives, i
met a crooked little man with
a gnickgnack paddy
whack in
his crooked little sack. leave
a guy alone, i declared
at customs far
too absurd to be remembered in
just a gnickgnack
paddywhack of time. i did
though recall the
thrill of the mall, when a buck went
as far as it could, farther than
i, if the truth may be known, but
nobody cares
about that any more, least of
all me, except on the 89th
of july, right after the storm of
the sesquicentennial,
when the
reign of cats and dogs ended, only
to start hailing cabs. sacred moley, i
yelped, too confused to
remember the secrets of ships trapped
forever in
finished off bottles of thunder
bird wine.

The Shapelessness of Things to Come

i went to shun
the gypsy, to learn
not of my fate. my
uncle's aunt was
tipsy, and got
there way too late. the
splotchy bocce bowlers whose
gutter talk was
spare, tormented the
high rollers by
spitting in the air. and
through it all, the hatters
got mad at one and
all, when all
who were the batters
refused to hit
the wall. then in
the darkest alley, the
sun declined to
shine. say this must
be where to
stick all
that stuff,
i told a friend of mine.

Yet Even More Haiku

Lo Mien Rip Off

oodles and oodles
of noodles surround my fork.
say, now, where's the pork?

Avian Roadkill

quacky the duck has
run flat out of luck, so it
seems. send me the bill.

The Latest Thing in TV

addlepated jerk
forced to choose among bimbos.
oh, wow, bfd.

Recycled Trash

paper goes in here,
plastic in there, but where do
yesterday's dreams go?

Sushi

pokey car ahead.
park it or drive it, grandma,
got fish not to fry.

Autobiography of Somebody Else

let us get
off on the wrong
foot, you and i, as
we gladhand our
way through the zoo. then,
too, there
was a time i recall
we could only
be seen by fools too
scrambled of brain to go
out in the rain in
october or sometime like that.
whereas i, totally unlike
the rest of you,
wish to thrive on the
remnants of once-shattered dreams,
now made
into ditties, of towns
without pity. insomniac jack would
wallow in bed 'til his
sores were too livid to count. then,
without so
much as a how-dee-doo, he'd flop
from the sack at the hiney crack
of dawn. sure beats sleepin', he
said to his stuffed
shirts as he waited in time
immemorial for another
sock to drop

Let's Talk Hollow Turkey

they asked in
a hush and a blush, did
you get the stuff? believe it, i
sneered, for
today there's a lost
our lease sale on
dead bread at the local
Smash 'n Grab. i made
off with a haul, shouting put
it all on my tab. enough of this
hooray and who shot
john, said the veep. we got particulars
to mention, for
which i will need your un-
subdivided attention. count me in
like errol flynn, called out a blind
tennis hustler, an anthracite
brunette whose memoirs,
titled endless love, once
made the best
binder list. move along, miss, there's
nothin' to see, proclaimed the fat
cop in the detritus shop. but, flat-
foot, you can see me, she
replied. ha! what a burn. when
will you pigs ever learn? hit the
bricks, suggested the cop as he lobbed
them, one
by one past her flailing racket. up yours, she

exclaimed. say, asked the law, was that
a bribe? pardon
me, boys, i said at last, now awash in stale bread, i
know the chattahoochee choo
choo when i smell it, so you need
not tell me why, but can
somebody show me the door? quoth the raven-
haired blind tennis hustler, never. more
tea, if you please, mr. coffee. death is
no excuse.

Landscape #4

a wet city
street in the dead of the
day, waits, glistening away,
for the next batch
of hamburger wraps and spent
drinking straws. the
distant honking of
foghorns in traffic is
relished at
the old hot dog
stand. a newspaper
truck with cheap
plastic tires, stands guard by
the toothpick palace atop the
big rock candy
pile of rubble.

Lambsy Takes a Dive

mayors, they say, eat
oats, by the boatload i think. but,
if forced, just for once to yodel
the truth, i'd swear that i never
was there. oh, tante jemimah,
regardez your oncle jûles. he's in
le bathtub, drooling into the pool. 1st
i do the backstroke, then i
crawl to the safety net of
an abandoned game of volleyball, whilst
a diarrheic seagull flies off in search of more
mischief to make. help, i've
been fouled, i called to
the ref, who turned a blind
eye into a silk purse. go
team, go, he cheered, or at
least go away, i have far
bigger fish i must fry. i could have told
him what happens on
days when the buffalo roam in
your home, but seldom was
heard a dyspeptic word, so i
gave it all up for the scullery life, where the
suds and the plates mingle
free. living at peace and
surrounded by grease, now
that is the life meant for me.
now i'm under
water, buckin' against the tide.

Sonnet to an Aroma

The wafting scent of cabbage boiling up
Or that of beans awaiting in a pot
The subjects of this sonnet, they are not.
Though, if I were to eat but just a cup
Of either one, I'd soon be on the mark
Of that fair thing I pay the homage to.
For, once the eating part were done and through,
A part that's not my mouth will start to bark.
The volume of the noise may shrink or swell.
Thy fury could know limit not or bound
In no proportion measured by the sound.
I do not mean the noise, I mean the smell.
You put my gut at ease for days and weeks,
My friend, you are the wind between my cheeks.

Ode to a Grecian Spoon

you best unpack
your picnic lunch, the crypt
sweeper said. this one's going
to run long and hardly
worth the trouble. armed only with a shovel in
the hovel of what was once home
to the bean and the
codpiece, i dwell in the
depths of saltshaker heights, waiting
for someone like me to turn
off the sound and turn on the
lights. desperately
needing the proof of what i heard so
very long ago, i made the
walk from kalamazoo to
timbuktu and back, only to
find it was indeed a waste
of space, to say nothing
of cold, hard print and tack. better
luck next time, i jeered at
myself, since no
body else would bother. oh,
yeah? i retorted, well,
let me invoke the glorified
nose hairs of your
father. what
have we come to, i axed lizzie
borden's mom, in a fit
of quandary too ghastly to

mention. why, kalamazoo, you
3-legged fool, have you
not been paying any attention? and
while good men do nothing but
play dominoes in the
old pizza park, storm
trooping babies in their
hobnailed booties go traipsing
across the land of old
counterpane, laying
waste to the formfitting
conventions of yesteryear,
silencing forever the
pacifiers of the far
and near. there will
be a lesson, quacked the wise
old vulture, let it be. just
don't let it be me. we
interrupt this
poem for a brief
commercial message: to get a
healthy mouth, complete
with big, strong
teeth, massage your
gums at madame lulu's
massage parlour. offer
not valid with
proof of the pudding or pie. all
work, despite what
you may have heard, coupled
with no play,
does not a
dull boy johnny make: he was

simply born that way. and so it
seems, the girl of my dreams will
ever stay fixed in
my thoughts much too jumbled
to sort. but, unlike the
girl of your real life and
limb, mine is a really
good sport. i tell her on nothing much more than
a whim, let's
go far away on a trip. i'll even pack my own
grip, for i never have needed
a flunky. we'll journey off
to the brand new spanking zoo, where
often i've gone to
seek out the monkey.

Doin' the Lambeth Backpeddle, Yo!

come into my
parlor, said the ice
cream huckster to the fly. hell
no, i won't go said willie 'the fly' mosca.
that stuff'll kill
you if you let it, that
is, when you can
get it.
then eat
leaden death, our
flavour of the month, jeered the
pistachioteer, as he hurled
a horseshoe vaguely in the fly's
direction, knowing that here is
where close still counted
for something. i
tell ya, that's all i need today, he
grumbled and groused.. then, before he
knew it (don't get
smug, it was before you
knew it too), a good
humor truck pulled up. humor
me, he said.
how's an eskimo, pie, excuse
me an inuit pie,
grab you? the trucker muttered into his
bullhorn. don't know,
cut me a slice.

99

the song of our trek, so
rudely halted at just forty
bottles, plus a chocolate malted, on some
flimsy pretext,
died in mid-chorus, right
there before us, just
because we reached
our destination unscathed, undone and
under-panting, despite our greed
for speed. the rhododendron, proclaimed
the talking rag doll,
is paved with good
intentions, did i not fail to mention? i dream of having all the
toppings on my pie, confessed the weary pest
comptroller to the priest, because it gives
me pizza mind. what
's that you say? there are
no bottles of
beer on this never seen but still
acclaimed in song forever wall? no
bottles of beer? boy, the old man
chuckled 'til he bled, if I had a nickel for every time i
had a nickel, why, I'd have
me some nickels i
guess. well, ya
go to the store, ya buy
some more; there's 99
bottles of beer on
the wall.

Those Old Weary, My Lamborghini's in the Shop, Blues

the hacks in
the back of the saccharine
shack all wore black when
bazooka
joe bit the gum. how did
they know this was
going to be so, or who they should ask not to
come? it was easy as pie, 'cause
they all knew the guy who
once used to spy for
the lord of
a fly. when they
stood in the
way on that terrible day of
the play in the fields
of the bored, you
somehow just knew that
before this was through, in
a decade or two, that some
joker's ox would
be gored. 2 points for
a win and a bottle of gin, or
at least a free spin, and
one for the time you
swapped spit with your
sister and wound up with a
feverish blister: that's how
they say a violin scherzo
is scored.

Travelin' Light

i'm travelin'
light tonight; lighter than the
strain on a debutante's brain on
how to save the endangered whooping
cough;. lighter than dark, well, i guess that's for
sure; lighter than dusk and purer than pure, i just
thought you'd like to
know, which, now
that i've blabbed,
you do. i'm travelin' lighter
than a wikki pedia salesman,
shuffling door
to door with
hours to kill and marbles
to spill; than a matter of no consequence and a consequence
of no matter, no spatter, no messy batter, no muss,
no fuss; just hop
on the bus, caractacus, and by
the by, don't
forget to dry-
clean your uniform. no
washee, no tickee.

A Winter's Head nor Tale

congrats, kid we'll just
have to see if ulation is
yet to come. but never
mind that, said the wily old
lender, just back from a
seven-day bender, here is your makes-
platinum-look-like-swiss-
cheese card. in the words of st. vitas,
welcome to the big dance. and, oh,
by the way, we'll just keep all that
cash you can't spare, for
your convenience of
course, he forthrightly
mentioned as he slapped with
his free hand, the flames that had
sprouted anew from his pants. and out
in the yard, all three of the feet were
jockeying to win place and
show in the midst of the county's
eleventh worst snow. i've tasted
better, old frosty allowed, though self-mastication is
hardly my thing. now, I hate to melt and
run, because, trust me, it's not quite
the fun they all sing that it
is every year. take it from me, the
guy with the yet even older silk hat,
it seems that i, who
was chosen amongst all of
the frozen, ought to know.

Glub's Nursery Rhyme

jack & jill were so
over the hill, for they both had long since
moved on.

the memories of
all past spills were, like most of
the refried cells that once had been
beans or, rather, brains, mostly dead
and gone.

so the path of righteousness and
truth, to travel
is the very thing to do that
they are loath.

instead they
sit all day and night in bars too
dimly lit to
sense or
even show

the way to san
diego or jose, to
say nothing of
the cruel vichyssoise of life and
all the things they know.

and they all lived
happily ever
after,
throwing down beers,
wiggling their ears,
it don't make sense but,
what the hell, it rhymes.

SECTION II
THE LOST SONGBOOKS OF GLUB DZMC

Zeke the Chicken Strangler

Oh Zeke the chicken strangler
Was not a rustler nor a wrangler,
But when it came to killin' birds, he knew his stuff
Yes and Zeke the chicken choker
Never could learn how to play poker,
But I bet no chicken ever called his bluff.

Now Zeke the poultry throttler,
He had the brains of a two-year-old toddler,
But in chicken chokin' circles, he had clout
Yes sir!
Well he was not very subtle,
And his mind was no trick to muddle,
But I'll bet a lot of chickens never managed to figure him
out.

Oh he couldn't choke a horse
With a Wall Street banker's cash,
And he could not stay collected
If you took him out with the trash.
Ah, but Zeke the chicken strangler,
He was above that sort of thing.

Now Zeke the chicken strangler,
He'd grab a hen by the neck and he'd dangle her,
Then he'd say, that's what I call a job well done.
Well now he wasn't very handy
And he didn't look too crafty,
But I bet a lot of chickens thought he wasn't too much fun.

Oh Zeke the pullet snuffer
Was not the last of a red hot lover,
But he loved to send them chickens to they doom.
And though it got a little smelly,
Well he would not miss his telly,
So he did the job right in his living room.

Well now he couldn't skin a cat
With a set of Ginsu knives,
And he couldn't even keep a bee
If you gave him a case of hives
Ah, but Zeke the chicken strangler,
He had strange ways of his own.

All Dressed Up

Grab your ball gown, got my tux
Everything will be deluxe.
Diamond studs in every cuff,
You can take your ermine muff.
Here's my top hat, there's my cane
Only fancy, nothing plain.
You're my belle and I'm your beau
When we're all dressed up,
Dressed up with no place to go.

Whip your lorgnette out to see
What there might be on TV.
Cocktails will be served right here.
That is to say, we got lite beer.
Though my couch is worn and old,
It has some tales that could be told.
Our night will pass so very slow
When we're all dressed up,
Dressed up with no place to go.

Some folks like to shop in malls,
Others like to stare at walls,
My wallpaper is the best.
See one room, you've seen the rest.
My bathroom is a joy to see,
Just the place you'll want to...be.
We'll be ones they'd like to know
When we're all dressed up,
All dressed up,
Dressed up with no place to go.

Porter Parody #66,532

You're the top, you're the big banana.
You're the slop in a pig's nirvana.
You're the nimble splat of a pratfall by a clown
You're Mr. T's best jewelry,
You're Tinseltown.

You're the best, you're the BeeGee's rocking.
You're the test of a queen size stocking.
I'm the news that lines the shoes
Of some whisky sop,
But if, baby, I'm the bottom,
You're the top.

You're so great, you're a TV dinner.
You're the weight of the derby winner.
You're the driven snow up in Buffalo at night.
You're a race-car crash, you're succotash,
You're hockey fights.

You're Champale, you're the Ruffles' ridges,
You're the sale of Old Brooklyn's bridges.
I'm a wasted shot at an empty
Can of pop,
But if, baby, I'm the bottom,
If, baby, I'm the bottom,
If, baby, I'm the bottom,
You're the top.

Whoopsie Daisy

I like to eat the pizza pie,
A large, with all the stuff.
Roughage is OK with me,
I like to play it rough.
A leg of lamb goes down the hatch
With a quart of Guinness Stout.
Then pretty soon that tasty chow
Is comin' right back out.

Whoopsie daisy,
Call me crazy,
But the stuff's as good goin' out
As comin' in.
Whoopsie daisy,
Call me crazy,
If you bring it all right back,
Then it's no sin.

At breakfast time, a little ham
My appetite will spank
A modest portion is OK,
Say, maybe just a shank.
Throw in a dozen scrambled eggs
And a poppy-seeded roll,
It doesn't matter 'cause it's going
Right down the toilet bowl.

Whoopsie daisy,
Call me crazy,

But the stuff's as good goin' out
As comin' in
Whoopsie daisy,
Call me crazy
'Cause it isn't pigging out,
It's pigging in.

I always super size my food
When I go out to dine.
I like to think that briefly, then,
That grub was once all mine.
If in a pet store, I were locked,
I'd kibble all the bits.
Then I'd toss my biscuits up,
Before I got the...trots
Whoopsie daisy,
Call me crazy,
But the stuff's as good goin' out
As comin' in.

Whoopsie daisy,
Call me crazy,
The porcelain pond's a place in space,
Where I have often,
Really coughin',
Downward facin',
Hasten, Jason,
A place
Where I have been.

A.A.'s Dark Side

Jonathan Joe, with a mouth like a zero,
Was everyone's foe and nobody's hero.
He'd steal anything that wasn't nailed down.
He'd steal the brass ring from the nose of a clown.
He'd steal half the laces from all of your shoes.
He'd unhook your braces, then pilfer your booze.
Jonathan Joe was a man of renown
Jonathan Joe was the mayor of the town.

With a hey nonney nonney
But a cold cha cha.
It even takes money
Just to sing fa-la-la.

Jonathan Joe with his cart full of plunder
Had secrets to know and nothing to wonder.
He had everything you thought you might need,
From an emerald ring to a shiny glass bead;
If you wanted a bat or nothing like that,
He was the cat who knew where it was at.
Far more than any, it's fitting to say,
He knew to the penny how much you would pay.

With a nay honey honey,
But a cold cha cha,
It even takes money
Just to sing fa-la-la.

Jonathan Joe, with a mouth like an oval

Was not living low in a shack or a hovel.
He lived in a mansion, festooned with antiques,
With a recent expansion for a circus of freaks.
With a pen for his goose and a birdbath to boot,
All from the use of his ill-gotten loot.
Jonathan Joe was awash in cold cash.
Jonathan Joe liked to pick through the trash.

With a say sonny sonny
But a cold cha cha,
It even takes money
Just to sing fa-la-la.

Stevie Foster's Rough Draft

Oh, Lenora, don't say to drop dead,
For I come from Gloccamorra
With a snare drum on my head.

Well, I come from Gloccamorra
With a snare drum, like I said,
For to see my fair Lenora,
And to paint this city red.

Oh, Lenora, don't say take a hike,
For I rode from Gloccamora
With a bell upon my bike.

I dreamt I went without a cup
Inside my overalls,
When sweet Lenora marched right up
And kicked me in the veranda

Oh, Lenora, don't say toodle-oo,
For I come from Gloccamorra
Tootin' into my kazoo.

With anxious heart, I gave a rose
To my Lenora, dear.
She went and punched me in the nose,
And said, get out of here.

Oh, Lenora, don't say to drop dead,
For I come from Gloccamorra
With a snare drum on my head.

bin go

here it came, there
it went. count the slashes
on your tent
don't forget to pay the rent, and
bingo was his name-o
b-i-n-g-o b-i-n-g-o b-i-n-g-o b-i-n-g-o-b-i

'f i knew now what
i knew then, write it
with a fountain pen,.
don't know where
and don't know when, but
bingo was his name-o
n-g-o-b-i n-g-o-b-i n-g-o-b-i n-g-o-b-i-n-g

one and one might be 2. i
just haven't thought
it through. but do not think that i'd
tell you and
bingo was his name-o
o-b-i-n-g o-b-i-n-g o-b-i-n-g o-b-i-n-g-o-b

high upon a window
sill, two bald eagles coo
and bill. maybe they are
up there still, and
bingo was his name-o
i-n-g-o-b i-n-g-o-b i-n-g-o-b i-n-g-o-b-i-n

there, you see, my fuzzy friend,
it all comes out right in the end.

The Happy Song

You can keep your happy days
Which once were here again.
For I am even happier
Than you were, way back then.
I don't see how it's possible
My joy will ever stop,
When I'm happy as a clam,
Yes, happy as a clam in slop.

I used to have the weepy blues
Until my eyes were red,
But that is yesterday's bad news,
You heard what I just said.
The tables now are turned around,
And I'm coming out on top.
How happy do you think I am?
I'm happy as a clam in slop.

There's no need to hustle
For an oyster or a mussel,
When you're happy as a clam,
Just like I am,
You're happy as a clam in slop.

Ode to Felix Navidad

Oh, give us some Figgie pudding,
Oh, give us some Figgie pudding,
Oh, give us some Figgie pudding,
Or we'll burn your house down.
Amen

The Fight Song of Gomorra Falls High

the colors we raise for
gomorra falls high. on behalf of
our team we swear we
will die. as, for our
great school, every
one of them fights, we
cheer on and on for our
brave sodomites.

we are the sodomites,
mighty mighty sodomites. every
where we go-oh, people want
to know-oh, what we
do-ooh, so we show them. then the
game is always
canceled, 'cause there's
no one left to watch it. they
all run home to
get busy, leaving some
folks in a tizzy. as to
forfeit they have
ceded, we remain still
undefeated. we
are the sodomites, mighty
mighty sodomites.
mighty
mighty
mighty
mighty

Da Glubsta Channels Irving Berlin to Say
Why He Won't Play the Simple Melody

Musical pranksta,
Won't you play me some gangsta,
'Cause my baby loves rap.
Just change that old bebop jive
To some hip hop that's alive.
If you will play but a scrap
Of a tune that is crap,
You will get all my applause,
And that is simply because,
I like to listen to rap.
Peace out.

SECTION III
THE LOST SEA SHANTYS OF GLUB DZMC

Barnacle Phil

Now I'll sing ye a song that'll give ye a fright
Or a busted knee or a chill
When I finally get down ta the details
Of the saga of Barnacle Phil.

For it's barnacles ta you, boys,
And it's barnacles ta me.
It's barnacles ta the keel haulor
And more ta thee keel haulee.

Say, of all the gobs ever decked a swab,
Never was and there never will
Be a man alive under five-foot-five
Could stand up ta Barnacle Phil.

Still it's barnacles ta you, boys,
And it's barnacles ta me.
It's barnacles ta the keel haulor
And more ta the keel haulee.

I could tell ye 'bout the fine times he had
In Salem and Portsmouth until
He drowned in a tub, for a real land lub-
-ber was the man they called Barnacle Phil.

And, yes, it's barnacles ta you, boys,
And it's barnacles ta me.
It's barnacles ta the keel haulorrr
And more ta the keel haulee.

Captain Biscotti

Captain Biscotti they say was quite dotty,
Though at piracy he was the best.
No dog of the sea took more loot than he,
But his put-upon crew got no rest.

In between clashes with foes and mad dashes
To flee from the hangman's garrote,
To his crewmen he sang until their ears rang,
But to tell him to stop, they dared not.

And then woe betide all those not on his side
If, when captured, they griped like a crank.
When the captain sang opera, he said, don't make me stop
or I'll
Send you right out on the plank.

Some captives would squirm and others confirm
They'd never heard such awful tones.
They'd pray to the Lord, then jump overboard,
Preferring to meet Davy Jones.

His clothes were but tatters, in all other matters,
The captain was humble as pie.
When it came to his voice, there was no other choice,
Said Biscotti from way upon high,

Amongst every corsair who breathes the salt air,
My singing is surely supreme,

When, truth be to tell, he sang so unwell
It even made killer whales scream.

As he sipped sarsaparilla, he let a flotilla
Of enemy ships gather 'round him.
Stations of battle! to his crew did he prattle
When the cannons had started to pound him.

His ship quickly sank as onto a plank
He tried hard to desperately cling.
Then off on a stage, far away from this rage,
A fat lady started to sing.

In Search of a Bruisin'

If I were on a whaler,
I'd go and hunt the whale.
I'd be the smoothest sailor
That ever made a sale.

If I were on a shrimper,
I'd eat my fill of shrimp.
Then stagger off much limper,
And fly home in a blimp.

If I were on a freighter,
I'd bag my share of freight,
There would be no one greater
At pulling my own weight.

If I were on a trawler,
I'd learn what is a trawl.
Then I'd stand much taller
When I had caught them all.

But I am on a cruiser,
Now here's the nasty news.
The work that I must do, sir,
Makes this one lousy cruise.

The Voyage of the *Starfish*

Now gather ye 'round and hearken this tale.
Bring a light snack or some cold ginger ale.
Set yourself down in a comfortable spot,
And realize this story is all that I've got.

'Twas on a day dismal and chock full o' gloom,
When the specter of danger was lookin' to loom,
That a ship called *The Starfish* was soon to set sail
On a voyage with a mission to somehow not fail.

Hard by Miami she was ordered to go,
Although why that was, no one there seemed to know.
Shiver me timbers and shiver them well,
For at ninety degrees, it was colder than hell.

The wind blew so hard that it puffed the sails out,
So to make yourself heard, you oft' had to shout.
And if that by itself did not bring enough thrills,
They'd forgotten to stock up on seasickness pills.

With sharks in the sea their ship had to mingle,
And for breakfast, they ate you-know-what on a shingle.
They'd lost all their sun block in a right shady deal,
So all they could do was to burn and to peel.

And with their fair port just comin' in sight,
The crew and the captain all had a great fright.
The bowline hitch on a rope come undone,
Though the rope led to nothing, nor secured anyone.

With a last desperate dash, *The Starfish* bore down
On the port of that fair-weather Floriday town.
And for all the sad ships that lay down in the drink,
She got there somehow and did not even sink.

The Sealubber's Dislament

Going to the zoo to applaud caribou,
Or shooting the skeet for their pelts,
That kind of thing may be just right for you
Or just right for somebody else.

But, if it might be, you're referring to me,
I'll tell you in terms not uncertain,
The place that I'd be is away out to sea,
With danger and mermaids a-flirtin'.

Having to pay to attend a soiree
Might be neither crafty nor arty,
And while you are snatching hors'doeuvres from a tray,
I'll be in a hot boarding party.

Just imagine the joy of this lucky boy
To be given the wonderful job
Of getting to holler out loud, Ship ahoy!
Or cleaning the deck with a swab.

Seeming polite, you say I'm not bright,
And sometimes I'd have to agree.
But, though you are right, you can go fly a kite.
Just give me the life of the sea.

Spinach Jubilee

so you're pop.
aye, the sailor, man. do
you live for the garbage
can? if these
words are shantys, i'll
eat your mom's
pantys, mister pop.
aye, the sailor,…….. man.

SECTION IV
THE LOST AD COPY OF "BUD" DZMC

Fast Food

as in days past
when oft i rode that train
in pain 'til at last I told them,
this is where
i get oft, i note to
self and all self-serving sayers
of the sooth, the uncouth
know of things we fumble
and stumble for in the dark
of the park at twilight time again.
AND YET WHEN ("Shift! Shift!", Waller, Thomas,
Yo Feets Too Big, op.cit.)
and yet when all is said and
done, there
remains nothing
more to be said and only to
give the elephants their weekly
enemas, you
who are so enamored of show
biz,
before all is done. there is
no way out but the weigh-in: walking
backwards, talking backwards, chalking blackboards.
and while you are about it, re-
member, it may be about you,
hurtling toward your place in line, not
on the cycle of
life, but the pogo-stick of death.
when all has

come to this, what hope
remains but mcporky's swineburger,
specialized sauce at
no extra cost. all
is not lost.

White Sale

who would have
thought amidst those who could be so easily
bought, like some
bloated blowhard whose pain was all feigned in the throes of
counting his toes, that whatever it is would soon
be ordained as
this, that + the other thing. not
i, said the cat in
the hat rack, nor did the bear in
thin air. say, what
ever happened to big
boy pete? was he left in the
lurch or just the back seat?
the mind can
but boggle at such holy
untruths or at
least it can figure the
odds maker's spread. and
that's just a thing
among many at
crazy fred's sale, sale,
sale-a-bration.
wash
clothing and towelage, fit
for a margrave.

Love Potion #8

side
effects may include little
green men writing
names with your pen on a
scroll meant for eyes and
nose only; blood on the stool and
the ottoman too, pink elephants
at parade rest; white knuckle
head trips and scabs on your spleen, not
to mention irregular blinks; rapid
recall or perhaps none at all; a
desire to hop with a limp. visions
of sugarplums dancing around the
blazing bonfires of
yesterday's tires; failure to heal
on the part
of your dog when commanded
to get well and bark. an urge to wear neckties
that make you look just like a
dork and cuffs much too
big for your britches; stoppage
of breath and startage of death, a chance for your
teeth to turn black.
a craving
for liquor, when lacquer will
do just as well; blindness
and deafness and dumbness and
sloth; a hole in the back
of your digestive tract, resulting in

some peristalsis; way too
much gentle on
what's left of your mind and a
need to yell smut at the moon.
artichoke heart and kidneys
akimbo; at least two left
feet, plus the one in your mouth;
incontinent sight and the dry
sweats as well; maudlin yearning to
be dead and in hell. for
encapsulate moments when
life could be grand, try hal's happy
caps, they're the best in
the land.

Beach Wear 'n Tear

sing me no
songs and i'll tell
you no lies, no
threequarter-truths, no fibs or
replies to your
letters, too few both in
number and gender to
answer. at two
hundred kilo, poor
venus d. milo was an underarmed,
underemployed ballet
dancer.
only a walrus with
carpentry skills could out-guess
the beans in the jar. so burn your
tuxedo and stomp on
your hat, this
party is come
as you are. that's quite
enough stuff, said lord
houghandblough to the wiener
dog racing a slinky down
stairs. that foppish cream
puff was quite right to get tough, but i
don't think that any
one cares. i come around
here but once
every year, to
collect all the lost chicken

bones, that self-righteous
tarts had been saving in carts, when
those without sin had
all run out of stones. still, as you grope for
that last pinch of
dope to stick up your
nose and then smoke, remember
giustini's self-waxing bikinis. they
were not meant to be such
a joke.

A Deal on Wheels

do i have the
car for you? tell me, is the
pope a jew? look it over, through
and through. it also comes in cobalt
blue. am
i going too fast for you? now, feature
this, if my
guess i miss, you
get power brakes and power
steering; power mirrors, just
made for peering. the power
seats are e-z folders, and, check
this out: for all your cups, we
got power holders. you'll have lots of
sticker shock and awe. you'd
be stumped to discover a single
flaw, from rich
corinthian pleather seats to
the funny way the
car's horn bleats. she runs with the power of a horse, but
a fast one, 'tis a far better model, of
course, than the last one we sold
you five weeks in the past
no, this one'll last,
if you really drive slow, which i know you can
do in your
sleep. am i right or
is the end i've gone off
of too deep?

airbags? sure,
without a doubt, both on
the inside and the out. now, is that
cool or possibly
what? hey, speaking of cool,
if your honey does
swelter, and the
heat might just melt her, then check
out this baby's a c.
a cool frigid blast from
the vents, not the past, will
set her right, try it &
see. with cold air so nice,
she'll be covered with ice, from
her dye-
job clear down to her knee. go ahead and find
out what everyone knows. when you
factor in the factory air,
you'll say, my, but, this car really blows!

Financial Advice for a Price

i look all about the
poorly arranged brown
debris at the bottom
of countless dry lakes and
i ask, whose big
idea was the fake
rubber snake, not
mine, I will wager a
pie. perhaps some
misguided pit
bull for the blind was
the reason the
priestess of
oysters in season decreed only
mortals may die.
the wild side of a walker
with wheels, is
still fairly
tame compared to a shark in
a battlefield
tank. what self serving bobber for
apples in slobber could
hope to compete with
o'shaughnessy's bank?

Parts

like an unfaithful
fishwife, ditching
her fish for a
chance to live high and
dry on the hog, i am
looking for easy amends. but
nobody said it was going
to be easy as this.
i cannot but
wonder aloud about you and
your one silly earmuff when
the Gardol's long gone
from my teeth. perhaps, then, the
time has come
when thrills could
be had at a dozen a dime. even
then, the
youth added, for subtraction
was banned, it was
probably too much to pay. i'll
have you to know, young
fellow, i said, this is all
my own hair, what's
it to you or me, anyway? when
everything else smells like
overripe clams on
casino night, then
nothing is fishy and all
truth is the same. a dime

for a dozen, once
more, is the price for knowing
such knowledge, or maybe
perhaps something nice, like
a magnetic statue of Old Man
Christ Himself. all this and
more, we have waiting in store at cousin
eddy's used auto part shoppe, across form
the corner of 18th and main. can't miss it with a bb
gun.

The Hots to Trot

embroiled, perhaps or maybe just
half baked in a roiled up mob of
the unwashed and most unimpressed, i
elbow my way or, if not
mine, then someone's, to
the front of the line in
the sand. this sure
is livin', i say to the
gnome whose seersucker
socks were pulled up
to his chin. when you
are right, you are right, the
old frogcatcher said with a
chortle very much unlike a sneeze. doodah,
doodah. it has been my ambition, naked
as the day i
was born, to grow up and become
a galoot. how'm i doin', i asked an
order cook who was so very short. if words
were salami, i'd be richer than
raspberry flan, now don't i, he
sneered. oh, doodah day. it's highly
past time to get
yourself gwine to bringham downs racetrack, the
home of the fix and
the trots. where ladies
eat free on a mad betting
spree, and then they can go
play the slots.

Breath Mints

The germs in your mouth
Will retreat to the south
When they see what's in store for your tongue.
Lucky Dog Breath Mints, the mints that I mean.
They taste a lot better than dung.

They'll make your breath shine
As though a big pine
Needle got caught in your throat.
They're fresher than fresh and cleaner than clean,
Great for when you've been sick on a boat.

If hobnob you must
With the top upper crust,
These breath mints you'll want day and night.
And with but a small hint of amphetamine,
They're just what you need in a fight.

Tell the clerk at your store
To lay in some more
Lucky Dog Mints for your use.
If his store sells cabanas or just kerosene,
Tell him that that's no excuse.

Say you and your crew
Will do what you do,
Which is burn his gyp joint to the ground.
Unless Lucky Dog Breath Mints will soon make the scene,
Like the next time you see him around.

Lucky Dog Breath Mints.
Ask for them by name, you lucky dog.

The Bookend

the dark at the
start of the tunnel was
nothing compared
to the light at the
end, so they say, though it little
behooves, let alone even
moves, a skeleton
key in the tarpitted ground that
somebody found, on
shadow boxing day. buy
gum, the old stock
picker shouted out loud deep
inside of a brown
paper bag. sell crack, he then
added, well under his
hat. while, slipping alone on
a wet, mossy stone that had
managed to gather in spite
of not rolling an inch, a
frantic pedantic professor of
panic cried, give me
the liberty, give someone
else death. in
raspberry fields, the
right of way yields to
the traipsers, forever, as well
as the flouncers.
if you've
taken a number and awaited

your turn at the book
burning fest, you still
need to get past the bouncers.
worry not as their
basketballs rapidly
pound the pavement in search
of a decent day's wages of
sin. try hippie giuseppe's holistic
hair color. it will make you
so youthful, they'll
let you right in.

Risk Management

is it not
always the way, the wise
old fool who
had persisted in his folly, getting
his f.s. degree (that's
sawbones of filosify) from a. & also from
m., so
now we have
to call him, get
this, doctor, told the
gathering mob of 2. i
would not put that stuff up
my nose if i weren't you.
the all you
can eat at the end of
the street was closed for saint
swithington's day, while
a dove in the sky ate
a bug on it's way to a
house all afire, from which all the
buglets had just
run away. i surely
don't mean in the
midst of my crash,
said old casey
jones to the slick
sumo preacher, to
throw you so far off the track. like
a fairly good

neighbor, the feelings
mutual calamity and
casualty company will
gather your money and work
very hard not
to give any back.

The Cure for What Ails

the bright brassy light of the
next day in line that
barges right in to
your memories of gin,
none too fond by the
way, reminds
you in tones you can
feel in your bones that
you took more than
just a small nip. if
you had to reckon, right
there on the
spot, how much of the
old piddydoodah you
had, your answer would
likely be zip. and
the truths that you
held to be self
evident went out with the
cookies, not the salad, you
recently tossed. whatever
it was that had made so much
sense in the dark of
the night where the spark of
your brilliance once
bloomed, is now lost. forget
truth eternal and whether it strayed
off to regions infernal, how do i stop
all these heaves, now as dry as a

bone all alone in the desert at
noon? try nellie the
zealot's bad hangover pellets,
for sale slightly
cheaper in
places around and
within saskatoon.

"Bud" Dzmc's Very Last Ad

say
there, bunky, ashamed that
you don't belong on
the showroom
floor, looking at all those
mighty fine guzzlers, just
because you're carrying
paper still on that
old jalop you
drive? banish all
fear and look away,
look away, dixieland, for
your lucky day
is here.
pick out a
big one to suit your
style, and forget all that
stuff about gas per
the mile. and, as for the dough
that they say
you still owe, honest stan, the
caravan man, will fold it into the
loan he'll make you right now
and at no extra charge, you
heard me right, mr. smart shopper. now
how's that for
a show stopper? you get a
free rollover with the purchase
of any SUV.

APPENDIX TO THE APPENDIX
THE LOST MINSTREL BALLADS
OF GLUB DZMC'S GREAT-GREAT-GREAT-
GREAT-GREAT-GREAT UNCLE,
DECIUS BRUTUS DZMC

Doodly Dandy

In those old days of yere, that is to say here
And now, if you please just the same,
Lived a freebooting grandee named Doodly Dandy
And soldiering, that was his game.

He was not alone, though he had not a phone,
He'd assembled a smart looking squad
Of brigands and braggarts and goons and poltroons
Who after him gladly would plod.

Now the King, you can bet, was badly beset
With tidings of carnage and war
For his rival, the Rook, that shifty-eyed crook,
Had made him exceedingly sore.

How dare that mad varlet attack me by starlight
And burn all my beans to the ground?
I'll get up a force, the King said, of course,
And teach him what goes comes around.

By tens and by fives, for the sake of their lives,
His vassals and villeins declined
The King's great invite to come out and fight
For glory as yet undefined.

Mercy no, we won't go, they chorused as one,
In the pay of that awfully tight wad,
When, to the King's glee, as you plainly can see,
Came Doodly Dan and his squad.

Have no fear, Old King Leer, he heard Dandy say,
We're fighting for glory and beer.
Just show us the way right into the fray,
For Doodly Dandy is here.

To arms, Dandy'd say, now into that fray,
Attack them and hack them to shards.
He commanded his throng who did not get along
Well with others, especially bards.

The foe soon did swoop down on Dandy's sad group
And gutted them each like a cod.
The King faced defeat because, I repeat,
He didn't have Doodly's squad.

The Maid and the Garden

To draw back the bow and lay a buck low
Is something as old as your hat.
But to sweetly discover
Your first gentle lover,
There's only one first time for that.

In a bright little dwelling that was always sweet smelling
Dwelt a maiden so lovely and fair.
Her garden, she tended
And her dresses she mended,
But she never had let down her hair.

In a village nearby, lived a lad young and spry,
Who had known every girl in the town.
With lust he was laden
To have that fair maiden
Whose beauty was of such renown.

In a moment or less, as I'll bet you can guess,
The young man was off to her house.
She should be glad I'm
Going to be her first time,
Thought the youth, who was somewhat a louse.

Black was the night when the lad came in sight
Of the fair maiden's cottage, so small.
To make himself set
For the fun he would get,
He'd entered with no clothes at all.

I care not for rapes, you foul jackanapes,
Whispered the maid from behind him.
With her dagger raised high
She said the time's nigh,
If you have any teeth left, to grind 'em.

Oh prithee spare me, the devil did dare me,
The young man cried out in despair.
Tho' if with you I'd sleep,
My heart's yours to keep,
If you'll just let yourself to go there.

You sweet, handsome guy, alas 'tis not I
With whom in love's ways you shall slumber.
For this did you strip:
Touch your ankles and grip,
And acquaint thee with my fat cucumber.

To take up a torch and burn down a porch
Is something as old as your hat.
But to sweetly discover
Your first gentle lover,
Ah, there's only one first time for that.

Ye King of Comedy

You can't fool a fooler, declared the mad ruler,
King Rameses Trojan deTroppe.
The jokes all he knew, and he'd done quite a few,
As he gave a hot foot to the Pope.

'Tis all well and fine, he said, pouring brine
In the bulb of a bright squirting flower,
To sit on the throne as you gnaw at a bone
While mulling the feeling of power.

But would it not be, I'm thinking, for me,
More fitting to act like the clown?
Better to jape than have men bow and scrape
On their knees with their heads to the ground.

He said to his jester, say I don't mean to pester
You while you are having your tea,
But could you impart how you practice your art
To a most willing subject? That's me.

I suppose that I might, in fact I'd delight
In showing the tricks of the trade
To a king so renowned that he's even been crowned,
Said the fool as he grinned in the shade.

To juggle the balls or dance on the walls,
Is pretty tough stuff for a start.
To give you a hand up, let's have you do stand up,
Your chance to sound funny and smart.

I'll tell you the word, there just has occurred
A spot, said the fool, and in fact,
I got you a gig with a tap dancing pig,
Your stand up will be next act.

Asked the king, will this work, for I do not a jerk
Wish to seem in the view of this crowd.
Said the fool, trust me, sire, your act is afire.
I'm certain these folks will be wowed.

I'll tell you once more as we walk through the door,
The king told the jester, we're here
For high cockamamie, so don't try to play me,
Or I'll throw you in jail on your ear.

Your Majesty's fright on this wonderful night,
With the truth is so far out of touch,
Said the fool, oh, and try very hard not to drool,
It's classier, though not by much.

The king had his page hoist him onto the stage,
As he lifted the megaphone high.
Is everyone glad? Well, that is too bad,
He said with a laugh and a sigh.

If I'm saying this right, how many a knight
Does it take to lay waste an estate?
To round up the heathen and make sure they're not breathin',
Then to burn and to loot should be eight.

Please hold your applause, said the king without pause,
Til I've done my entire routine.

When I've finished the funny, you can throw me your
money,
And say what a pleasure it's been.

Exclaimed the king then, tell me why did the hen
Try to climb up and over a fence?
The answer is three, though it still puzzles me,
How that riddle can make any sense.

And so the night went, as he tried to present
The funniest jokes in the book.
He used his best stuff 'til the crowd cried, enough!
And the innkeeper gave him the hook.

The days that remain in the miserable reign
Of King Rameses Trojan deTroppe
Are horrid and grim, not to say dull and dim
While the fool yet still flees from the rope.

Old Thunderclap

Old Thunderclap could be a handy old hound
To have close at hand, lying around,
In spite of the fact that he smelled of manure.
Where Thunderclap went, you could always be sure.

With children and tots he was not very nice,
He'd bitten them all once or twice.
In the dead of the night, he would bark and then bay,
And he would not shut up 'til the breaking of day.

He'd chase away cattle who wanted to graze,
Then out in their pasture he'd laze.
He liked to do battle with people's prize pets,
And gloat as their owners trudged off to the vet's.

How was it a dog so incredibly bad
Could live the sweet life that he had?
Though many to hang him would have gladly elected,
He was by the gentry completely protected.

So lend me an ear, or buy me a beer,
That would be still better yet,
And I'll tell you the tale, say, make that an ale,
Of how fortune befell to this pet.

It took place at the festival, there in the town
To honor their cabbage, renown.
Though much of the stuff was exported afar,
Some like to feast on it right where they are.

And on festival day all the people came out
To wallow in cabbage and kraut.
A contest was held by the festival's host,
To see who could shovel down cabbage the most.

Said Beer Barrel Bill from the local grist mill,
I plan to keep eating until
The moon fades away and the cock crows at dawn.
Then, if there's more, I will keep going on.

Everyone knew that the game was all done.
For nobody else ever won.
But out from a carriage that was fancy and fine,
Marched a stern lady up to where Bill reclined.

Consider, sirrah, your challenge now met,
Up off your...bench you must get.
However much cabbage you think you can eat,
She said, I will best you and not skip a beat.

All this time Thunderclap lay in the shade
Not caring much how this was played.
As he gnawed on a bone he'd dug up from a grave,
He paid little heed to how people behave.

The contest commenced with a fanfare so loud
It did the old village right proud.
Then a couple of goons, armed with big wooden spoons,
Served up the food amidst dancing and tunes.

Now Beer Barrel Bill, he could sure eat his fill,
His appetite nothing could kill.

But across from him sat a determined old dame,
Lady Castor de l'Oiel, of medicinal fame.

Though she ate up a lot more than anyone thought
She could eat with a figure so taut,
Beer Barrel Bill left her far in the dust,
As the townspeople knew that he certainly must.

But still Lady Castor had eaten much more
Than only one plate, more like four.
A terrible pressure was building inside
To let out a thing not conducive to pride.

A look of sweet innocence played on her face
As she surveyed the lay of the place.
Then, with very small noise, but still quite a medley
Some tunes were let out that were quiet but deadly.

Good God, this is awful, the host sharply cried.
It smells as though something has died!
Bad dog! Lady Castor was quick to point out
As she leveled a finger at Thunderclap's snout.

Your Ladyship's pardon I beg and I hope.
We shall dangle this mutt from a rope.
Said the host, very vexed at this turn of events
As he prayed that the lady would not take offense.

Unhand that dog, you miserable cad,
She swiftly commanded the lad
Who had taken Old Thunderclap up in his grip
While a noose 'round the neck he was starting to slip.

Though the smell from that mongrel is so awfully bad,
I think it would be rather sad
To ruin this day by hanging up there
An innocent creature, who just fouled the air.

Should the life from this dog any man try to strip,
He'll get a fair taste of the whip,
Proclaimed Lady Castor, not the last one to log
The blame for that thing against some nearby dog.

Sir Gallidan Pallidan Jones

A slayer of dragons and fixer of wagons
Was Sir Galladin Pallidan Jones.
Fearing not man or beast,
He would roam west to east,
Converting his foes all to bones.

No knight with a lance stood even a chance
When pitted 'gainst Jones in a fight.
He once slew a dragon
While sipping a flagon
Of mead in the dark of the night.

The love of his life (but don't tell his wife)
Was a lass known as Lorelei Lee.
With whom he would dally
While bananas she'd tally
In the very first known A&P.

How sadly he'd stew, parts of him blue,
As the lovely Miss Lee heeded not
His heartfelt entreaties
Mid boxes of Wheaties,
And pies that were made from a pot.

Pray listen, Sir Knight, though try as I might,
I care for thee not, said Miss Lee,
'Cause my heart, so it seems,
Beats for him of my dreams,
The sack boy named Stooey McGee.

That simpleton lout is what it's about,
Your spurning my love and romance?
I'll duel with the dope
Or else from a rope
I surely will make him to dance.

I challenge you, sir (you miserable cur),
Thundered the knight to McGee.
The combat you choose,
For you're certain to lose.
I'll bet now you wish you were me.

I don't wish to die for sweet Lorelei,
Said the sack boy while fouling his pants,
So let us jump in
And race for to win
'Cross the lake, that's my only small chance.

Said the knight, small it is, for I'm quite a whiz
At stroking the old butterfly.
While you're doing the dog paddle
I'll be in the saddle,
Riding off with the fair Lorelei.

No doubt you are right, said the sack boy contrite,
It was foolish of me to suggest it.
Through the lake, let us plow,
We two, here and now,
Though I'm stupid to even contest it.

On my mark, get set, go! called the knight down below,
As into the water he sped

Then he sank like the stones,
Did Galladin Jones,
For his armor he'd not stopped to shed.

Bye, bye, gentle knight, said McGee with delight
To the corpse in the depths of the pool.
Though a sack boy to some,
I'm someone whose mom
Did not care to raise up a fool.

The Lady and the Emperor

On a cold winter's day that was quite far away
From the warmth of the summer's sweet mirth,
Came a lass on a horse, named Godiva, of course,
All done up in the suit of her birth.

Before you get smug and say not to bug
You about that poor tired old yarn,
You may yet be perplexed by what happened next,
Ere her horse was returned to the barn.

From our sight she had gone, as she kept riding on
With no one to come to her aid,
When she stumbled into, and nearly rode through,
A rather peculiar parade.

Said a lout, yay hey hey, but you still must make way,
Fair lady of little attire,
But feel not dejection, because your selection
Of 'clothing' I greatly admire.

E'enso, spake the lout, there is not any doubt
That way is the thing you must make.
The emperor's sleigh will be coming this way,
And of that there can be no mistake.

Let me spare you the task of stopping to ask
If this was the one with new clothes.
It was one and the same, now please do not blame
Me for telling what everyone knows.

Called the emperor, hark! I think you must park
My imperial sleigh in the snow.
For I have just seen, and my sight is quite keen,
A damsel I'd soon like to know.

To Godiva he said, how it fills me with dread
To see you like this in the snow.
To dress in the buff is hardly enough
When the temperature's twenty below.

Said she, look who's talking, not even a stocking
Are you wearing to cover your toes.
At least my long hair makes me not quite as bare,
As you are right now, heaven knows.

The snow, I'm inclined to think, made you blind
The emperor said in a flash.
I'm oh so resplendent, from my crown to my pendant
And my shoes with my gloves do not clash.

I'm a generous man and a really big fan
Of a spirited lady like you.
While your ease on my eyes is an extra nice prize,
For the thing that I'm soon going to do.

I shall take from my back the cape that you lack
And allow you to huddle within it.
Just know I don't mind being so very kind,
Though I never had been, I'll begin it.

Well, hip hip hooray, said Godiva that day,
Thanks for nothing, you horny old fraud.

Your 'cape' is a warm as a reptile's charm,
And it still doesn't cover my bod.

Cried the great man with glee, it has just come to me,
Who you are and for what you are known.
It's the chocolates you make, for which I'd forsake
A date with a plump chicken bone.

Seeing that I was so nice, out here in the ice
And the snow of this miserable day,
I wonder if I for a favor could try:
That you might throw some chocolate my way.

Said the lady, of course, it so happens my horse,
You handsome and kind lucky boy,
Has left a great load, right here in the road,
Of chocolate. Dig in and enjoy!

Did his majesty bite on that equine delight?
The truth of it nobody knows.
But then this was the guy who did not have the eye
To see he was wearing no clothes.

The Cure for Matrimony

A fellow named Joe was quite sick of his life,
Chiefly because of his wife.
If only, he thought, I could find without sin
A way I could do the old battle axe in.

Remedy, then, was the thing that he sought,
As he searched for the counsel and thought
Of those who had actually once gone to school.
I am, he observed, going to be no one's fool.

The Barrister proved to be no help at all,
Saying he was busy 'til fall.
The Priest told him this was no way to behave,
For anyone not a full Certified Knave.

So with his sad lot did poor Joe feel stuck.
He guessed he was fresh out of luck,
When he happened upon a most fortunate sign
Attached to the shop at the end of the line.

On it he saw a duck making a din,
Which meant that the doctor was in.
I've tried all the others, so why not one more?
Joe wondered aloud as he passed through the door.

Say, Doctor, I'm hoping and wishing you might
Help find relief for my plight.
My wife's quick demise is my most fervent hope,
But I cannot end up with my neck in a rope.

Said the Doc, I believe I can find you a cure,
In fact, I am certainly sure.
The way that you give that old harpy the shove
Is to take her to bed several times, and make love.

Do it twice daily, I mean with your spouse,
And the light of her life you shall douse.
The strain that she suffers will make itself clear.
She'll be breathing her last at the end of a year.

How clever and smart, exclaimed Joe with glee,
Worth every bit of your fee.
Now let me get started to work on this stunt,
And before very long, I'll be rid of that woman.

Homeward he ran and launched into his plan
To again be an unmarried man.
I'm here, he announced, for my husbandly chore,
And later that night, he would do it once more.

Day after day, he twice did the deed,
Sowing the Grim Reaper's seed.
Or that's what he thought he was doing to her,
But a passing observer might not be so sure.

For the old girl looked better with each passing day.
She ceased to feel withered and gray.
Her complexion became quite robust and fresh,
And the bags and the wrinkles were gone from her flesh.

Poor Joe had not been so lucky, I fear,
Still, he knew this would take a full year.

His knees grew more weak, and his back became bent.
His get-up-and-go had gone up and went.

It happened the doctor was passing Joe's way,
In exactly a year less a day
From the date when they hatched their nefarious plot.
Going well was the thing that it clearly was not.

Joe, you're a wreck, did the doctor proclaim,
Like an ember that's run out of flame.
If you do not your lusty behavior abate,
I fear you may meet a most horrible fate.

It's true that I'm weak, and I shake like a leaf,
But with fate I do not have a beef.
For tomorrow, he said with a glint in his eyes,
Is the glorious day the old harridan *dies.*

Nate's Lucky Day

Nasty Old Nate, that renowned reprobate,
Ate limburger cheese for his breath.
And tortured the peasants, just by his presence,
By talking them all half to death.

Sometimes he'd stick with the pockets he'd pick
To keep him in whisky and wine.
And then he would squeal on whomever he'd feel
He could frame for his most recent crime.

Quite often the itch to go strike it rich
Made him indulge in dognapping
Or robbing the till at the local gin mill,
With most of his crimes overlapping.

The people would flee (and that includes me)
Whenever he came through the gate.
No good thing could come from being close to that bum,
As many found out, but too late.

One day a young lass Nate's way happened to pass.
He greeted her nod with a wink.
And told her, say, Miss, it would be my own bliss
To buy such a beauty a drink.

Well, if you mean me, I should say I'm quite free,
She notified Nate then and there,
To throw down the schnapps or some fermented hops
In the warmth of the balmy spring air.

Hooray and hot dig, thought that lusty old pig,
For this surely is my lucky day.
I'm in the right spot for some good you-know-what,
And for it I won't have to pay.

Here's to life, fun and free, he bellowed with glee
As he raised high his glass in a toast.
And here's to the lass, who is raising her glass
In response to the skills that I boast.

Despite what Nate thought, her charms had been bought,
'Though the girl practiced not prostitution.
The folks all around that poor, blighted town
Had chipped in for Nate's retribution.

As he went on to gloat, he did not make note
Of the potion she poured in his gin.
He threw down the booze, 'til he started to lose
The knack to keep anything in.

As his face turned so pale, he said to regale
You with more of my wit I would like,
But a man I must seek, 'bout a dog, so to speak,
Then he fled as if riding a bike.

Before you could twitch, he was off in a ditch
Squatting and feeling quite ill.
How sadly he groaned, and how madly he moaned,
And he may be down there, squatting still.

The Beanstalk of Nothing Else

There once came a giant, much bigger than me,
Bigger than you, and he liked to yell Fee!
Later would come the Fie! Foe! and Fum!
For the guy was quite smart, due to not being dumb.

He lived high atop a stalk, made for beans,
Tho' he couldn't care less if you ate all your greens.
In fact, if the thing I am saying be quite true,
The stuff he preferred most to snack on was you.

And if you were English, well, that just went double,
Since grinding your bones could lead only to trouble.
Be you alive or, in any case, dead,
The big guy was fond of his whole-marrow bread.

It so happened a nearsighted boy known as Jack
Had spilled three small beans near his house, in the back.
When finally he noticed the beanstalk so tall,
He imagined those seeds were the cause of it all.

I knew they were magic, said Jack with a snort,
Now let me climb up this thing, just for the sport.
With a heave and a ho and a grunt and a sigh,
He began his ascent to that place in the sky

Where the beanstalk left off and the giant began.
If Jack had the brains of a goose, he'd of ran.
When he got to the top, he did not make a peep,
As he spotted the giant, lying down, fast asleep.

In a bold voice, Jack hollered, Fum, fee foe fie!
You have just met your match, sir, and that match is I!
For I am a young man, and you are so old.
After I've whipped you, I'll make off with your gold.

The fight, if there was one, was simple and sound,
And one of them only returned to the ground.
To the giant townspeople said the big man, don't fidget,
For somehow I've managed to vanquish the midget.

The Bee

In a world where the mobsters all got to eat lobsters
While honest folks settled for gruel,
The very worst thug, just released from the jug,
Was a fellow named Eddie the Cruel.

No sheriff or cop could manage to stop
The shenanigans he liked to pull.
At the bank, he'd say, Honey, take all of the money,
And fill up my sack 'til it's full.

He kidnapped some geese, and, for their release,
Got cash and some valuable stones.
Then he turned his men loose for a feast of roast goose,
And all he returned were the bones.

Can nobody make this tiresome rake
Once more to reside in our jail?
Said the mayor, sore afraid that whomever he paid
To do the job, surely would fail.

Your jail might not work to impede such a jerk
Said a clever young man to hizzonor,
But I have a plan to make certain that man
Will instead wish that he were a goner.

Get warlocks and witches and son-of-a-bitches,
Magicians and wizards and quacks
To practice their voodoo; I mean, what can you do,
Other than raising our tax?

Amongst all that batch, someone's bound to unlatch
The door to this man's place of rest.
We'll hold, don't you see, a great spelling bee
To see who can hex him the best.

They tackled the task and gave all one might ask,
But none of them Eddie could rout.
Their bold incantations and multiplications
He could not have cared less about.

Fiddle deedee, he said (not to me),
I care nothing for anyone's trick.
The magic you brought has all gone for naught,
So why don't you go suck a lime.

When Eddie had left, the group felt bereft
Of all their magnificent skills.
Then up popped a guy with a gleam in his eye.
I'll get him without using pills

Or potions or frogs or three-legged dogs,
He said. They are so awfully lame.
Now, no one guffaw, I will lay down the law,
And, by the way, Murphy's the name.

Quite soon Eddie's life became very rife
With ailments and troubles galore.
Why I'm so blistery is surely a mystery,
He said as he rubbed every sore.

He knew not the reason why life was displeasin'
And plagued by misfortune and pain.

When he washed his fine buggy, one day hot and muggy,
And finished, it started to rain.

Any bread that he dropped, on the floor always plopped
With the butter side facing the ground.
When he needed a mate to carry a crate,
There was never a soul to be found.

Alas and alack, the safes that I crack
Have nothing worth more than a rag,
He said, while the others that all of my brothers
Get into are loaded with swag.

At last he said, Fine! I will fall into line
And return to the jail to eat swill
If that'll prevent this guy Murphy's intent:
If something can go wrong it will.

Ready for Freddy

The times were not easy for Wilbert the Queasy,
King of what little he'd own.
Any punk potentate with an army of eight
Could have toppled this guy from the throne.

His navy was small, for he had none at all,
While his army was usually drunk.
His royal dragoons were afraid of raccoons,
And were once put to rout by a skunk.

Oh give me a man who has a great plan
To help keep the crown in my hold,
The King would declaim without any shame,
And I'll pay him his measure in gold.

Did someone say gold, if I might be so bold,
Inquired the Sycophant Royal,
A fellow named Freddy who was not all that steady,
And who sat upon many a boil.

There must be a way, he heard himself say,
To turn the King's fear into gold.
Though yet I've no clue as to what I should do,
I'm sure it will be something bold.

For Freddy could creep to the top of the heap
In any king's court you could name.
Though his faults were immense, he had plenty of sense
To know how you play at the game.

He knew how to flatter, as he laid down his patter,
Ever praising the King's falling stock.
This guy did it all. He could sure crawl the crawl,
And he really could talk the fine talk.

Though Your Majesty's might will bring fear in the night
And the late afternoon to your foes.
We must stay vigilant, 'til your treasury's spent,
For that is the way that it goes.

I've heard some bad things from neighboring kings
About the Mad Prince of the Sand,
He explained to his lord, lest the man should get bored,
They say that his weapons are banned.

And, if that weren't enough, he plans to play rough,
To invade your backyard with a bang.
And if my best guess is not lacking or less,
I think he will come with his gang.

Oh, what can a king but do, with a wring
Of his hands did poor Wilbert despair.
I guess I could flee to the Caspian Sea
Or perhaps disappear in thin air.

Said Freddy, Tut tut, I will tell you what's what,
How you're going to defeat the Mad Prince.
There was never a guy who was smarter than I,
And I'm sure there has not been one since.

Now our troops are but fit for slobber and spit,
So I'll set them to polishing shoes.

And the soldierly togs I will put on our hogs,
Then I'll tell the Mad Prince the bad news.

The Prince of the Sand and his dastardly band
Will flee from that pork on the hoof.
When our pigs make their charge, the retreat will be large.
Why, they'll try to climb up on a roof.

To fight with our swine, I'm quite sure they'll decline,
For they think that our pigs are taboo.
Their terror and fright will be our delight,
Then the Prince of the Sand will fear you.

I like it a lot, but is that all you've got?
Inquired the King with a sigh.
I won't be caught nappin', so let's make it happen,
He commanded his Chief of the Sty.

The King gave the word and then a great herd
Of hogs ventured forth to attack
They met the foe's troops, who first hollered, whoops,
But would not be taken aback.

At the dining room table, they were clearly unable
To partake of a porcine delight.
But here in the fray, just to keep them at bay,
They'd stop them however they might.

And if that meant to cook and to eat those they took,
While reluctantly donning their bibs,
Such things must be right in the heat of the fight,
So they feasted on barbecued ribs.

Now Your Majesty's might will bring fear in the night
To all those against you who planned,
Said Sycophant Freddy, always willing and ready
To praise the Mad Prince of the Sand.

EXDEX

A

Aardvarks, 3, 317-19
    with bubble gum, 64
    without bubble gum, 78-85
    without bubble baths, 189
Additions, 21-23, 418-19
    to, 17-76, 194
    from, 23-24, 25
    it's called "subtraction," nitwit, 103, 106, 109-112, 419
Aesop, 5, 94, 419
    -'s fables, 22-23
    -'s whoppers, 41, 83
Antelopes, 127-29
    playing with deer, 13
    playing with fire, 42-43
Antoine the Creep, 4, 8, 64, 73, 102-09, 527
Ape, ya big, 24-26, 419
Arbuckell, Phatty, 19-21
    goes on trial, 36
    gets job as spokesman for coke, 121, 419
    goes incognito as "Chubby Carbuncle," 225
Association, 29-73
    guilt by, 34
    shame by, 44
Atlee, Sir Clement, 139
    Sir Innocent, 153
    Sir Urban XVI, 278

B

Balance of payments, 123-25
    of spinning plates, 192-93

C

F

I

M

N

O

P

T

removed during uneven sandwich fad, 73-74
Utah, 1-3, 14, 92, 419
    as the cradle of jazz, 64
    outlaws monogamy, 72
    then outlaws mahogany, 72-73
    outdraws New Mexico, 88-89

V

Valentine, Saint, 15, 25-30, 122, 419
    gets no cards, 18
    goes and eats worms, 119-20
Vanity, The Iron Pyrite, 64
Versailles, Treaty of Zoilo, the, 27-28, 30, 105
    Flip Wilson and, 123-24
Vim, 46-48
    vs. vigor, 56
    vs. rigor, 59-60
Vines, grape, 272, 601-08
    as a hearing aid, 339
Vinnie the Poop, 62, 65-68
Vicissitudes, the cruel of life, 38-39, 40
    of lasagna, 94
VoteFraudpalooza, 19, 35, 43
Voting with your feet, 17, 44-45, 86, 419
    difficulty of working levers with toes, 31-32

W-X

Wait a minute, 232, 287
    wait a minute, 303
    you ain't heard nothin', 304
    yet, 305

Y

#!!%

ACKNOWLEDGMENTS

I am not going to do proper justice to everyone I ought to, I am quite sure of that. Why? Because, as I try to write this page, I am 63 years old. When I heard my first shaggy dog story, I was ten. When I got the idea of putting together a collection of them, I was twenty-one. A lot of time has flown the coop, and, while I will not yet claim to be a victim of Alzheimer's, I am, without question, in the savage grip of CRS.

Let me begin and end with the most important acknowledgments and work my way inward. First, I have my parents to thank, not only for the DNA, but for the upbringing that went with it. Let me not gush too mushy and sentimental. If my brother and I acted like brats, we got the back or the front of their hands. At the same time, my brother and I were allowed to let our wit run rampant, even if it poked into adult institutions that little children were supposed to hold in awe. And, where other children our age would have been spanked or, at the very least, told to shut the hell up, we were encouraged to keep rolling along.

As to the stories and the stories-within the stories, many of them came from the written word, anything from gag-a-day calendars to the internet. Let me try to remember the people who took the trouble to bend my ear.

I got The Wonderful Cake from a very classy lady I met at a cocktail party held by some friends of my parents. I have lost track of them all, and I cannot remember her name, which is a pity. It is probably my favorite shaggy dog story, and it was one of the most fun to write.

The True Meaning of Life, which is the shell of a series of three concentric shaggy dog stories, I got from my best friend and college roommate, Tom Caceci, who is, as of this writing, a professor of veterinary medicine at Virginia Tech University. He is also responsible for the innermost gag. I do not remember who told me the second layer, but, I don't know that I was ever actually introduced to the guy. I think I sort of overheard it. Anyway, we will hear from the troublesome Dr. Caceci again.

The Ten Dollar Suit, I got from the late Paul Herndon. He is, without question, the greatest unheralded author I have ever read, and I am including myself in that category, as I write this article. The story is not a piece he wrote, but rather, a joke that he casually rattled off in the space of two minutes, while we were killing some time. If you can read it in two minutes, then you should tell Evelyn Waugh he needs to attend *your* speed-reading school.

As for The Red Horse, I picked that one up in the army, either from a Specialist Dyer or Specialist Dryer. There's that old CRS kicking in. Well, to one of you two, I'm sorry to have dragged you, kicking and screaming into where you obviously do not belong. To the other, thanks for a rollicking good yarn.

The next story, Yet Another Vampire Tale, I got from a human source. I do clearly remember the source and the setting. The fellow's name was Chip Woods and he was an overnight campmate. In a setting where feeble stories are the order of the day, his was, almost certainly the feeblest one I had ever heard in two summers within two different camps. Not just in spite of that, but because of that, it was very shaggy of dog. Still, it presented a challenge. It also presented an opportunity. Thanks to Chip (Considering he is my age, first, I hope he is still among us; then I wonder if he still goes by "Chip" rather than "Charles" or "Chutney" or whatever his real name is.), I developed an interest in the minstrel ballads that inevitably accompanied the tale, which led me to the mysterious balladeer, Decius Brutus Dzmc, which, in turn, led me to his even more mysterious great-

great-great-great-great-grand nephew, Glub Dzmc. You can see the dispoetic results for yourself if you are so masochistically inclined.

Our Man in the Street came from my brother, about which I will go into further detail later.

The final and worst story, The Tizz Bottle, is the work of the ever-malevolent Dr. Caceci. The wonder is, considering how long it took for him to tell the story and for me to listen to it, that either of us graduated from Kenyon—a school that did not allow a great deal of leisure time for the swappage of long, pointless jokes.

Within the shaggy dog stories there are many more short jokes than I can count and more people than I can acknowledge, from my kindly, but very bright, Aunt Irma, who gave me a joke to put in the original Shaggy Dog, to my dad, who gave me a joke for The Ten Dollar suit. Least but not last, and to whom I do not extend any gratitude at all, there is the jerk who gave me the joke about the wrestler, for the ten dollar suit. It's a good joke, but the guy is a first-class jerk. Of course, I heard it years ago, so the teller may no longer be alive, as I have known others younger than he to have passed on. If that may be the case, let me amend my remarks: perhaps he *was* a first-class jerk. Anyway, let me thank everyone else for the shorter yuks.

As to my brother, Burt, I have him to thank, not only for that dubious tale but for years and years of love and support that have never wavered. When we were younger, I always enjoyed being the straight man, while he played the goof. Somehow, over the course of time, the roles have reversed and the stakes have risen, but he has stepped into his new role with grace and aplomb. His wife, Jennifer, is all I could ask for in a sister-in-law and a good friend, and my two rambunctious, but ingenious nephews, Gavin (a/k/a Gavininininininin) and Alec (a/k/a Mr. Kazzam, but his real name is Alistair) are a joy to behold. In fact, it was young Gavin who helped me discover the Lost Notebooks of Glub Dzmc, but that is, as they say, a long story. We have enough of them in this book already.

Finally, I want to thank my editor, Vanessa Weeks Page. I did pay her to actually edit this piece—not pretend edit the way I did—and she did a truly remarkable job, to the extent that, when you factor in all her time and her effort against the amount I paid for it, though not picayune by any means, it amounted to a bean picker's wages. Vanessa found stuff that I would have overlooked if I had sat transfixed, staring at a given page for a decade. I do consider myself to be somewhat erudite, though I will admit to the spelling skills of a third-grader (I apologize, all you 3rd graders; please excuse my presumption, but I did win a tootsie pop in a 2nd grade spelling bee. So there.) and the typing skills of a chimpanzee.

And, really finally, I want to thank the members of Cochrane's Saloon, new and old, present and past, living and dead. The group—a writers' support forum—has been around since the 1970's. I joined in 1981, so I am a comparative "newbie." It is named as it is after the poet, Shirley Cochrane, who taught courses both in poetry and creative writing at a facility in the former Glen Echo Amusement Park in Washington, DC, where I lived for 22 years. (In Washington, not the amusement park. It's not like I got my mail sent to me c/o the Tilt-a-Whirl, mind you).

In addition to the excellent story of The Ten Dollar Suit (my second favorite of the batch) that I got from Paul, who was a member up until he died, I have heard a great many shorter gags from several of the members. Speaking of The Ten Dollar Suit, the first thirteen words of it are not mine. One of the members—Caroline Keith—wrote them in an effort to free me from a particularly confining writer's block, and, she seems to have succeeded. I think she did in a big way, but then, I am a little prejudiced.

But I owe more to my writers' group than a few good gags.

They have offered me support of all kinds. They have provided very useful criticism and advice which, though they imagine I shun it all out of hand, has had an enormous influence in shaping these pages. If I could gather and print out all the words I had deleted—and rightly so—at their behest, it would make their collective eyes pop or, at the very least, snap and crackle. I am a great deal like my mother in that I care very little what others think about me. (Which may seem odd for someone whose avocation is performing on stage, but not really. At the curtain call, I do not much care whether you are on your feet or on your buns, as long as I am satisfied with how I performed). That said, there are worse things than hearing from your peers that you have produced an excellent piece of work. I would by lying if I said I did not relish the positive input I get from my writing companions.

If I single two people out in the group, I do not wish to imply that the others are nothing more than furniture. I count every person in Cochrane's saloon as a friend and have been saddened by the death of all the members we have lost. That said, I especially want to thank Peter Modley, not just because he is my second-cousin-in-law, but because he is a good and true friend, and the aforementioned Caroline Keith. My association with these two people goes well beyond the Saloon. It was Peter who introduced me to this wonderful group at a time when I was too blocked even to write a grocery list and was smoking way too much of mother nature to get around to much of anything. I would not necessarily say that my return to the keyboard was the sole source of my return to sobriety, but it was a somewhat huge factor. Caroline, the person with whom I most enjoy trading insults, has never been anything but completely loyal. As a hawker of real estate, she sold my Tilt-a-Whirl cab for a pretty penny, which was no small boon indeed, but, even if she were a toll-taker at the Tydings Bridge (which I never use), she'd still be a good and close friend.